URBAN INFORMALITY

An Introduction

Melanie Lombard and Philipp Horn

First published in Great Britain in 2024 by

Bristol University Press
University of Bristol
1–9 Old Park Hill
Bristol
BS2 8BB
UK
t: +44 (0)117 374 6645
e: bup-info@bristol.ac.uk

Details of international sales and distribution partners are available at bristoluniversitypress.co.uk

© Bristol University Press 2024

British Library Cataloguing in Publication Data
A catalogue record for this book is available from the British Library

ISBN 978-1-5292-1916-6 hardcover
ISBN 978-1-5292-1917-3 paperback
ISBN 978-1-5292-1918-0 ePub
ISBN 978-1-5292-1919-7 ePdf

The right of Melanie Lombard and Philipp Horn to be identified as authors of this work has been asserted by them in accordance with the Copyright, Designs and Patents Act 1988.

All rights reserved: no part of this publication may be reproduced, stored in a retrieval system, or transmitted in any form or by any means, electronic, mechanical, photocopying, recording, or otherwise without the prior permission of Bristol University Press.

Every reasonable effort has been made to obtain permission to reproduce copyrighted material. If, however, anyone knows of an oversight, please contact the publisher.

The statements and opinions contained within this publication are solely those of the authors and not of the University of Bristol or Bristol University Press. The University of Bristol and Bristol University Press disclaim responsibility for any injury to persons or property resulting from any material published in this publication.

Bristol University Press works to counter discrimination on grounds of gender, race, disability, age and sexuality.

Cover design: Hannah Gaskamp
Front cover image: Top photograph: Philipp Horn, bottom photograph: Tatiana Pinzón.
Bristol University Press uses environmentally responsible print partners.
Printed and bound in Great Britain by CPI Group (UK) Ltd, Croydon, CR0 4YY

To Alfredo Stein Heinemann, our shared mentor

Contents

List of Figures, Tables and Boxes		vii
About the Authors		x
Acknowledgements		xi
1	**Introduction: The Global Significance of Urban Informality**	**1**
	Setting the scene: why urban informality?	1
	Approaching the multiple and interrelated dimensions of informality	9
	Analysing responses to informality	13
	Engaging with representations of informality	15
	Using this book and chapter summary	18
	Recommended reading	20
	Exercises	20
	Alternative representations	21
2	**Understanding Urban Informality**	**23**
	Origins of urban informality	24
	Conceptual and policy debates in the 20th century	28
	21st-century debates	35
	Postcolonial urban theory	41
	Informality at a global scale	42
	Chapter summary	42
	Recommended reading	43
	Exercises	43
	Alternative representations	43
3	**Living Informally**	**45**
	Living informally: manifestations and factors	46
	Elements of informal living: land, housing, services	55
	New developments	62
	Chapter summary	65
	Recommended reading	66
	Exercises	66
	Alternative representations	66
4	**Working Informally**	**67**
	The informal sector: historical roots and conceptual approaches	69
	From informal sector work to informal employment	72
	Towards a comprehensive approach on the urban informal economy	80

	Chapter summary	85
	Recommended reading	86
	Exercises	86
	Alternative representations	87
5	**Governing Informally**	**89**
	Politics and informality	90
	Governing informally, (post)colonial development and the urban	92
	Articulations of governing informally	95
	Chapter summary	107
	Recommended reading	108
	Exercises	108
	Alternative representations	108
6	**Responses to Living Informally**	**111**
	The emergence of a global urban agenda	112
	State-led responses	114
	Citizen-led responses	123
	Chapter summary	131
	Recommended reading	132
	Exercises	132
	Alternative representations	133
7	**Responses to Working Informally**	**135**
	Responses as seen through different conceptual lenses	136
	Conventional top-down responses	138
	Embracing informal work	144
	Chapter summary	153
	Recommended reading	153
	Exercises	153
	Alternative representations	154
8	**Emerging Alternatives**	**155**
	Beyond informality?	156
	New policy and practice approaches to informality	164
	Engaging with informality	172
	Chapter summary	180
	Recommended reading	180
	Exercises	180
	Alternative representations	181
9	**Conclusion: For Trans-Local, Multi-Voice Understandings of Urban Informality**	**183**
	Overarching arguments and conceptual framework	183
	Evaluating responses to urban informality	187
	Future directions	190
Notes		193
References		197
Index		221

List of Figures, Tables and Boxes

Figures

1.1	A word cloud of informal practices from different parts of the world	2
1.2	Mukuru informal neighbourhood in Nairobi, Kenya	3
1.3	'Close, No. 118 High Street', by Thomas Annan	4
1.4	Regional dimensions of informal employment (percentage of informal employment in total employment)	7
1.5	Room in a tenement, New York	16
2.1	Overcrowded housing in 19th-century London	26
2.2	*Barriada* near Pachacamac, Lima, Peru in 1970	29
2.3	Sugarcane juice vendors in Lucknow, India	32
2.4	Self-help processes in Xalapa, Mexico	33
2.5	A home in Mumbai, India	39
3.1	Ponte Tower, an example of inner-city informal living in Johannesburg	48
3.2	Informal neighbourhood in Xalapa, Mexico	50
3.3	What do we mean by informal? The branching tree of irregularities in housing	54
3.4	Informal housing diversity	58
3.5	Consolidation of a neighbourhood in Xalapa, Mexico, 2006–11	61
3.6	Informal development in a middle-income neighbourhood, Nairobi, Kenya	63
4.1	Examples of informal work in Bolivia and South Africa	68
4.2	Home-based work in a rented home in an informal neighbourhood, Bogota, Colombia	73
4.3	Informal market scenes in El Alto, Bolivia	79
4.4	The informal economy by region measured by percentage of gross domestic product contribution	83
4.5	Value chain of ready-to-eat chickens in informal markets in Tshwane, South Africa	85
5.1	Ciudad Bolivar, Bogota, Colombia	95
5.2	Signs evidencing community and lynch mob justice in El Alto, Bolivia	98
5.3	Land invasion at the edge of an established informal neighbourhood in Xalapa, Mexico	104
5.4	Mukuru informal neighbourhoods in Nairobi, Kenya, a street view	105
6.1	Evictions in Cape Town, South Africa	116

6.2	Villa El Salvador in Lima, Peru, past and present	117
6.3	Costs of regularization	123
7.1	Banner promoting cleanliness in the inner-city streets of Durban, South Africa	140
7.2	Malecón 2000 in Guayaquil, Ecuador	141
7.3	Informal street vending activities in the Warwick Junction area in Durban, South Africa	146
8.1	Responses to food insecurity in informal neighbourhoods in Cali, Colombia, during the COVID-19 pandemic	159
8.2	Women undertaking informal neighbourhood mapping in India	161
8.3	Members of Mum's Mart savings group from Wythenshawe, Manchester, UK, visiting the Ladies of Hope group in Mukuru, Nairobi, Kenya	168
8.4	'Two different ways of life' from *How to Plan for Informality: The Experience of Catalytic Communities*	171
8.5	Photo of neighbourhood school taken by resident in Xalapa, Mexico	176

Tables

2.1	Characteristics of informal and formal economic sectors	31
4.1	A taxonomy of informal economic activities	82

Boxes

1.1	A note on the term 'global South'	5
1.2	'Illegal' by Patrick Magebhula Hunsley (1958–2014)	8
2.1	19th-century slums in England	27
2.2	Contrasting accounts of informality	35
3.1	The history of an informal neighbourhood in Cali, Colombia: an account by Alexander López, Asomevid	51
4.1	Heterogeneous motivations for street vending in Guangzhou, China	72
4.2	Home-based informal employment as depicted in the novel *A Fine Balance*	74
4.3	Capturing informal sector employment	77
4.4	Informal workers in El Alto, Bolivia: many are young and some are rich	79
4.5	Economic informality and COVID-19	81
4.6	Different causal explanations for the informal economy	87
5.1	Hyperregulation in Bolivia	103
5.2	Unequal clientelist politics in Dhaka, Bangladesh	107
6.1	Titling in Mexico, the case of the Commission for the Regularisation of Land Tenure	121
6.2	Supporting communities in Karachi, Pakistan: a conversation with Arif Hasan, Urban Resource Centre	124
6.3	Supporting affordable housing in Mumbai, India	130

7.1	Malecón 2000: promoting Guayaquil to tourists while reproducing urban colonialism	141
7.2	Formalization of the informal economy: a comprehensive approach	143
7.3	Amplifying the voices of informal workers in Durban, South Africa: a conversation with Richard Dobson, AeT	144
7.4	Key organizations supporting informal workers	148
8.1	Working with social leaders in Rio de Janeiro, Brazil: a conversation with Theresa Williamson, Catalytic Communities	169
8.2	Representations of informality in fiction	173
8.3	'Development' by Arif Hasan	178

About the Authors

Melanie Lombard is Senior Lecturer in the Department of Urban Studies and Planning at the University of Sheffield, UK. Her research explores aspects of urban informality, relating particularly to housing, land and place, through a focus on urban residents' everyday constructive activities, in cities in Latin America, Africa and the UK. She has published widely in journals and contributed chapters to several edited collections.

Philipp Horn is Senior Lecturer in the Department of Urban Studies and Planning at the University of Sheffield, UK. His research focuses on inclusive urban development, Indigenous urbanization, youth rights, and participatory planning in the global South, with a regional focus on Latin America and Africa. He has published numerous journal articles, books, book chapters and working papers.

Acknowledgements

Our paths first crossed at the former Global Urban Research Centre in the School of Environment, Education and Development at the University of Manchester. Here, we both had the privilege to work under the mentorship of Alfredo Stein Heinemann. Alfredo is not only an urban development planning specialist with more than 37 years of experience in providing practical solutions to urban low-income residents living informally; he is also a dedicated researcher, teacher and mentor. With his door always open, we both had the privilege to spend hours chatting, listening and learning with him about the challenges of and solutions to urban informality, and the need to put first the interests and priorities of those who live, work and govern informally. Many ideas shared in this book stem from these discussions, and it is for this reason that we dedicate this book to Alfredo.

This book heavily draws on our teaching experiences. At the University of Sheffield we jointly convene 'Urban Informality', a module for Master's-level students in the Department of Urban Studies and Planning. Long before we started teaching this module in 2018, urban informality had evolved into a critical field of study for those working on urban issues in the global South and, increasingly, the global North. It is the subject of ongoing debate in academic and policy circles, and is now on the curriculum of many built environment and global development programmes. However, when putting together our module, we noticed that little was available in terms of introductory guides. By writing this book, we hope to contribute to filling this gap, offering a comprehensive introductory overview of urban informality and related theoretical, policy and practice debates, illustrated with empirical examples throughout. Inspired by our own teaching and research, we have written this book to be accessible to advanced undergraduate students, postgraduate students, academics, policy makers and practitioners. It is likely to be relevant for readers engaged in the interdisciplinary fields of urban studies and global development, particularly those concerned with planning and the built environment, which are so intimately connected with urban informality.

Writing this book took over three years (including a global pandemic), often in parallel with preparing classes for our students, from whom we have learned so much during lectures, seminars, workshops and field trips. We therefore would like to thank our past and current students on the module 'Urban Informality', as well as contributors, Sam Burgum (University of Sheffield), Sophie King (Community Led Action and Savings – CLASS) and other Sheffield- and Manchester-based community leaders associated with the Community Savers network, and Lindsay Sawyer

(University of Sheffield), who provided different perspectives and helped us develop some of the ideas discussed in this book. For example, in the first teaching session in 'Urban Informality', we ask students to upload and share alternative representations of urban informality, including fiction, poetry, films, first-hand accounts and photography. This inspired us to incorporate non-academic representations of urban informality in this book, and some of the 'alternative representations' included at the end of chapters are based on recommendations from our students. Special thanks go to Tom Goodfellow, a regular contributor to the 'Urban Informality' module, whose ideas on political informality we have drawn on in the chapter on 'governing informally'. Beyond this specific course, we have engaged with many other students and colleagues on learning and teaching about urban informality, at undergraduate, Master's and PhD level; they are too numerous to list individually but we are grateful for their inputs.

In the different chapters of this book, we draw heavily on empirical, theoretical and practical examples from previous and ongoing research projects and collaborations we are involved in. In our research, we both work and collaborate with people who live, work and govern informally, and we also collaborate with researchers and practitioners with expertise on urban informality. We would like to thank people who accompanied us on our research journeys. We both thank the many people who are engaged in living and working informally with whom we have discussed these issues and from whom we have learned so much. At Sheffield, we thank our colleagues and collaborators (current and former), including especially Sam Burgum, Olivia Casagrande, Vanesa Castán Broto, Steve Connolly, Tom Goodfellow, Paula Meth, Beth Perry, Lindsay Sawyer, Leon Tellez Contreras, Simon Rushton, Juan Mario Diaz, Juan Miguel Kanai and Glyn Williams. We would both thank former colleagues, mentors, and peers at the University of Manchester who inspired our work and thinking around topics discussed in this book, including: Nicola Banks, Tanja Bastia, Sally Cawood, Michael Hebbert, Jessica Hope, Kirsten Howarth, Diana Mitlin, Caroline Moser, Alfredo Stein and Matthew Thompson. In Latin America, Philipp thanks his long-term collaborators Katherine Illanes and Carlos Revilla at the Instituto de Investigación y Acción para el Desarrollo Integral (IIADI) in La Paz, Patricia Urquieta and Windsor Torrico (formerly at the Universidad Mayor de San Andres in La Paz), and all urban Indigenous activists, academics, students and practitioners from Belo Horizonte, Concepcion, El Alto, La Paz, Pucon, Quito, Rurrenabaque, Santa Cruz and Sucre with whom he had the privilege to collaborate and co-learn. In Kenya, he thanks Kimani Joseph, Jack Makau and Patrick Njoroge from SDI Kenya, as well as community activists and practitioners linked to Muungano wa Wanavijiji and Akiba Mashinani Trust. Melanie thanks colleagues and activists in Colombia, particularly Jaime Hernández García, Carlos Andrés Tobar Tovar, Alexander López Angulo, Betty Alarcon Afiuni, Sandra Sarria, Jefferson Jaramillo Marín and Adriel Ruiz Galvan; and in Mexico, Mauricio Hernandez Bonilla and Clara Salazar. She also thanks the leaders and members of the Community Savers network, Sophie King and fellow CLASS board members.

This book is interspersed with testimonies from expert practitioners who share their insider perspective on urban informality from different geopolitical contexts with our readers. We thank Arif Hasan (Urban Resource Centre, Karachi, Pakistan), Richard Dobson (Asiye eTafuleni, Durban, South Africa), Alexander López (Asomevid, Cali, Colombia) and Theresa Williamson (Catalytic Communities, Rio de Janeiro, Brazil) for engaging with us in interviews and for agreeing to share their testimonies in this book.

We also thank those who provided us with permission rights to publish or reproduce photos, figures, illustrations and poems in this book, including Tatiana Pinzón (front cover image from Aguablanca District in Cali, Colombia), the International Labour Organization (Figure 1.2), the late Patrick Magebhula Hunsley and Joel Bolnick (Box 1.2), Cornell University Library (Figure 2.2), Dinodia Photos/Alamy (Figure 2.3), John Wiley & Sons (Figure 3.3), Eunice Nthambi Jimmy (Figure 3.6), Friedrich Schneider (Table 4.1), Lorena Guerrero (Figures 5.1 and 4.2), the International Monetary Fund (Figure 4.2), Elsevier Journals Limited (Figure 4.3), Daneel Knoetze/Groundup (Figure 6.1), Panther Media GmbH/Alamy (Figure 6.2), the Lincoln Institute for Land Policy (Figure 6.3), Diego Grandi/Alamy (Figure 7.2), Asomevid (Figure 8.1), SDI (Figure 8.2), Community Savers (Figure 8.3), Arif Hasan (Box 8.3), Theresa Williamson (Figure 8.4) and Azucena Jiménez (Figure 8.5).

The production of this book has also benefited from the unwavering support of our publishers at Bristol University Press, and here we would like to thank Zoe Forbes, Philippa Grand, Rebecca Tomlinson and Stephen Wenham for their patience, guidance and support throughout. We also thank the anonymous reviewer for their helpful comments and suggestions.

On a personal note, Melanie would like to thank Martyn, Arthur and Frieda for holding the fort at home, and Mary Lombard for her steadfast support throughout this and always. Philipp would like to thank family and friends, especially Sally, for support and putting up with him in the different stages of writing this book.

Let us finish by thanking each other: It has been a real pleasure working on this book together. Both of us contributed equally to the writing process and any errors are entirely our own.

1

Introduction: The Global Significance of Urban Informality

'Looking for opportunities has been my parents' main reason for coming to El Alto. They didn't have much money at the time and what they had was only enough to buy a plot of land in a very remote area. Here we built our own house. At that time, we were the only ones in the area. As the years went by, more people started buying land and built their own homes. Now, our neighbourhood is completely urbanized and forms part of the city of El Alto. But this neighbourhood wasn't developed and planned by the authorities in the municipality. It was built by us residents, using our hands. It took years to demand services from the local government. Now at least we have electricity, water, and gas, but the roads and the central avenue are still not paved. ... Many of the people who live here, myself included, work informally. For some this brought profits, but many of us struggle with poverty. ... My dream is to live in a place that is no longer synonymous with poverty and discrimination, but in an El Alto where the residents are respected and recognized for their entrepreneurial spirit. We are not lacking aspirations here, but many of us require resources and some support to move ahead, to improve our homes and businesses. I dream of a moment where those in power recognize and invest in our potential.'
 A young woman in her 20s, reflecting on the consolidation of her informal neighbourhood in the city of El Alto, Bolivia[1]

Setting the scene: why urban informality?

This book takes a global approach to informality. The opening testimony illustrates how, for many people in diverse urban settings around the world, informality is characteristic to the way they live, work and govern (or are governed). It is associated with both positive and negative connotations as well as a variety of policy and planning responses that produce varying outcomes for different people. In this book we draw on examples from distinct urban contexts and diverse theoretical approaches, and, by moving beyond academic representations, we emphasize the voices and perspectives of people who are directly affected by and involved in responding to informality. In this way, we highlight that informality is a phenomenon that affects us all directly and indirectly in different ways. Perhaps most importantly, we argue for recognition of informality as an urban phenomenon that is here to stay.

So, what precisely is informality, and why does it matter? According to the *Cambridge Dictionary*, informality can be defined as 'the fact of not being formal or official' or 'of being suitable for friends and family but not for official occasions'. When understood like this, most human beings have probably experienced informality or engaged in informal practices in one way or the other. Reflecting on everyday practices in our own countries of origin, informality seems to be omnipresent. For example, in Germany (Philipp's country of birth) people often refer to the fact that they gained a personal favour due to their *Vitamin B* (with B standing for *Beziehung*, meaning relationships). The equivalent of *Vitamin B* in the UK (Melanie's country of birth) is perhaps *pulling strings*, a colloquial term that refers to practices whereby people achieve or gain something by making use of their personal contacts. These different practices can be considered informal as they refer to getting things done in an unofficial way. In each society, informal practices have their own terminology and unwritten rules. In Figure 1.1, we have pulled together a collection of terms for such informal practices from all over the world.

In this book, our focus is predominantly on articulations and characteristics of, as well as responses to, informality in urban settings. We recognize that urban informality is complex and 'can be just about anything to anyone' (Marx and Kelling, 2019: 495), a situation which has led to recent debates attempting to theorize informality more precisely (such as McFarlane and Waibel, 2012; Boanada-Fuchs and Boanada, 2018; Acuto et al, 2019). While we draw on some of this work, in this book, we do not attempt to provide a definitive conceptual characterization of urban informality; rather, we aim to present an account of key theoretical, policy- and practice-orientated debates in this field, illustrated by empirical examples.

Figure 1.1: A word cloud of informal practices from different parts of the world

Source: Philipp Horn and Melanie Lombard

Figure 1.2: Mukuru informal neighbourhood in Nairobi, Kenya

Note: We discuss this neighbourhood and recent upgrading efforts in further detail in Chapters 5, 6 and 7.
Source: Philipp Horn

Among other issues, we pay attention to the role of informal processes and practices in the context of housing and settlements, basic services such as water and electricity, and public infrastructure such as roads and transport networks. According to the United Nations Human Settlements Programme (UN-Habitat), one in eight people, meaning around one billion people, live in informal neighbourhoods (such as the one seen in Figure 1.2). Here, they often live for many years with insecure land tenure, inadequate housing and access to basic services, and a lack of influence in urban governance and planning.

While most people who live informally reside in the global South (a contested term used to denote parts of the world associated with Latin America, the Caribbean, Africa and Asia, discussed in Box 1.1), we demonstrate in this book that informal housing has existed historically, and continues to exist, in many cities of the global North (the parts of the world associated with Europe, North America and Australia) – be that in the form of refugee camps, backyard sheds or irregular housing developments of the ultra-rich. In fact, the term 'slum', a derogatory word often associated with informal neighbourhoods, has its origins in 19th-century Victorian Britain, particularly in cities like London and industrializing towns in Northern England and Scotland (see Figure 1.3). Writing on Victorian Britain, the industrialist and philosopher Friedrich Engels (1969 [1887]: 45) described 'slums' as the 'worst houses in the worst quarters of the towns; usually one- or two storied cottages in long rows, perhaps with cellars used as dwellings, almost always irregularly built'. Throughout the chapters of this book we use a historically grounded perspective to trace continuities in and changes

Figure 1.3: 'Close, No. 118 High Street', by Thomas Annan

Source: www.gla.ac.uk/myglasgow/library/files/special/exhibitions/month/Mar2006.thml

of urban informality over time in different geopolitical settings. In particular, we discuss the evolution of debates around informality further in Chapter 2.

Irregular building and inadequate housing conditions remain a key feature of informal neighbourhoods across the globe, an issue that we discuss in Chapter 3, on 'living informally'. Addressing irregularity and inadequate conditions in informal neighbourhoods represents a key challenge for people involved in the governance and planning of cities globally. This challenge is recognized by the United Nations Sustainable Development Goals, which include as one of their core targets the aim to reduce the proportion of people living in informal neighbourhoods and to improve the lives of people who live informally (as part of Goal 11, 'Make cities and human settlements inclusive, safe, resilient and sustainable', which is discussed further in the next section).

Box 1.1: A note on the term 'global South'

Here we want to briefly consider the idea of the 'global South' and what we understand it to mean, as it is a key term in this book. The 'global South' is often used to refer to countries defined by the World Bank as being low- and middle-income, which were sometimes referred to as 'developing' or 'third world' countries in earlier development discourses. They are generally located in the Southern hemisphere, primarily in Africa, Asia and Latin America. The term is sometimes used to denote countries with common characteristics of economic poverty, which can be understood as the result of a dependent economy based on the production of export commodities and colonial heritage, but also geopolitical power relations.

However, 'global South' is a contested term. It has been critiqued as simplistic, reductionist and divisive (Potter et al, 2008), as well as geographically loose: for example, Australasia is geographically in the global South, but is counted as part of the North, while China is sometimes included in the 'South' even though it is in the northern hemisphere and has experienced rapid economic development. Nevertheless, despite these inadequacies, the terminology is helpful in capturing both the challenges of economic poverty which still exist in many countries, and their historical disadvantage as a result of colonialism (Potter et al, 2008: 32). In this sense, it is a 'signifier of structural inequalities', expressive of global power hierarchies, but also of the possibilities for resisting these (Sud and Sánchez-Ancochea, 2022: 1137). This potential for resistance is captured in recent theoretical debates on postcolonial and Southern urban theory, discussed further in Chapter 8.

Most saliently, the term 'global South' risks homogenizing diverse areas and regions, as it flattens the richly varied contexts found within its territorial scope. In this book, while we attempt to draw on a wide variety of empirical and theoretical examples, we have inevitably had to sacrifice empirical richness in some places, partly due to our own regional areas of research focus, which are primarily in Latin America (although both of us have also conducted research in other contexts, including African, Asian and European countries). In the different chapters we draw on research and other sources from diverse contexts, and also from conversations with expert practitioners from specific regions, in order to broaden the book's geographical and intellectual scope.

Urban informality also refers to economic practices by unregistered enterprises or to employment configurations that lack legal and social protection (as is often the case for self-employed street vendors). Such informal economic practices form a major part of the global economy. According to the International Labour Organization (ILO, 2019), more than 60 per cent of the world's working population engage in informal economic activities, with 93 per cent of such activities occurring in the global South. In India alone, informal work counts for 90 per cent of employment (Chen and Vanek, 2013). The informal economy makes a significant contribution to gross domestic product (GDP) in many countries, particularly in the global South where it often represents more than 50 per cent of GDP (see Figure 1.4).

Informal economic practices are not confined to the global South but also appear to be on the rise in the global North. In North America, approximately 9 per cent of GDP is accounted for by activities in the informal economy (Chen and Vanek, 2013). The rise of the so-called 'gig economy' has in recent years led to an additional increase in informal employment in both the global North and South, as companies hire independent self-employed workers often without offering workplace protections such as sick pay. In the UK alone, it is estimated that the proportion of workers employed in the gig economy almost doubled from an estimated 2.8 million people in 2016 to 4.7 million people in 2019. Informal economic practices can also be observed in irregularities by companies who seek to avoid paying taxes to the government of the jurisdiction in which the owner should be a taxpayer. We explore these issues further in Chapter 4, on 'working informally'.

Informality also takes place within and is shaped by the realm of politics and governance. This may occur through the use of *Vitamin B* or *pulling strings* to secure positions of power or personal favours by political authorities – practices often associated with corruption or clientelism (concepts explored throughout this book and particularly in Chapter 5, 'Governing Informally'). Meanwhile, informality does not simply appear out of nowhere but is often the result of politics. States may deliberately declare certain things (for example, types of housing, modes of infrastructure and service delivery) or practices (for example, patterns of production, trade or employment) as legal, illegal, irregular, or indeed informal. Any articulation of urban informality must therefore be considered inherently political.

Building on these insights, our book develops an agenda for studying urban informality that is based upon the following arguments. First, informality affects us all in direct and indirect ways. Second, an urban informality lens helps to make sense of patterns of inequality, poverty and exclusion in different cities, peri-urban areas and places affected by urbanization. Third, moving beyond North/South binaries, our book frames urban informality as a global issue characterized by a series of interrelated characteristics, which we define here as living, working and governing informally. Each of these characteristics must be understood and addressed in a context-specific way. This can only be achieved by deploying a transdisciplinary lens, and to make sense of informality in its complexity this book draws on insights from different disciplines, particularly from social science and the humanities. Fourth, engagement with academic representations is insufficient to make sense of informality. Instead, there is a need to engage with more diverse representations, experiences and bodies of knowledge (see Box 1.2). For this purpose, we draw on fiction, film, poetry, photography, interviews and other media, alongside current theoretical and policy debates, in order to bring in diverse voices and perspectives from social movements, non-government organizations (NGOs) and, of course, people living informally and working in the informal economy (such as the testimonies at the start of each chapter, drawn from our own research). We explore the issue of representations further in the penultimate section of this chapter.

Figure 1.4: Regional dimensions of informal employment (percentage of informal employment in total employment)

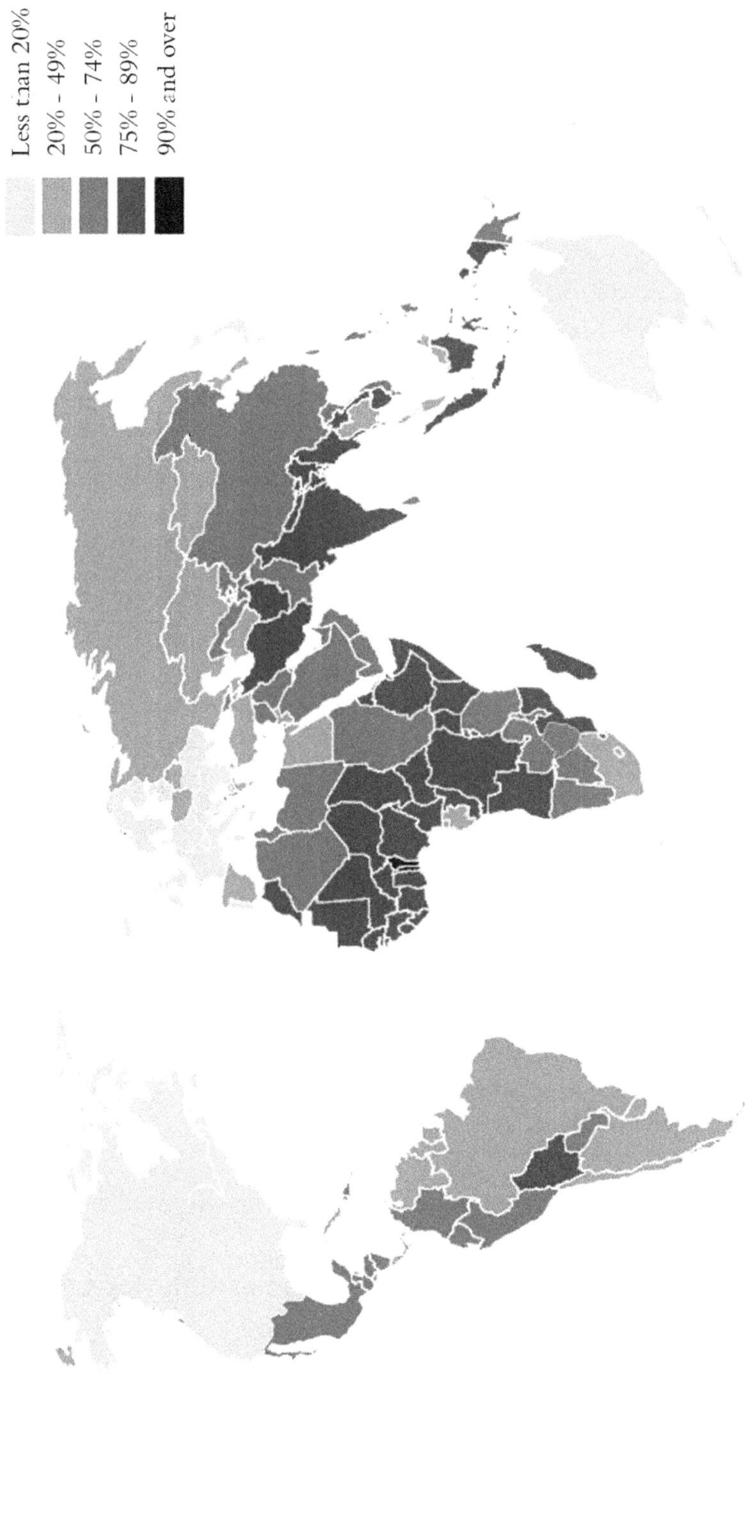

Source: ILO (2019)

Box 1.2: 'Illegal' by Patrick Magebhula Hunsley (1958–2014)

By now, you have already learned a bit about informality from an academic and policy perspective. Here, we would like you to expand your understanding by reading a poem written by someone who lived and worked informally. When reading this, think about the following questions: What does this representation tell us about informality? How does it differ from other representations?

The rent is too high
So I move to build my own shack.
'It is illegal' they say.

The house they planned and built for my parents is too small
So I move and build my own house.
'It is illegal' they say.

Violence destroyed our homes
We flee and end up on no man's land.
'It is illegal' they say.

We are not employed.
So we make ways and means to provide for ourselves.
'It's illegal' they say.

They sell vodka. We sell gaveen.
They sell Heineken. We sell Jubas.
They have bars. We have shebeens.
They have their supermarkets. We have our spaza shops.
They build casinos. We have our own gambling dens.
'It's illegal' they say.

Their methods of survival are correct, honest and proper.
Ours are not. That's what they tell us anyway.
They follow us with dogs and with bulldozers
To sniff out our Permissions to Occupy and to demolish
our shacks.
If we bribe them they let us sell our gaveen and our dagga
Then they chase us and shoot us for cars they say we stole.
But when they have caught us they take bribes
And sell the cars for themselves.
'It's legal' they say.

They promise jobs, houses and education
But in the end we get evictions, threats and corruption.

> So I guess we settle for the right to survive.
> Since we cannot ever meet their standards
>
> We set our own.
> They lock us up.
> 'You are illegal' they say.[2]

Throughout this book we will point you towards a multiplicity of alternative representations of informality within and beyond academia. We hope that this will provide you with a more nuanced understanding about this phenomenon that ultimately affects us all.

Individually, these different arguments are perhaps not novel – they have been elaborated in different and disparate academic, policy and alternative formats – but by bringing them together in one book we hope to provide readers with a comprehensive and accessible overview of urban informality. We introduce these different arguments next, and elaborate them in further detail in the chapters of this book. In the remaining two sections of this chapter, we present the framework we use to make sense of informality's different dimensions, unpacking further the categories already introduced, and explore how the phenomenon has been represented in different ways, in order to contextualize our approach.

Approaching the multiple and interrelated dimensions of informality

Since urban informality was first observed, the question of how to understand it – often as the basis for responding to it – has occupied urban researchers, policy makers and practitioners. While we discuss these debates in detail in Chapter 2, here we briefly recap on how those concerned with informality have attempted to categorize it, in order to introduce our approach in this book. Initial mid-20th-century notions of informality as a problem gave way to its subsequent reframing as a solution. Divergent schools of thought on informality have been identified, including dualist, where informality is equated with marginal economic activities distinct from modern capitalism; legalist, which sees informality as practices excluded from the modern economy due to over-regulation; and structuralist, whereby informality includes subordinated economic activities which are exploitatively connected to the formal capitalist economy, such as subcontracting. While these conceptualizations remain influential, existing debates often focus on informal sectors (for example, housing or labour markets), informal settings (places where certain groups secure livelihoods or commodities) or informal outcomes (for example, practices which are determined illegal) (Banks et al, 2020: 223).

Banks et al (2020: 223) propose a concepualisation of informality underpinned by political economy, suggesting that seeing urban informality as a 'site of critical analysis' allows a better understanding of 'how resources are distributed and power secured and consolidated' in urban settings, across multiple scales and involving diverse actors, within and outside the state. In other words, paying attention to what is labelled informal, and how the idea of urban informality is deployed in a given context, can shed light on urban inequalities and resource distribution. They highlight three domains which encompass most informal activity, and which can be used as a way to organize our thinking and understanding of informality: spatial, economic and political. While these are heuristic categories, meaning they are helpful for analytical purposes, they do not always neatly map onto reality, an issue which we explore further in this section. Nevertheless, we suggest this approach is useful for making sense of this growing field of study, and the complex phenomena which it attempts to capture. Informed by this approach, we have structured the chapters in this book around three dimensions of urban informality – living, working and governing informally. In doing so, we build on Banks et al's (2020) categories of spatial, economic and political articulations of urban informality, deploying the terms living, working and governing to highlight the agency of people in shaping and experiencing these different yet interrelated spheres of informality. In the following sections we explain briefly what we mean by each of these categories.

Living informally

Living informally refers to practices and processes 'associated with informal housing and settlements involving a combination of informal land acquisition, self-help construction, and incremental service provision' (Lombard and Meth, 2016: 159). Living informally is often associated with informal neighbourhoods or 'slums', a problematic term we explore in Chapter 2. A commonly used definition of informal neighbourhoods is that of UN-Habitat, which highlights inadequate conditions of housing and/or basic services, specifically relating to five characteristics:

- inadequate access to safe water;
- inadequate access to sanitation and infrastructure;
- poor structural quality of housing;
- overcrowding; and
- insecure residential status.

This definition has generated critical debate, an issue further explored in Chapter 3. Nevertheless, such definitions can be helpful in identifying key elements and processes relating to how people live informally. In particular, these refer to land, housing and services, normally as part of the search for adequate shelter, and often (although not exclusively) on behalf of low-income communities.

Living informally has been the subject of much academic and policy-focused attention. For example, the Sustainable Development Goals include provision for different elements associated with living informally, such as clean water and sanitation, and Goal 11 ('Make cities and human settlements inclusive, safe, resilient and sustainable') explicitly addresses the issue through target 11.1: 'By 2030, ensure access for all to adequate, safe and affordable housing and basic services and upgrade slums'.[3] This ambitious aim goes beyond the core target 7.D of the Millennium Development Goals, which was to '[a]chieve, by 2020, a significant improvement in the lives of at least 100 million slum dwellers'.[4] In fact, this target was surpassed, as between 2000 and 2014, more than 320 million informal neighbourhood residents improved their living conditions, gaining access to 'either improved water, improved sanitation, durable housing or less crowded housing conditions' (UN, 2015: 60). During the same period, the proportion of urban residents in the global South living in informal neighbourhoods dropped from around 39 per cent to nearly 30 per cent. Nevertheless, despite these positive indicators, in this period the *overall number* of people living in informal neighbourhoods increased from 792 million to over 880 million people, in the context of wider population growth (UN, 2015).

While there are notorious difficulties in gathering reliable data on informal urban development (as with other forms of urban informality), it seems incontestable that '[i]nformal housing is the dominant mode of settlement' in many countries in the global South (Lombard and Meth, 2016: 159). Certainly, these figures suggest the continued need to understand how people live informally and what factors contribute to this phenomenon. In Chapter 3, which looks at informality as a way of living in the city, we discuss these issues in further detail; and in Chapter 6, we explore different responses to living informally.

Working informally

Working informally is commonly associated with the 'urban informal economy' in cities. This term is used to encompass both informal enterprises, such as street vending or taxi driving, and informal employment practices, which may occur in the formal as much as the informal sector (Chen and Vanek, 2013). Additionally, it often describes activities ranging from legal (such as cash-in-hand labour, which contributes to GDP but is unreported) to semi-legal or illegal economic practices, such as hustling, smuggling and so on (although our focus here is not primarily on criminal activities). Similar to living informally, working informally has historically been equated with the 'survival' activities of informal neighbourhood dwellers and rural–urban migrants (Moser, 1978). More recently, it has been recognized that it is not a specific sector of economic activity, but rather forms part of a continuum within the wider economic system: in other words, there exist strong and extensive linkages between the formal and informal economy, and it is questionable as to whether one could exist without the other. These links may be constituted by the trade of goods, raw materials, tools and equipment, services, and acquisitions of skills and know-how (Chen, 2012), among other things.

As Lombard and Meth (2016) suggest, the significance of the informal economy globally cannot be overstated. It is estimated that informal employment accounts for more than half of all non-agricultural work in countries in the global South (Vanek et al, 2014), and in some regions it accounts for the majority of employment. Experiences of working informally are highly diverse, and shaped by different contextual factors. Although conditions are often poor, particularly due to lack of social protection, employee benefits and adequate working environment, informal working also offers an opportunity for many to exist and sometimes to thrive in the money-driven urban economy. At the same time, experiences of the informal sector are also different depending on group characteristics, and the highly gendered nature of the sector has been recognized, with women often more likely to work informally as caregivers, in home-based economic activity or in unpaid work (Fox and Goodfellow, 2016: 125). Since at least the 1980s, the existence of informal activities in 'advanced economies' has been identified. For example, a report on the informal economy in the UK found that many small-scale entrepreneurs now bypass the formal process of company registration, due to the high entry threshold (Copisarow and Barbour, 2004). We unpack the phenomenon of working informally, and its articulation in different parts of the world, further in Chapter 4. Similar to living informally, there exist a variety of responses to working informally. We reflect on those in Chapter 7.

Governing informally

Finally, governing informally is defined here primarily in contrast to formal politics, in other words 'the operation and constitutional systems of government' (Painter and Jeffrey, 2009: 7). Governing informally may refer to political practices in everyday social interactions (forming alliances, exercising power, advancing specific goals or developing influence), which most of us engage in, one way or the other (Lombard and Meth, 2016). The distinction between formal and informal politics is very slippery, and both are influential in shaping everyday urban life. We follow other theorists who recognize clear ties between informality and the state. State power shapes informality (in its multiple dimensions) and vice versa (AlSayyad, 2004; Roy, 2009; Yiftachel, 2009). For example, in many urban contexts, including those where informality is prevalent, the state plays a fundamental role in setting the context for economic or housing activity, in terms of establishing or enforcing regulatory frameworks, providing infrastructure and facilitating investment. Meanwhile, often responding to context-specific constraints or opportunities, those involved in producing and operating within informality may engage with or in informal governing practices such as corruption, clientelism, patronage and paternalism. In many cases, the role of the state is a determining one, via enforcement or suspension of norms and regulations, for example, where state incapacity or unwillingness to enforce regulation leads to more tolerant attitudes to informal processes. In other words, 'informality is not the chaos that *precedes* order (like some kind of Hobbesian state of nature), but the situation that results from deliberate *suspension* of order' (Collord et al, 2021: 12, emphasis in original).

Governing informally is perhaps the least explored dimension of informality, but this does not diminish its significance. Institutional and social elements of urban informality, which relate to this political dimension, tend to have been overlooked by spatial and economic disciplines. Nevertheless, political scientists in the United States have long observed how elites employ informal relations within the formal functioning of the state to maximize their own benefit (Mills, 1956; see also Banks et al, 2020). In the global South, governing informally is often so widespread as to be considered everyday. But the differentiated outcomes of such processes, for example, in terms of clientelist distribution of benefits among specific households in a given settlement (Banks, 2016a), suggest the need to interrogate such informal practices alongside others, and for a stronger conceptualization of governing informally more generally. We explore this further in Chapter 5.

A word of caution about categories

While we present these categories as a framework to help us understand the different dimensions of urban informality, we do so with several caveats. First, these categories do not exist in isolation from each other. While they may be a useful analytical device, which we employ to structure our approach in this book, in reality we need to appreciate their interconnectedness and interdependence. Although we may be able to use such categories to organize debates on informality, and to identify what is going on in a specific urban context, it is also true that 'without recognising interconnections within and between these domains, we run the risk of overlooking vital phenomena, processes, and interactions' (Banks et al, 2020: 224). Second, we suggest that starting from a focus on these three domains enables looking within but also across them, in order to attain 'a more complex and nuanced view of the social and political relationships through which these [informal processes] function' (Banks et al, 2020: 233). Third, these categories relate to formal as well as informal practices, suggesting the co-existence of informality and formality, as argued earlier. Finally, it is worth noting that although informality has been studied for at least seven decades, in the last decade or so, new developments have been observed, including suggestions that different forms of informality are on the rise, and are increasingly prevalent in the global North as well as the global South, necessitating new and innovative conceptualizations and responses. We take these considerations into account in the chapters that follow, and in Chapter 8 in particular, we focus on emerging trends and alternative understandings of and responses to informality.

Analysing responses to informality

In addition to exploring articulations of urban informality, a core aim of this book is to critically analyse how different actors respond to this phenomenon, for example, via policy and planning interventions, donor campaigns, collective action or everyday coping strategies. In Chapters 6 and 7, we reflect on how responses to informality have changed over time and vary from context to context. We broadly distinguish between top-down (or state-driven) and bottom-up (or citizen-led) interventions, while paying close attention to the interrelations between such responses. As we explain in further detail in what follows, such a relational perspective is important as top-down and bottom-up interventions hardly ever exist in isolation; instead, they often overlap, co-exist, intersect or stand in tension with each other.

In our discussion on responses to living and working informally in Chapters 6 and 7, we critically reflect on the roles of and relationships between multiple actor groups in addressing urban informality, including national and local governments, international agencies and donors, private sector and civil society actors, and ordinary people who live and work informally. National governments tend to define and finance policies for land use and housing as well as economic policies that directly or indirectly address the issue of informality. National governments allocate resources to and define the responsibilities of local governments; they may also establish regulatory requirements for civil society organisations such as NGOs or community-based organizations (CBOs). At the international level, national governments come together in forums organized by international agencies such as UN-Habitat to collaboratively define global urban development commitments such as the New Urban Agenda (United Nations, 2017), which increasingly recognize the importance of addressing informality. In most urban settings, it is however local governments that play a key role in practically addressing informality as they tend to be responsible for provision of infrastructure and services, land use and public space regulation, and urban planning (Satterthwaite and Mitlin, 2013). Multilateral and bilateral agencies may issue loans and grants and provide assistance and support to governments and private enterprises around specific programmes that address informality. Civil society organizations such as NGOs, CBOs, citizen-led groups and social movements are also increasingly playing a key role in providing innovative responses to informality, supporting and sometimes helping to scale up existing 'popular' activities initiated by residents who live and work informally (Streule et al, 2020).

While there are numerous approaches to addressing informality, the distinction between top-down and bottom-up responses can be helpful in identifying the actors involved and the nature of processes. According to Devkar et al (2019: 332), top-down responses are those 'provided by the government or government agencies, which are usually characterised by central planning and implementation'. In contrast, bottom-up responses are usually carried out by 'non-government organisations (NGOs) and CBOs or other small-scale providers, which are characterised by a higher degree of decentralised planning and implementation' (Devkar et al, 2019: 332). While these definitions provide a useful starting point to distinguish between different types of responses and actor groups associated with them, we consider this distinction to be insufficient, especially in a contemporary context where many interventions involve some degree of cooperation between actors, including international agencies, government, private sector and civil society (Watson, 2016). As such, we argue that the main difference between the two approaches – top-down and bottom-up – relates to who *initiates* a response and defines roles and responsibilities for those involved in implementation. Top-down interventions tend to be initiated by international agencies, national and/or local governments who establish policies, regulations, rules and procedures that other actor groups should follow. In contrast, bottom-up approaches are usually initiated locally by citizen-led groups, NGOs and/or social movements, but often seek to influence and change the behaviour of other actor groups, including governments, operating at higher levels. In our discussion of responses, we therefore pay close attention to the relationship between top-down and bottom-up approaches, and to how each approach itself may shift over time and be articulated differently in distinct geopolitical contexts.

To better understand shifts towards more cooperative multi-actor responses to informality, it is important to reflect on changes in urban policy and planning over the last decades, often occurring in the context of democratization and neoliberalization. Until the 1970s urban government was mainly managed by national governments, with involvement of local authorities in urban administration limited to land use planning, tax collection and the delivery of some services (Freire and Stren, 2001). As a result of decentralization and devolution reforms occurring in many countries across the world throughout the 1980s and 1990s (Beard et al, 2008), local governments became more influential in urban management, responsible for the effective and efficient provision of services (Freire and Stren, 2001). Since the 1990s, governments have also been expected to facilitate good urban governance. This role requires them to be more accountable and transparent, more adroit at contributing to the transformation of diverse forms of local democracy, more willing to recognize the complexity of new forms of citizenship, and more capable of proactively involving different public, private and civil society actors (Pierre, 1999). Considering shifts from government to urban governance, top-down responses to informality are understood here as initiated and administered by governments, but may involve an array of other actors operating at different scales – be that international, national or local.

In the meantime, governments often do not give enough attention to informality, or continue to introduce responses – such as criminalization or eviction – that have negative consequences for those who live and work informally, leading them to engage in their own struggles 'for housing, services, inclusion and entitlements ... usually un-assisted' (Satterthwaite and Mitlin, 2013: 131). While implicitly a reaction to inappropriate top-down responses, such struggles may occur outside the realm of government, as they often start with a focus on local needs, but may ultimately seek to 'shift politicians, political parties, civil servants, state agencies and political institutions with their norms, values and ways of behaving' in such a way that local demands, needs and priorities are considered (Satterthwaite and Mitlin, 2013: 132). It is this type of response that we define here as bottom-up; beginning at the grassroots, in places such as informal neighbourhoods or street markets, while frequently seeking to achieve change at higher levels. Making sense of different responses and articulations of urban informality requires critically engaging with different sources of knowledge that seek to represent this phenomenon, an issue we discuss in further detail in the next section.

Engaging with representations of informality

Multiple and diverse representations of informality have accompanied its existence at least since Victorian accounts of 'slums', up to the present day, in a variety of different locations and contexts. This gives rise to questions such as: How do we know what we know about informality? How does existing knowledge frame informality as a phenomenon and related responses? Is a single concept able to adequately account for such diversity? These are especially pertinent given the association of illegality with informal living and working, meaning that gaps in (formal, official) knowledge about these processes and places are often accompanied by an interest in remaining 'invisible', although this is highly context-dependent. Different realms of knowledge production have attempted to capture these issues in diverse approaches to representing informality, which we introduce briefly here. We explore these in more detail in subsequent chapters.

Popular and artistic accounts have long been fascinated with the horrors of the slum. From Victorian-era novels by Charles Dickens and Elizabeth Gaskell, motivated by the desire for social reform in industrializing British cities, to Jacob Riis' (1997

[1890]) stirring photography of 'How the Other Half Lives' in American cities (see Figure 1.5), portrayals of informal living have been used to argue for social and political change in urban areas. Accompanying this, a more sensationalist strand of knowledge has condemned such areas. Examples can be found in newspaper stories associating specific areas or populations with increased levels of crime and immoral behaviour, reflecting apparent alarm among the middle classes at the potential for insurrection (past and present) in the context of rapid urbanization, whether in Europe, Latin America, Africa or Asia. What these accounts have in common – whether they lament or condemn informality – is their association of living, working and governing informally with specific people (for example, the urban poor), practices (for example, street vending and corruption) and places (for example, 'slums' or the global South). More recently, fictional accounts have tended to romanticize informality. Films such as *Slumdog Millionaire* (2008), and books such as Gregory Roberts' (2004) *Shantaram*, have been criticized for their stereotyping and voyeuristic approach to people living and working informally. This suggests the need to critically analyse and problematize such forms of knowledge production. As we will see, this is a recurring theme across different spheres of knowing informality.

Academic accounts have similarly struggled with the question of how we know informality, resulting in divergent framings. While social researchers such as Charles Booth (1889) captured 'snapshots' of London's slums with his poverty maps in the 19th century, and writers such as Charles Abrams (1960) outlined the reality of New York's tenements, the bulk of academic writing in this area has been concerned with informality in the context of urbanization in the global South. Reflecting entrenched hierarchies of knowledge production, much of the earlier writing in this field is associated with scholars from the global North, although this is now being rebalanced with work from the global South, intersecting with debates about Southern urban theory (discussed further in Chapter 8). Documenting the growth of *villas*,

Figure 1.5: Room in a tenement, New York

Source: Riis (1997 [1890])

tugurios and *poblaciónes* in Latin America, European and American researchers such as William Mangin (1967), John Turner (1968), Janice Perlman (1976) and Larissa Lomnitz (1977) were apparently among the first to present these issues to the wider academic community. In fact, they often worked alongside and drew on the work of Latin American researchers, whose contributions have been less well-recognized due to the dominance of Anglophone debates (an issue discussed in Chapter 2).

In this arena too, a tension can be detected between heroic and exploitative narratives of informality, with the diagnosis often dependent on the researcher's disciplinary and political orientation, which may be articulated implicitly rather than explicitly. In response, later publications have identified different strains of thought underpinning these debates, for example the dualist, legalist and structuralist approaches mentioned earlier (Rakowski, 1994), which are further discussed in later chapters. More recently, academic debates have interrogated how informality is framed, problematizing the concept and related terminology, particularly the word 'slum', such as Alan Mayne's (2017) book *Slums: The History of a Global Injustice*. Adding to these debates, scholars aligned with 'Southern theory' approaches have suggested alternative conceptualizations such as '*jugaad*' (Chatteraj, 2018) and 'popular economy' (Gago, 2018). Such accounts often stem from critiques of, or dissatisfaction with, policy responses. We discuss them further in Chapter 8.

Policy, and related to this, practice-based accounts of informality are often linked to and reflect the spectrum of possible government responses to informality, from eviction to tolerance to support. While a generalized punitive response detected in 1950s Latin America has been superseded by more supportive and progressive approaches, eviction and/or displacement (usually entailing loss of livelihood) is still a real concern for many people living and working informally, across both the global South and North. Underpinning many policy responses has been a more generalized concern with the morality of (urban) poverty. This was overt in the Victorian and industrial era, seen for example in social reformist endeavours of middle- or upper-class activists such as Octavia Hill in London and Jane Addams in Chicago (Hall, 2002). In more recent decades supportive responses such as conditional cash transfers in Brazil and Mexico, which have had a significant effect on populations living and working informally, have nevertheless reproduced ideas that informality and poverty need to be solved or corrected through actions on the behaviour of those living in these conditions. This is despite involvement in policy responses from a wider and more diverse group of actors, including NGOs, donors, international agencies and private corporations, reflecting the shift from government to governance in many urban contexts worldwide. However, despite the long engagement of urban policy and (planning) practitioners with informal processes and phenomena, knowledge production tends to be partial and politicized, often serving the policy goals of those gathering data. This reiterates the need to understand informality from the view of those most intimately engaged in it. We discuss responses further in Chapters 6 and 7.

As a counterpoint to policy-based accounts, *community-focused accounts* of informality are necessary for a full understanding of these issues, while bearing in mind critical debates which problematize community and particularly the idea that communities are homogeneous (for example, Chambers, 1995). This is especially relevant in contexts where local authorities do not have the capacity or political will to engage adequately with people living and working informally, or where problematic policy responses such as eviction prevail. Methods of gathering data often rely on community knowledge and skills, although some organizations (for example, Shack/Slum Dwellers International) are now training community researchers in geographic information system techniques to record information on population and geographic layout about their own settlements. As well as providing information to the community about informal living and working conditions, this form of knowledge production may also bolster the capacity and autonomy of local communities, for example, by giving them a basis from which to negotiate with local authority and other actors. It should be balanced against the interests of those who live and work informally to remain invisible, fearing losing their livelihood or shelter, or heavy financial burdens via tax, service payments or bribery. Some of these issues are discussed in later chapters, particularly Chapters 3, 4 and 8. Paradoxically, this desire for invisibility may often be more acute in the global North, where regulatory enforcement is often (although not always) stronger.

As well as introducing different approaches to representing informality, the discussion here highlights the need to move beyond different geographical locations, spheres or silos of knowledge production – whether popular, academic, policy or community-focused – to take a global focus which transcends binary thinking in both geographical and conceptual terms. This does not mean jettisoning the categories of South and North or informal and formal, but rather exploring how phenomena and experiences across different contexts may resonate, providing a basis for shared learning or revealing similarities, while acknowledging contextual specificities. It also suggests going beyond disciplinary divisions to forge a global and interdisciplinary understanding of informality, which critically engages with diverse representations.

Using this book and chapter summary

The book provides an introductory overview to urban informality, with a focus on the evolution of this concept and phenomenon, its main characteristics, and related responses. Because of this, it is likely to be particularly helpful to students of these issues (at postgraduate or advanced undergraduate level), as well as researchers and practitioners. As previously discussed, each chapter engages with conventional academic texts from different disciplinary orientations in order to examine historic and current theoretical and policy debates, but also go beyond academic accounts through the inclusion of fiction, poetry, photography, interviews and other media, bringing in diverse voices and perspectives from social movements, NGOs, and people living and working informally. While we encourage readers to engage with the full text, some might prefer to explore specific thematic chapters as they align more with their interests. To guide the reader, we provide a brief overview of chapter contents here.

Chapter 2 offers an account of understandings of informality from the first observations about the informal sector and settlements to informality as an everyday component of life. We start with a brief contextualization relating to the longer history of informality, focusing on debates around the colonial cultures of planning, as well as fears about 'slums' in the context of industrialization in the global North. We then provide an overview of conceptual and policy debates on informality over the last 50 years, reflecting on ideas such as self-help housing, marginality and legalization. We also look at more recent and current debates and controversies, around the 'return of the slum' and the importance of language, postcolonial and Southern theory, and informality as practice.

Chapters 3 to 5 focus on the core features and characteristics of the three core components – living, working, governing – of urban informality. Chapter 3 looks at living informally, providing an overview of definitions and meanings related to urban informal neighbourhoods, as well as their form, evolution and causal factors. Emphasizing three core elements of informal neighbourhoods, namely land, housing and basic services, the chapter pays particular attention to land acquisition, housing development and service provision. It also examines more recent trends such as the emergence of informal tenement housing, innovations in service provision in African cities, elite and middle-class informal housing in Asia, Latin America and the Middle East and informal housing developments in the United Kingdom and other global Northern contexts.

Chapter 4 focuses on working informally, tracing historical shifts from an initial focus on the informal sector towards more broader understandings around informal employment and the informal economy. It discusses the contribution of the informal economy towards economic growth within cities of the global South, in terms of GDP, employment, income generation and other factors related to socio-economic development. The focus opens out from the home and individual business, to the street level and street markets, to the global economy, to explore how debates evolved but also to allow us to establish connections with living informally. Attention is paid towards contemporary articulations of the informal economy, including the gig economy, platform urbanism and digital labour in both global South and North.

Chapter 5 explores governing informally, which has received less explicit attention within the urban informality literature than living and working informally, despite being intimately linked to both. The chapter starts with tracing the conceptual roots of governing informally in the political sciences literature. It discusses why governing informally is prevalent particularly (though not exclusively) in global Southern contexts affected by (post)colonial development and rapid urbanization. The chapter then explores different articulations of governing informally, and its relations with living and working informally, broadly distinguishing between informal politics initiated by state and elite actors and by ordinary people who live and work informally.

Having established what is meant by living, working and governing informally, Chapters 6 and 7 explore top-down, or state-led, and bottom-up, or citizen-led, responses to urban informality, as well as approaches that combine elements of both. Focusing on living informally, Chapter 6 explores different approaches to providing or improving access to land, housing and services in contexts characterized by informal provision. The discussion distinguishes between responses to living informally as undertaken by international agencies, state actors and civil society organizations.

Chapter 7 focuses on responses to working informally. It begins with a discussion on the implications of dualist, legalist, structuralist and voluntarist conceptual approaches for related responses. Attention is then paid to responses such as eviction and revanchism that treat working informally as a problem, before focusing in closer detail on top-down, bottom-up and co-productive interventions that seek to embrace working informally in efforts to create more just, inclusive and sustainable cities.

In Chapter 8 we focus on emerging trends and alternative understandings of and responses to informality. We explore conceptual alternatives to informality, including popular urbanization, collective life and solidarity economies. We also pay attention towards how informality is represented increasingly as a global, and not just as a Southern, phenomenon, something that is evident for example in the New Urban Agenda. We introduce emerging avenues for researching informality, offering a brief overview on ethical principles of conducting research on informality as well as innovative methodologies.

In the final chapter, we summarize the previous chapters and sections, and explore 'what next', in theoretical, empirical and practical terms.

At the end of each chapter, we provide a set of additional resources for readers to draw on if they wish to explore the topic further. These include recommended readings, which are drawn on in the chapter; some self-guided exercises that readers may wish to undertake to deepen their understanding of the issues discussed; and a set of alternative representations which go beyond academic texts, allowing readers to consider other ways in which informality is understood and portrayed.

Recommended reading

- AlSayyad, N. (2004) 'Urban informality as a "new" way of life', in A. Roy and N. AlSayyad (eds) *Urban Informality: Transnational Perspectives from the Middle East, Latin America, and South Asia*, New York: Lexington Books, pp 7–30.
- Banks, N., Lombard, M. and Mitlin, D. (2020) 'Urban informality as a site of critical analysis', *The Journal of Development Studies*, 56(2): 223–38.
- Mayne, A. (2017) *Slums: The History of a Global Injustice*, London: Reaktion Books.

EXERCISES

- We recommend you look at *The Global Encyclopedia of Informality*, a two-volume open access book (and associated website: https://www.in-formality.com/wiki/index.php?title=Global_Informality_Project) edited by Alena Ledeneva (2018a; 2018b) that provides an explanation of informal practices from across the world. You may want to choose an example from the country or region in which you were born or where you are based currently. Explain to what extent, how and why this entry represents an example of urban informality, and whether it contains characteristics of living, working and/or governing informally. When doing this, you may want to reflect on the introductory definitions provided in this chapter.

- Have a look at the following list of alternative representations. This is really just an initial list of possible resources. Reflecting on your reading of this chapter, you could begin and create

> your own list of alternative representations. You may want to think about films, novels, blogs, podcast series and other material you have engaged with in the past that captures the notion of informality. When revisiting this material, please note down answers to the following questions that you might like to consider when aiming to make sense of different representations of informality: Who wrote this? From what perspective and place? How did they gather information/knowledge? Who, what or where is being represented? How might this information be used for different purposes (for example, commercial, activism or political)?

Alternative representations

- A vivid and absorbing fictional representation of living, working and governing informality is Rohinton Mistry's 1995 novel *A Fine Balance*, set in India in the 1970s and 1980s.
- For different representations of informality in film, you might want to watch movies such as *City of God* (2002), *City of Joy* (1992), *Metro Manila* (2013), *Nairobi Half Life* (2012), *Slumdog Millionaire* (2008) or *Tsotsi* (2005).
- If you want to learn more about the young woman – whose testimony opened this chapter – and other young people who live and work informally and experience informal governance in the city of El Alto, Bolivia, we recommend you watch the documentary film *The Roots Ahead* (https://vimeo.com/797441920?share=copy) produced by Philipp Horn.

2

Understanding Urban Informality

'The people of Bajamar reconstructed land claimed from the sea, the people themselves; we helped to build by filling in with rubbish, with waste. I remember that people used to quarrel over the rubbish cart, or people who had rubbish or building debris would tip it in order to claim land from the sea, starting to fill in and construct streets, and that's how it was built. I remember in Morrocoy a street that was just wasteland and water, and the community filled it in and now it is a paved street. ... It destroyed the social fabric when we heard that people from Bajamar would be relocated to Ciudadela San Antonio, and people around here think the worst of us, they say: "Here come those people from those violent neighbourhoods, they have weapons, they have all sorts of problems." ... Local universities saw us as thieves, our young people were robbers ... our children were the most violent, and they wouldn't accept them.'

Social leader in Ciudadela San Antonio, Buenaventura, Colombia, reflecting on the representation of informal neighbourhoods and their residents during a process of relocation[1]

Urban informality is a slippery concept.[2] Over the last 50 years, it has become increasingly present in academic disciplines interested in urban issues; yet paradoxically, this has made it harder rather than easier to define. One of the most common conceptualizations identifies urban informality with processes and practices which fall outside urban regulatory frameworks. But often, as we have already seen, informal processes may at least interact with, or occur partially within, these frameworks, suggesting this definition is not clear-cut. This definition also accepts the idea of regulatory frameworks as the defining element of informality; but what about places where it precedes these frameworks, or simply does not relate to them? This has led some theorists to question whether the idea of informality is helpful. It is perhaps partly because of this definitional complexity that the field of conceptual debates about urban informality has mushroomed in recent decades, as theorists in urban studies, planning, geography and other disciplines attempt to get to grips with what informality is, and what it is not.

This chapter introduces key theoretical debates and conceptual currents, in order to set the scene for discussions throughout this book. While it discusses diverse conceptualizations of urban informality, it also highlights the definition complexity of this term, and controversies relating to this. The chapter structure shows how debates on urban informality, and specific articulations of living, working and governing informally, have evolved over time. It opens with a brief review of the history of informality debates, exploring the idea's roots in colonial planning practices in the global South as well as in discussions about 'slums' in industrial era cities in the global North. We then give an overview of conceptual (and policy) debates from the mid-20th century, in which informality became a subject of study in its own right, relating to patterns of rapid urbanization in Latin America, Asia and Sub-Saharan Africa. Ideas such as self-help housing, marginality and legalization, alongside concerns about 'slums' which echo earlier debates, again influenced planning policy and practice in this era. Finally, we explore 21st-century debates and controversies, including around 'the return of the slum', informality as practice, postcolonial urban theory and informality in the North.

Origins of urban informality

Despite the fact that urbanization throughout history has been accompanied by the phenomenon of unregulated processes and practices, the term 'urban informality' did not become prevalent until around the turn of the current century. Nevertheless, urban informality is not a new phenomenon, and must be understood in historical context.

Colonial urbanism

In Latin America, understandings of the formal (planned) and informal (unplanned) city have their roots in Spanish colonialism, which lasted from the end of the 15th century until the 19th century. The colonizers not only eradicated almost half of Latin America's Indigenous population but also restructured the region socially and spatially. The colonizers destroyed most pre-colonial cities and, relying on forced labour from Indigenous peoples and Black slaves, constructed new urban centres (Hardoy, 1973). Cities served as administrative centres of the colonies and were inhabited mainly by 'White' Spaniards. Following 15th-century European models of architecture and planning, colonial cities were structured according to a grid model and contained roads and public infrastructure such as sewer networks (Morse, 1978). In contrast, 'non-White' populations such as Indigenous peoples were denied from inhabiting cities and predominantly inhabited the countryside where they engaged in semi-feudal labour (Platt, 1982). In urban settings, Indigenous peoples were confined to the 'unplanned' periphery where they predominantly lived in self-constructed houses and lacked access to roads and public services – features which we today associate with informal neighbourhoods.

Colonial spatial divisions were, for example, evident in early 16th-century La Paz – today's seat of Bolivia's national government. The 'planned'/'formal' city, which was home to wealthier residents predominantly of Spanish descent, was in the urban centre and surrounded by the 'unplanned'/'informal' neighbourhoods of San Sebastian, San Pedro and Santa Barbara that were inhabited predominantly by poorer residents of Indigenous descent (for a more detailed history of these ethno-spatial divisions see Arbona and Kohl, 2004; Horn, 2019). Research on La Paz and other Latin American cities highlights how socio-spatial and ethnic divisions continued as part of urban growth in the post-colonial period, with low-income groups and rural-to-urban Indigenous migrants often living in self-constructed houses in peripheral informal neighbourhoods (Kingman, 2012; Horn, 2019). As Hernández (2017: ix) suggests, in the region, 'the extension of informal development that we see today in most cities ... are a magnified expression of the conditions of urban growth initiated by the Spanish and Portuguese with their segregationist approach to urban planning and design during the colonial period'.

This pattern of racial segregation was repeated in urban colonial settings in Asia and Africa, during later waves of European colonialism between the 18th and 20th centuries. It can be seen for example in the '*cordon sanitaire*' that surrounded the central, White/European area of colonial cities (Home, 2014), separating it from the outer areas or 'townships' to where local populations had been removed (Demissie, 2007). These later processes of colonialism, particularly in Asian and African countries colonized by European powers, were entangled with industrialization in Europe. European powers, especially Britain where the Industrial Revolution started, accumulated wealth on the basis of goods extracted from the colonies, including not only coffee, tobacco and sugar, but also enslaved peoples. This wealth and these goods supported processes of accumulation and industrialization which led to mass urbanization and the emergence of 'slums', another form of early informality.

19th-century slums

The 'slum' emerged in the context of the rapid urbanization of European and North American countries which accompanied industrialization towards the middle and end of the 19th century. Industrial development attracted increasing numbers of workers to urban centres, including those working in newly erected factories but also tradespeople and vendors, such as shoemakers, tailors, carpenters, bakers and fruit and vegetable sellers. The low and often irregular wages earned by the poorest sectors of urban society, who represented a significant proportion of the population, were only sufficient to afford very poor housing, with one or more families inhabiting a single room in privately rented houses, in areas where housing was often tightly packed together (as seen in Figure 2.1). The cause of this situation was a lack of decent housing for the poor in locations close to the sources of casual labour on which they depended (Hall, 2002), namely the centrally located factories and warehouses.

One of the best-known works on 'slums' in the industrial period is Engels' (1969 [1887]) *The Condition of the Working Class in England in 1844*, published in English in 1887, which stressed the spatial nature of urban segregation resulting from the dislocating effects of industrialization and urbanization. This can also be

Figure 2.1: Overcrowded housing in 19th-century London

Source: Blanchard Jerrold and Doré (1872)

seen in Booth's well-known poverty maps of East End London, published as the *Inquiry into the Life and Labour of the People in London from 1886 to 1903*, which characterized different areas according to their residents' living conditions and labour status. The maps depict levels of poverty and wealth street by street using coloured shading: purple denotes a mixed area with 'some comfortable, others poor'; light blue 'poor, 18–21 shillings per week for a moderate family'; dark blue 'very poor, casual ... [c]hronic want' and black the 'lowest class ... [v]icious, semi-criminal'. Other studies such as Mearns' *The Bitter Cry of Outcast London*, a pamphlet published by the Congregational Union in 1883, conveyed similarly shocking descriptions of the physical and moral outrages of London's slums, which included acutely overcrowded and unsanitary living conditions, accompanied by criminal and immoral behaviour as rational responses to the prevailing destitution. Box 2.1 details some of these descriptions.

Such accounts reinforced middle-class understandings of these places as 'plague spots' and 'dens of vice' (Yelling, 1986: 10–11), and the social and environmental decrepitude of slums was viewed by Victorian society as both 'a moral and sanitary problem' (Yelling, 1986: 2). In the leading industrial countries, inquiries into urban poverty were underpinned by fears of social instability stemming from a mistrust of the city and its concentrating effect on poverty (Hall, 2002). These fears are apparent in the work of Jacob Riis, a Danish American journalist, whose photographs of the appalling living conditions in slum tenements of New York in the 1880s, which housed three-fifths of the city's population, caused an outcry on publication. Moreover, they

Box 2.1: 19th-century slums in England

Engels (1969 [1887]: 86) describes the Old Town of Manchester as characterized by 'filth, ruin and uninhabitableness, the defiance of all considerations of cleanliness, ventilation and health'. He describes a working-class area off Long Millgate (near present-day Piccadilly Station):

> Passing along a rough bank, among stakes and washing-lines, one penetrates into this chaos of small one-storied, one-roomed huts, in most of which there is no artificial floor; kitchen, living and sleeping-room all in one. In such a hole, scarcely five feet long by six broad, I found two beds – and such bedsteads and beds! – which, with a staircase and chimney-place, exactly filled the room. In several others I found absolutely nothing, while the door stood open, and the inhabitants leaned against it. Everywhere before the doors refuse and offal; that any sort of pavement lay underneath could not be seen but only felt, here and there, with the feet. This whole collection of cattle-sheds for human beings was surrounded on two sides by houses and a factory, and on the third by the river, and besides the narrow stair up the bank, a narrow doorway alone led out into another almost equally ill-built, ill-kept labyrinth of dwellings. (Engels, 1969 [1887]: 59–60)

Similarly, Mearns describes working-class housing in South and East London:

> Every room in these rotten and reeking tenements houses a family, often two. In one cellar a sanitary inspector reports finding a father, mother, three children and four pigs! In another room a missionary found a man ill with small pox, his wife just recovering from her eighth confinement, and the children running about half naked and covered with dirt. Here are seven people living in one underground kitchen, and a little dead child lying in the same room. Elsewhere is a poor widow, her three children, and a child who had been dead thirteen days. Her husband, who was a cabman, had shortly before committed suicide. Here lives a widow and her six children, including one daughter of 29, another of 21, and a son of 27. Another apartment contains father, mother and six children, two of whom are ill with scarlet fever. ... Where there are beds they are simply heaps of dirty rags, shavings or straw, but for the most part these miserable beings huddle together upon the filthy boards. The tenant of this room is a widow, who herself occupies the only bed, and lets the floor to a married couple for 2s. 6d. per week. In many cases matters are made worse by the unhealthy occupations followed by those who dwell in these habitations. Here you are choked as you enter by the air laden with particles of the superfluous fur pulled from the skins of rabbits, rats, dogs and other animals in their preparation for the furrier. Here the smell of paste and of drying match-boxes, mingling with other sickly odours, overpowers you; or it may be the fragrance of stale fish or vegetables, not sold on the previous day, and kept in the room overnight. Even when it is possible to do so the people seldom open their windows, but if they did it is questionable whether much would be gained, for the external air is scarcely less heavily charged with poison than the atmosphere within. (Mearns, 1969 [1883]: 13–15)

were seen as evidence that '[t]he sea of a mighty population, held in galling fetters, heaves uneasily in the tenements' (Riis, 1997 [1890]: 296). You can see one of these photos in Chapter 1 (Figure 1.5).

The term 'slum', first used to describe marginalized places (and the people who live in them) in the context of industrial urbanization, has been critiqued by many (Mayne, 2017: 15). We explore these critiques further in this chapter, given its current resurgence in the context of late urbanization; yet as Hall (2002) points out, these accounts of 'the city of dreadful night' also highlighted the poverty and lack of housing for the poor which had created this situation, emphasizing the need for action. 'Slum' in this setting can thus be seen as a political rather than a scientific term, containing 'a condemnation of existing conditions and, implicitly at least, a call for action' (Yelling, 1986: 1), even while reflecting a deterministic view of the urban poor based on their living conditions and location. Indeed, such studies gave rise to investigations influencing subsequent policies for housing regulation and improvement, in some cases entailing slum clearance, which sought to address the unprecedented need for decent housing. Such policies were nevertheless limited in their effectiveness as they often displaced poor populations (Hall, 2002). These processes resonate with later attempts to understand and address urban informality in the global South, to which we now turn.

Conceptual and policy debates in the 20th century
Rapid urbanization and fears about 'slums'

Echoes of these accounts of 'slums' can be found in debates on urbanization and its effects in Latin America in the mid-20th century, at the start of the period of 'late urbanization' identified by Fox and Goodfellow (2021).[3] For the first half of the 20th century in many Latin American cities, private renting was the dominant tenure for low-waged households needing cheap and centrally located housing, often in dilapidated, formerly elite residences converted into tenements for multi-household occupancy (Ward, 1990). The rapid urbanization that occurred in the region from the 1950s onwards was linked to industrialization and mass rural–urban migration, as rural workers saw the possibility of improving their livelihoods and living conditions in industrializing urban centres. The increase in urban populations, accompanied by a lack of adequate affordable public or private housing, led to the development of informal neighbourhoods in central areas, and increasingly at the edges of cities where land was more readily available. For example, writing on Lima, Peru, Matos Mar (1966) highlights how rural-to-urban migrants, often of Indigenous descent, started to establish their own informal neighbourhoods – referred to as *barriadas* – on the desert hills at the periphery of the city.

The 'urban explosion' that this period of urbanization entailed saw the increase, between the 1950s and 1985, of the global South's urban population from 285 million to 1.2 billion, or from 16 per cent to 30 per cent of the total population (Kasarda and Crenshaw, 1991: 467). Given the 'ever-growing horde' of people 'swarming' and 'pouring' into cities (Abrams, 1964: 2–3), increasing housing demand in contexts where cheap, well-located residential options were scarce, people took matters into their own hands, occupying or 'squatting' on vacant,

Figure 2.2: *Barriada* near Pachacamac, Lima, Peru in 1970

Source: Billie Jean Isbell Andean Collection, #6710. Division of Rare and Manuscript Collections, Cornell University Library

unserviced land in order to build their own housing informally, with services often initially provided through 'pirating' illegal connections to electricity and water networks (see Figure 2.2; for a fuller outline of this process, see Chapter 3). These early informal neighbourhoods, initially characterized as 'slums of despair' (Stokes, 1962), were seen as potential breeding grounds for aggression and militancy, as rural–urban migrants who arrived 'without income or skills' were destined to remain 'marginal' within the city, living in overcrowded 'slums' of insecure tenure (Abrams, 1964: 3). Fear of social disintegration and revolution in the 'teeming slums' gave rise to questions of 'whether political stability can be maintained while productivity is developed and the painful shift to industrialization is effected' (Abrams, 1964: 287–8). Rural–urban migration was seen as the cause of social problems such as the breakdown of stable structures that characterized rural life – particularly the family (Lewis, 1952).

These portrayals were indicative of a generally negative view of urban informality. It was characterized in crude, simplistic and politicized terms, using words for people living and working informally such as 'urban informals' (Abrams, 1964) or 'human flotsam and jetsam' (Lerner, 1967 in Lloyd, 1979: 209). Such prevailingly negative views underpinned widespread systematic policies of eviction of informal neighbourhoods in the 1950s and 1960s, on the basis that these places presented a problem, rather than a solution to housing need (Mangin, 1967). Government and public opinion condemned settlements as 'disorganised products of outside agitation' (Mangin, 1967: 67), the product of political manipulation of rural–urban migrants, characterizing inhabitants as '[l]iving almost like animals ... overwhelmed by animality' (Schulman, 1966 in Mangin, 1967: 66–7) and suggesting eradication and displacement as a solution. In some cases, governments also attempted to implement policy 'solutions' of preventing rural-to-urban migration and further urbanization, in keeping with anti-urban bias which affected investment and urban policy in African cities later in the 1970s (Fox, 2014).

An example of how these negative views of low-income neighbourhoods were bolstered by academic debates can be seen in Lewis' work on the 'culture of poverty', based on his studies of Mexico City and Puerto Rico's inner-city slums. Such places, according to Lewis (1967a: xiv), were characterized by 'family disruption, violence, brutality, cheapness of life, lack of love, lack of education [and] lack of medical facilities'. He offers a portrayal of life punctuated by hardship, conflict and casual violence, aiming to convey 'what it means to grow up in a one-room home in a *vecindad* (slum tenement) in the heart of a great Latin American city ... undergoing a process of rapid social and economic change' (Lewis, 1961: xi). This influential theory has been accused of reproducing particular stereotypes of the urban poor (Harvey and Reed, 1996) in terms of their 'moral destitution' or irrational behaviour (Portes, 1972: 269). Although Lewis later clarified that the 'culture of poverty' referred to a design for living in stability and cohesiveness amid difficult circumstances, its association with social disorganization reinforced the orthodox view that 'the informal housing area was by definition a slum, therefore – again by definition – an area of delinquency, breakdown and general social malaise' (Hall, 2002: 272–4).

Identifying informality and conceptual controversies

Alongside these early observations of informal processes of housing provision, the identification of informality as a separate yet interrelated (economic) sphere or sector is strongly associated with the International Labour Organization (ILO), the branch of the United Nations responsible for setting labour standards globally, who addressed it as 'a concept and an economic reality' (Bangasser, 2000: 1). In the 1960s and 1970s, prevailing economic orthodoxy suggested that 'Third World' economies were at a different stage of development to those in the 'First World', and that in order for them to catch up, 'development planning' was necessary, focusing on the provision of formal jobs. However, the failure to provide sufficient numbers of jobs, particularly in the context of increasing urbanization, became an 'increasingly evident paradox' (Bangasser, 2000: 5).

In response to the paradox of urbanization occurring without full employment, throughout the 1960s the ILO conducted a series of 'missions', gathering unemployment data in specific developing economies to produce national employment plans. The Kenya Mission's report (ILO, 1972) was particularly significant for its exposition of 'traditional' or 'informal' economic sectors, ignored by employment statistics which covered wage-earners and some self-employment but omitted 'a range of wage earners and self-employed persons' (ILO, 1972: 5). The report argued that the informal sector's economic significance had been underestimated and unfairly stigmatized, limiting its potential, arguing: 'Though it is often regarded as unproductive and stagnant, we see it as providing a wide range of low-cost, labour-intensive, competitive goods and services' (ILO, 1972: 21).

Table 2.1: Characteristics of informal and formal economic sectors

Informal sector	Formal sector
Ease of entry	Difficult entry
Reliance on Indigenous resources	Frequent reliance on overseas resources
Family ownership of enterprises	Corporate ownership
Small scale of operation	Large scale of operation
Labour-intensive and adapted technology	Capital-intensive and often imported technology
Skills acquired outside the formal school system	Formally acquired skills, often expatriate
Unregulated and competitive markets	Protected markets (through tariffs, quotas and trade licences)

Source: ILO (1972)

The report identifies a set of characteristics associated with the informal sector (see Table 2.1), which included jobs such as 'carpenters, masons, tailors and other tradesmen, as well as cooks and taxi-drivers' (ILO, 1972: 5). The ILO advocated for a more positive government attitude towards this sector, which would encompass discontinuing demolition of informal housing, reviewing licensing practices, and improving articulation between the formal and informal sectors. It is important to note that the concept popularized by the ILO originated from research undertaken by researchers at the University of Nairobi, a fact that is often overlooked (being mentioned only in a footnote of the ILO report), but that is likely to have bolstered its take-up in contexts where it was applied (Bangasser, 2000).

A similar approach can be found in the work of Keith Hart (1973), an anthropologist at the University of Manchester strongly associated with the emergence of the 'informal sector' concept. In his influential article, 'Informal income opportunities and urban employment in Ghana', Hart (1973) observed how standard categories used to describe economic activity in 'Western' countries, such as unemployment and underemployment, seemed unhelpful in this context. For example, in Accra's Nima district, an informal neighbourhood which housed 8 per cent of the city's population, 40 per cent of men and 95 per cent of women were not classed as in waged employment, falling instead into the categories of self-employed, non-wage earning, unemployed or not economically active. For those unable to access formal employment or sufficient wages, the 'world of economic activities outside the organised labour force' (Hart, 1973: 68) was represented by the informal sector, characterized by temporary, irregular work with variable rewards. Previously dismissed as insignificant and small-scale, Hart (1973: 68) showed that '[i]n practice, informal activities encompass a wide-ranging scale, from marginal operations to large enterprises', including farming, transport, petty trading (seen in Figure 2.3), tailoring, medicine and begging. Often, households depended on several sources of income, with the informal sector acting as a 'buffer' against formal unemployment. Instead of dismissing and stigmatizing it, Hart argued, governments should pay greater attention to the informal sector, incorporating informal goods and services in economic analysis. This issue is discussed further in Chapter 4.

Figure 2.3: Sugarcane juice vendors in Lucknow, India

Source: Alamy/Dinodia Photos

The term 'urban informal sector' superseded 'urban unemployment' during the 1970s, and could be said to have 'entered the development paradigm' by the millennium (Bangasser, 2000: 12). Yet critics such as Bromley (1978: 1033) saw this two-sector approach as conceptually simplistic, inconsistent and unclear, confusing informality with the urban poor while 'boosting' existing institutional analyses of so-called 'Third World economies' without threatening the status quo. Indeed, it has been argued that these conceptual debates did not lead to changes in labour regulations and standards to more proactively incorporate the informal sector because of their lack of transformative ambition (Bangasser, 2000), seen in their depiction of the informal sector as 'having a present but no future' (Bromley, 1978: 1034).

Several researchers working on and from the global South (particularly Latin American countries) challenged the negative characterizations associated with informal living and working in the 1970s (for example, Peattie, 1970; Lomnitz, 1977; Lloyd, 1979). Perlman (1976) was particularly influential, arguing that 'marginality', a condition which was practically synonymous with informal neighbourhoods and their populations, served in Brazil and across Latin America as 'both a myth and a description of social reality' (Perlman, 1976: 242). Contrary to the popular view of the urban poor living in shantytowns characterized by social disorganization and radical politics, she found that *favela* dwellers were socially well-organized and cohesive, culturally optimistic with aspirations for their children's education and their housing, economically hard-working, and politically neither apathetic nor radical: 'In short, they have the aspirations of the bourgeoisie, the perseverance of pioneers, and the values of patriots. What they do *not* have is an opportunity to fulfil their aspirations' (Perlman, 1976: 242–3, original emphasis). In fact, the myth of marginality was used

Figure 2.4: Self-help processes in Xalapa, Mexico

Source: Melanie Lombard

for the social control of the poor, who far from being marginal, were integrated into society in ways that resulted in them being 'economically exploited, politically repressed, socially stigmatized and culturally excluded' (Bayat, 2000: 539; see also AlSayyad, 2004).

A similar rejoinder came in the idea of 'self-help', referring to housing where the owner-occupier constructs some or all of the accommodation, with or without (professional) help (Turner, 1968; 1972; see Figure 2.4). The lack of government will, resources and flexibility to provide the right kind of shelter, combined with a great potential resource in the desire, energy and initiative of families to house themselves, led to the prescription of 'greater user autonomy in the provision of housing' (Turner and Fichter, 1972: xi). In response, international agencies (in particular the World Bank) and governments came to accept that self-help housing could be a 'solution'. The idea was widely influential in policy terms, with sites-and-services and upgrading policies implemented in many countries during the late 1960s and early 1970s, relating respectively to state provision of basic infrastructure on dedicated plots of land for self-help housing, and in-situ improvements to existing infrastructure. These processes are explored further in Chapter 7.

Beyond Anglophone debates, significant regional debates were taking place relating to informal living and working, as alluded to earlier. For example, publications in Spanish by Latin American researchers constitute an important strand of early accounts of urban growth and informal development. Jose Luis Romero (1976), in his historical account of the Latin American city, identifies the 'divided city' which was constituted by the influx of rural–urban migrants. Jorge Montaño (1976) showed how in Mexico City, the 'reciprocal obligation' of clientelistic relations between the urban poor and the Mexican authorities responded to community demands while maintaining stability and avoiding conflict (discussed further in Chapter 7). These debates informed later work on Latin American cities such as Azuela and Tomas (1996) on informal urban land markets, Cordera et al (2008) on urban poverty, and Salazar (2012) on legalization's effects on informality. More broadly, regional debates on Latin American cities also influenced understandings of urban informality globally (AlSayyad, 2004).

The widespread adoption of 'self-help' meant that improving rather than replacing informal neighbourhoods became the priority for intervention (Davis, 2006), amid growing recognition that 'the unnamed millions who build, organize and plan illegally are the most important organizers, builders and planners' of cities in the global South (Hardoy and Satterthwaite, 1989: 15). Nevertheless, these ideas also generated considerable criticism (Ward, 1982). In particular, critics attacked the double exploitation of labour at work and in housing construction, which subsidised formal labour costs as 'access to low-cost shelter reduces the wage level required for subsistence' (Moser and Peake, 1987: 5). Some argued that this paved the way for a more entrepreneurial approach to urban informality.

Entrepreneurial informality and explanatory frameworks

Approaches to informality that followed the era of self-help built on its focus on the power of individuals and households to address their informal, often challenging, living and working conditions. An entrepreneurial approach to poverty and informality emerged, strongly associated with the work of Hernando de Soto. In his influential book *The Mystery of Capital*, de Soto (2000) argued that provision of legal titles is the solution to informality and poverty: creating property ownership (through titling) and legalization of assets gives poor people the security of tenure they need to invest in their homes and businesses, and hence invigorate the economy. This was based on calculations suggesting that the urban poor hold up to US$9.3 trillion in informal assets, which is labelled as 'dead capital' as it cannot be exchanged or used to raise credit. This capital can be 'brought to life' by property titles which allow its exchange or use for credit, thus invigorating the wider economy.

The influence of this idea can be seen in the prevalence of tenure legalization programmes, which aimed to formalize informal property and neighbourhoods. The widespread nature of title legalization programmes in many developing countries, particularly in Latin America, means that evictions and removals have been replaced by relative tolerance of illegal tenure developments. However, such approaches have been critiqued as 'micro-entrepreneurial solutions to urban poverty', which pave the way for further withdrawal of government support (Davis, 2006: 71–2). These programmes have also been criticized for their over-simplification of complex issues, including the structural causes of poverty (Fernandes, 2002), their political usage, and their failure to generate the promised wealth (Miranda, 2002). Ultimately, then, legalization has not offered a 'solution' to poverty or informality. We explore these issues further in Chapter 7.

To make sense of these debates, Rakowski (1994) suggests dividing them into two broad tendencies: 'structuralist' and 'legalist'. Structuralists view informal neighbourhoods as the result of capitalism's uneven development (for example, Mangin, 1967; Perlman, 1976; Davis, 2006). Legalists see informality as an alternative, rational and entrepreneurial or even 'heroic' economic survival strategy (such as Turner, 1972; de Soto, 2000). We explore these frameworks later in Chapters 4 and 7, where we also introduce other concepts such as dualism and voluntarism (Chen, 2012). However, it is important to note that, whether crisis or heroism, such framings tend to view formality and informality as fundamentally separate (Roy, 2005; Alfaro d'Alencon et al, 2018). This negates the reciprocal relationship that often exists between formal and informal sectors, processes and practices (Bromley, 1978). In fact, the relationship is messy and tangled, and the sides not clearly delineated, leading some observers to question whether this binary categorization is too simplistic, or too broad to be meaningful (Moser, 1994).

Box 2.2: Contrasting accounts of informality

[T]he cities of the future, rather than being made out of glass and steel as envisioned by earlier generations of urbanists, are instead largely constructed out of crude brick, straw, recycled plastic, cement blocks and scrap wood. Instead of cities of light soaring toward heaven, much of the twenty-first-century urban world squats in squalor, surrounded by pollution, excrement, and decay. (Davis, 2006: 19)

The common perception of slums as locations of poverty, squalor, destitution, insecurity and danger tells one part of the story – but there are also stories of enterprising, hardworking slum denizens. Life in a shantytown is full of challenges and hardship, but shanties are homes, where conversations take place over dinner, kids do homework, and neighbors live next door. (Bendiksen, 2008: 5–6)

Consider the following questions:

- Which account do you agree with and why?
- Which conceptual approach to informality do you think these authors align with?

21st-century debates
Urban informality and the return of the slum

Since the early 2000s, there has been an explosion of interest in urban informality, leading to a proliferation of literature from diverse disciplines beyond anthropology, economics, and architecture and planning, which were traditionally concerned with such issues. This can be traced to some key publications, notably Roy and AlSayyad's (2004) *Urban Informality: Transnational Perspectives from the Middle East, Latin America and South Asia*. This edited book was one of the first to present case studies beyond disciplinary boundaries, bringing together examples of living, working and governing informally from diverse contexts. It is notable for its introduction of the term 'urban informality', which had been less frequently used in English language publications to describe articulations of living and working informally. Tracing it back to Juan Pablo Perez Sainz's work on the informal economy (in Spanish) in the 1980s, AlSayyad (2004: 28) uses it to denote 'social and economic processes that shape, or are manifest in, the urban built environment'. More precisely, urban informality is not associated with the poor, their labour or marginality; '[r]ather, it is an organizing logic which emerges under a paradigm of liberalization' (AlSayyad, 2004: 26). In other words, informality in the late 20th century can be understood as deeply entangled with processes of globalization and liberalization. We explore these questions further in Chapters 3 and 4.

The early 2000s also saw two further significant yet controversial publications on urban informality. First, the 2003 Global Report on Human Settlements, subtitled 'The challenge of the slums', was published by UN-Habitat, the United Nations agency with responsibility for human settlements (discussed further in Chapter 6), as part of a regular report series giving a global overview of shelter and urban development issues. The 2003 report is significant as it claimed to offer 'the first global assessment of slums', based on a newly formulated operational definition which enabled an assessment of scale, characteristics and policy responses globally. The contested definition of 'slums', along with the difficulty of undertaking such assessment due to the scarcity of reliable data, has meant that subsequent global assessments have been limited, although some attempt has been made relating to the 'urban' Sustainable Development Goal, in the annual United Nations Sustainable Development Goal Report. These issues are discussed further in Chapter 3.

Second, Mike Davis' (2006) *Planet of Slums*, mentioned in Box 2.2, described how 'much of the twenty-first-century urban world squats in squalor, surrounded by pollution, excrement, and decay' (Davis, 2006: 19). Drawing on the UN-Habitat publication, Davis (2006: 200–1) saw 'slums' as 'a fully franchised solution to the problem of warehousing this century's surplus humanity' in a world where exclusion occurs at local, national and global levels. The cause of this spatial exclusion, he suggested, can be traced to the imposition of Structural Adjustment Programmes in the 1980s by the World Bank and the International Monetary Fund, which made life unsustainable for millions of rural poor, forcing them to move to cities, with resultant explosive urbanization. In this way, 'cities have become a dumping ground for a surplus population working in unskilled, unprotected and low-wage informal service industries and trade' (Davis, 2006: 175).

These publications contributed to concerns about 'the return of the slum' in the language of international organizations, policy and academic debates (Gilbert, 2007). The resurgent use of the term 'slum' has been seen as evidence of a worrying trend towards a generally negative and over-simplified universal image of informal neighbourhoods (Gilbert, 2007: 698). As Varley (2013) and others have pointed out, the revival of slum terminology in the global South suggests a link between Victorian-era anxiety about working-class neighbourhoods and today's informal neighbourhoods. The discursive 'return of the slum' may signal an attempt to show the seriousness of the urban situation in the global South, also similar to Victorian debates. But focusing on the problems of urban informal neighbourhoods is risky as 'a generally negative universal image can be dangerous' (Gilbert, 2007: 698). The reproduction of terms like 'slum' or 'squatter' (for example, Neuwirth, 2005), indiscriminately applied to places and people under the 'informal' heading, obscures diversity and complexity.

Moreover, it is feared that the discursive resurgence of 'slums', which stereotypes residents and looks to environmental improvements to address poverty, may also provide local authorities with the justification they need for demolition and eradication policies. Indeed, it has been claimed that the UN's 'Cities Without Slums' campaign influenced the implementation of the 2007 Slums Act in KwaZulu-Natal, South Africa, which caused the removal of informal neighbourhoods and their residents (Huchzermeyer, 2007) before it was overturned in 2009, revealing unintended consequences of such negative discursive framings (Meth, 2013). This can also be seen in examples from Delhi which show how 'nuisance talk' by the middle classes – premised on their dissatisfaction with the aesthetic impact of 'slums' on their land and property values – has influenced policy and interventions, threatening displacement for one million informally settled residents due to legal action by middle-class residents' welfare associations (Ghertner, 2012). Similarly, Datta (2011) analyses popular discourses portraying Indian 'slums' as violent places, represented as a microcosm of the village, where out-of-place, peasant-like slum residents live.

Such accounts suggest the enduring nature of these discursive constructions of informal settlements, whose influence can be tangible for residents, despite a long tradition of contestation and resistance. Indeed, recent research suggests that we should delete this 'deceitful and miserable word' (Mayne, 2017: 15), which connects 19th-century to 21st-century accounts, from our vocabulary as researchers. Others have suggested the use of 'informal neighbourhoods' in preference to terms like slum or even informal settlements (McFarlane and Silver, 2017), an approach which we largely follow in this book.

Urban informality as collective opposition

The 21st century has also seen diverse attempts to reverse the normative inference of informality and use it to foreground the agency of marginalized populations, identified by Boanada-Fuchs and Boanada (2018: 404) as seeing 'informality as a form of collective opposition'. Similarly, Varley (2013) identifies a focus on informality as resistance in recent literature on and from Latin America (which nevertheless also perpetuates dualisms, for example, through generalizing tropes such as *favela* at the expense of local variation). This approach follows a tradition of ethnographic (and often longitudinal) studies by anthropologists and urban theorists in specific communities, exploring lived experiences of urban informality in the context of globalization from the perspective of those living and working in these conditions. In particular, studies by Moser (2009), Simone (2000; 2004b), Auyero (1999a; 1999b; 2000) and Bayat (2004) explore how global forces exert pressure on local informal neighbourhoods through economic crises, structural adjustment and neoliberal governance, while simultaneously emphasizing the importance of local determinants in shaping particular manifestations of liberalization in specific cities, and their effects on the urban poor. For example, Auyero (1999a: 47) highlights the interaction of rising unemployment, educational exclusion and welfare retrenchment through the lived experience of residents of an informal neighbourhood in Buenos Aires, Argentina, to show how 'these structural processes are perceived and translated into concrete emotions, cognitions and actions by the residents of the slum'.

As well as reincorporating local processes into debates about the links between globalization and urban informality, the detailed empirical research that underpins these studies explicitly challenges stereotypes emerging from essentialist understandings that endure in theoretical and policy debates on informality, resonating with wider debates on poverty. Responding to the 'decontextualisation' and 'technification' of poverty by international agencies (Moser, 2009: 23), ethnographic approaches reveal the heterogeneity of urban poor communities and the informal neighbourhoods they often inhabit (see, for example, Figure 2.5), thus highlighting the complexity of measuring, contextualizing and responding to urban poverty and informality. Foregrounding agency by emphasizing the views of urban communities confirms their self-reliance, echoing earlier debates on self-help, and highlighting their 'huge creativity, pride and resilience' (Moser, 2009: xvii).

This is not to romanticize the situation of people living and working informally. In the context of constraints and powerful elite interests, agency may be characterized by 'quiet encroachment', in the sense of 'largely atomised, and prolonged mobilisation with episodic collective action', rather than organized resistance (Bayat, 2004: 90, further discussed in Chapter 5). However, by highlighting the struggle and negotiation in which communities engage to obtain goods and services in informal neighbourhoods, these accounts 'find ways of making visible urban possibilities that have been crowded out or left diffuse or opaque' in debates that often essentialize the identities of those who live and work informally (Simone, 2004b: 14).

Roy (2011: 224) offers an incisive yet sympathetic critique of what she calls 'subaltern urbanism', which she locates in accounts of the slum as 'terrain of habitation, livelihood and politics ... [which seek] to confer recognition on spaces of poverty and forms of popular agency that often remain invisible and neglected'. While this paradigm offers an important challenge to apocalyptic portrayals of slums, assigning political agency to urban dwellers risks attributing them with an essentialist 'slum habitus' (Roy, 2011: 228). Rather than attaching a deterministic informal 'identity' to informal neighbourhood residents, Roy argues that we must aim to understand the conditions under which knowledge about slums is produced, in order to understand

Figure 2.5: A home in Mumbai, India

Source: (c) Jonas Bendiksen/Magnum Photos

the gaps in history and representations, 'the limits of archival and ethnographic recognition'; in other words, what is left out of urban theory (Roy, 2011: 231). Here, then, the question is less 'What is urban informality?', and more 'How do we know urban informality?'. We return to this question in Chapter 8.

Informality as state (in)action

The counterpoint to accounts of collective opposition and resistance is a focus on informality as a product of state action, or 'a direct product of the government' (Boanada-Fuchs and Boanada, 2018: 403). This approach to informality suggests that it is part and parcel of urban development in most, if not all, urban settings. In other words, informality is a necessary conceptual tool for understanding urban development, and is strongly related to attempts to regulate this. From a purely regulatory perspective, there are four reasons for informality (which may co-exist): residents may not be able to adhere to regulations; they may not want to; the state may be unable to enforce regulations; or it may be unwilling to enforce them (Harris, 2018: 273). This suggests that informality must be understood in relation to the state, as 'governments shape informality' through their role in creating, enforcing or failing to enforce regulations (Harris, 2018: 275). These regulatory weaknesses may be based on resource or capacity limitations, but they may also be strategic, suggesting that informality is 'an inevitable context of planning, a fact of social existence', and that regulation must therefore adapt to the 'messy character of urban life', which may necessitate varied regulatory approaches depending on the context (Harris, 2018: 278).

The idea that informality is 'ubiquitous' (Harris, 2018) also suggests that it is not simply the purview of low-income or marginalized groups, an argument that has been put forward by scholars for decades. The uses of urban informality in a given context may extend beyond the poor to encompass different sectors including middle- or high-income residents, the state and businesses. McFarlane's (2012) discussion of Mumbai's 2005 floods shows how popular debates at the time provided a window onto informal practices in the city, including not just encroachment by 'slums', but also the state's and developers' 'extra-legal' development practices, which bypassed urban environmental regulations and allowed construction on flood plains. In this understanding, informality represents 'a way of doing things' (McFarlane, 2012: 104), which moves away from value-laden approaches or labels for places or groups, towards a more open category which can be applied in a variety of different contexts and people. More recent scholarship on elite uses of informality is explored in detail in Chapter 3.

Some theorists assert that rather than viewing informal neighbourhoods as physical environments, deficient of basic infrastructure and services, they can be seen 'as complex and changing social processes that play themselves out in intricate spatial arrangements' (Huchzermeyer, 2004: 47). Seeing informal neighbourhoods as social processes allows a broader view of these places and the dynamic social and political relations which occur there, as well as more static spatial, technical and legal aspects. Similarly, Roy (2005: 148), picking up the thread of AlSayyad's

(2004) argument (discussed earlier), sees 'urban informality' as 'an organising logic, a system of norms that governs the process of urban transformation itself'. Here, the standard dichotomy of formal and informal is rejected in favour of the suggestion that 'informality is not a separate sector but rather a series of transactions that connect different economies and spaces to one another' (Roy, 2005: 148). Nevertheless, in most contexts, certain uses of informality are penalized, while others are not, reflecting an 'uneven geography of spatial value' (Roy, 2011), which tends to criminalize the poor's informal activities. Exploring this further suggests the idea of informality as a 'site of critical analysis' (Banks et al, 2020), as discussed in Chapter 1. Meanwhile, other recent theoretical debates suggest the need to 'transcend informal urbanism' (Acuto et al, 2019), an idea which we briefly consider in the next section, and return to in Chapter 8.

Postcolonial urban theory

What the theoretical approaches outlined here have in common is a rejection of the idea that informality is abnormal or even problematic. Moving away from the idea of the 'slum', they insist on seeing informality as part of life. This is not to suggest that living and working informally is not without difficulties, but this approach attempts to look beyond stigmatizing and simplistic labels and discourses, to understand the realities of urban life. An important element of this approach is its critique, whether implicit or explicit, of planning norms and regulations which condemn informality out of hand. This speaks to postcolonial planning approaches, which seek to understand how colonialism and its legacies have shaped cities in the global South, particularly through planning law and practice, which is often imported from other contexts.

Such perspectives seek to understand, from a historical perspective, how informality derives from structures and processes dating from colonial times, such as the segregation of the city along racialized lines (as discussed earlier in this chapter). Additionally, they are interested in how ideas and practices deriving from colonialism as a set of power relations continue to circulate and shape urban life; in other words, how '[p]lanning perspectives from one part of the globe have shaped a dominant and persistent planning rationality' (Watson, 2011: 151). This approach suggests that planning standards see 'normality' as relating to 'proper' living in clean, orderly and 'modern' cities, a paradigm in which informality does not feature, leading to the punitive policy responses (such as demolition) outlined earlier and discussed at length in Chapters 6 and 7.

Robinson's work on 'ordinary cities' has been significant as part of these debates. She suggested that dominant ideas in urban theory, such as 'global' and 'third-world' cities, limit imaginings of what cities are or could be, based on the experiences of a few Western cities (Robinson, 2006). Instead, she has argued for moving away from a developmentalist perspective that views cities of the global South in terms of what they lack, and towards an alternative view of cities as 'ordinary'; in other words, as 'diverse, creative, modern and distinctive, with the possibility to imagine (within the not inconsiderable constraints of contestations and uneven power relations) their own futures and distinctive forms of city-ness' (Robinson, 2002: 546). Her call for 'a cosmopolitan, postcolonial urban studies' (Robinson, 2002: 533) has led others to suggest transcending standardized categories by 'bringing into view and theorising a range of ordinary spaces' in the urban setting (Legg and McFarlane, 2008: 7; see also McFarlane, 2008). More recently, the call to 'decolonize' urban theory has been critically engaged with in debates on Southern urban theory, discussed further in Chapter 8.

Informality at a global scale

Within these moves towards a postcolonial urban studies, an important methodological tool has been comparative urbanism. This suggests the need to learn *from* the South, through making theoretical or empirical comparisons (South–North or South–South). This opens up the possibility of sharing insights across different regions, and questioning assumptions generalized from liberal democratic countries (responding to the postcolonial critique outlined earlier), but also enables working comparatively at a global scale, to uncover global material and political processes and relations (Watson, 2011). In particular, it has been suggested that in contexts of urban austerity, crisis and other shocks in global 'Northern' cities, informality has been on the rise, and is increasingly recognized. As Northern cities confront informality, 'reverse flows of theory' (Yiftachel, 2006: 216) may help to form new concepts, as in the case of Durst and Wegmann's (2017) application of 'informality' to new housing constructions in Texas (explored further in Chapter 3).

This can also be seen in work on 'beds in sheds' in London, which are illegally constructed or converted 'sheds', built in the back gardens of suburban housing, rented out to individuals or households, leading to issues of overcrowding and illegal connections to services (Lombard, 2019; Schiller and Raco, 2021), also discussed further in Chapter 3. Recent research has applied this comparative approach through the lens of relational comparison, for example exploring the positionality of San Francisco and Jakarta in global processes (Sheppard et al, 2020). There are significant contextual differences in such geographical comparisons, relating to the scale of and also responses to informality, particularly regarding the state's ability to enforce planning regulations, and willingness to do so (Harris, 2018). Nevertheless, while these vary in different contexts, it is clear that informality has long existed in many Northern contexts, and is likely to continue to do so, as shown earlier in this chapter in our discussion on 'slums' in industrializing Europe but also in recent work, such as Chiodelli et al's (2021) account of historic and contemporary informal urban practices in Italy.

Chapter summary

This chapter has provided an overview of debates on urban informality. We began by tracing the origins of urban informality, linking it to the rise of 'slums' during industrialization but also to its colonial roots. We then focused on conceptual and policy debates over the last 70 years. Earlier ideas including self-help housing, marginality, dualist framings, legalization and related policy efforts have been increasingly subject to critique and, more recently, attention has turned to efforts to reframe informality as collective opposition and state (in)action. Postcolonial (and Southern) urban theory have been particularly influential in more recent debates, mobilizing the 'slum' and other informal spaces as sites for urban theorization. It is now also clear that urban informality is by no means only a Southern phenomenon but one that emerges increasingly, and in distinct articulations, in the global North. The global nature of informality is slowly being recognized in agendas such as the Sustainable Development Goals and the New Urban Agenda, though it remains to be seen how global goals around informality are effectively translated into local policies and planning interventions, an issue which is explored further in Chapter 7. The chapter also paid close attention to how informality is represented within different academic, policy and public discourses – with all of them ultimately guided by specific political worldviews.

Recommended reading

- Hardoy, J. and Satterthwaite, D. (1989) *Squatter Citizen*, London: Earthscan.
- Roy, A. and Alsayyad, N. (2004) *Urban Informality: Transnational Perspectives from the Middle East, Latin America and South Asia*, New York: Lexington Books.
- Davis, M. (2006) *Planet of Slums*, London: Verso.

EXERCISES

Thinking back on your reading of this chapter, reflect on the following questions:

- Who defines key terms (such as informality), and how are they enacted by planners and people in their everyday practices?
- Whose voices are represented in debates in this field?
- How similar are different manifestations of urban informality in distinct contexts? What are the key differences?
- How can different places learn from each other about urban informality? Can experiences in the global South help to inform UK planning responses?

Alternative representations

- Watch this documentary, *A Roof of My Own* (United Nations TV, 1964, available at: https://vimeo.com/301298249), about the origins of Peru's barriadas.
- For bird's-eye views of inequality around the world, visit photographer Jonny Miller's website of his project *Unequal Scenes* (https://unequalscenes.com/projects).
- Watch this video which uses live action sketch techniques, *Are Slums the Global Urban Future?*, by Ananya Roy and Abby Vanmuijen (2013, https://www.youtube.com/watch?v=1xk7dr3VG6s).

- For more intimate portraits of people living informally in diverse urban contexts, see Jonas Bendiksen's book, *The Places We Live* (2008, https://www.jonasbendiksen.com/books/the-places-we-live).
- Read about how journalism portrays informal living and working in the annual *Best and Worst Reporting of Rio's Favelas* (https://rioonwatch.org/?tag=series-best-worst-reporting) round up, published by the non-government organization Rio On Watch.

3

Living Informally

'When we started self-building the neighbourhood, we organized the community. Many families were part of this, working to generate savings, selling empanadas, doing things to make some money. We had the support of a local charity, and a committee was formed, to take charge of carrying out and managing works. Everything was through self-help. So, they started by installing bathrooms, and people began to organize their spaces, because their houses were made of cardboard and wooden boards. So, through these self-help processes, we started with bathroom fittings. The charity gave us 70 per cent of the resources and we had to contribute 30 per cent … we developed a process, each group would go to someone's house, and work on the fitting. Then we would come back, get organized and go to someone else's house, and in this way we started to improve the housing. The streets were unpaved, there was no drinking water, you had to go to a nearby neighbourhood [to get water], so this was a really lovely process because people wanted to improve their conditions, and we got organized for that.'

Social leader recounting how self-help processes unfolded in Cali, Colombia[1]

Globally, it is estimated that up to one billion people live in informal conditions, often in urban informal neighbourhoods. The well-known image of the *favela* (a term used for informal neighbourhoods within or at the outskirts of Brazilian cities) is frequently held as the archetype of informal housing, with its steep and narrow streets, precariously perched houses, and lack of electricity or running water, nestling in the hillsides surrounding the large formal metropolis. In fact, as we will see in this chapter, living informally is a diverse phenomenon, which includes many different types of housing practices and neighbourhoods, almost always shaped by contextual factors. It occurs in Latin American, Asian and African cities – reflected in the diverse terminology for such neighbourhoods, such as *colonia popular*, *gecekondu* and *bidonville* – but is also increasingly recognized in global North contexts, for example, with the recent phenomenon of 'beds in sheds' in the UK. People may live informally in the inner city, as well as at the urban fringe; and living informally is a practice which is not restricted to lower-income urban residents, although informal practices by middle- and upper-income groups are often less studied.

Informal housing is related to land and service provision, and we explore these issues in this chapter. For example, the way in which land is informally acquired by urban residents – who often lack other formal housing options – can shape the neighbourhood and determine its future prospects, depending on the type of land which is settled, as well as the nature of the (informal) transaction by which it changed hands. In particular, the dimension of tenure security is understood to be critical for informal neighbourhood consolidation, affecting the provision of formal services, although as we discuss in this chapter, this relationship cannot be universally assumed. In fact, the slow process of collectively and informally providing services (such as illegal connections to the electricity network), followed by incremental formal provision (such as a formal connection for street lighting, and subsequently for individual households), may also help to determine how secure residents feel in their neighbourhood.

This chapter explores how places develop and how people live through the lens of informality. It looks at the definitions and meanings related to urban informal neighbourhoods, as well as their form, evolution and (debates around) causal factors. The chapter explores three core elements of land, housing and basic services, focusing on how residents are often key agents in processes of land acquisition through invasion or illegal subdivision, incremental and self-help housing construction, and provisional followed by improved service provision. It also looks at how living informally is changing, in terms of elite and middle-class informal housing, the emergence of informal high-rise housing, and manifestations of informality in the global North.

Living informally: manifestations and factors

In this book, as explained in Chapter 1, we use the term 'living informally' to refer to a range of experiences and processes which are usually associated with housing and neighbourhoods developed informally, in other words outside regulatory frameworks relating to land use, building regulations or housing standards. Such houses (or neighbourhoods) are often developed through a combination of informal land acquisition, self-help construction and incremental service provision. However, it is difficult to offer a general definition of informal living, as there are vast differences in location, design, quality and so on, as well as in regulatory frameworks and approaches, meaning that what may be considered informal in one setting may be acceptable in another.

Nevertheless, following Hardoy and Satterthwaite (1989), we can identify several distinct manifestations or forms of informal living that occur to a greater or lesser extent in many urban contexts, particularly in the global South: namely pavement dwelling, inner-city 'slums' and urban informal neighbourhoods. We briefly explore these in turn in the following sections.

Manifestations of informal living
Pavement dwelling

Pavement dwelling is a phenomenon found in many cities, predominantly in South Asia.[2] While often linked to street homelessness, which implies transience, in some cities it has become an established manifestation of informal housing. This type of informal living has been particularly associated with and studied in Indian cities, although it has also been observed elsewhere in cities such as Manila (Dovey and King, 2011). Research on Mumbai suggests that although pavement dwelling originated in the early 20th century, its dramatic increase in the 1970s derived from rural–urban migration due to food shortages and agricultural reform (Menon, 2018). Pavement dwellers live on footpaths and pavements, often adjacent to formal housing or other buildings which are usually situated in or close to city centres, with dwellings constructed of materials such as cardboard, wood, plastic sheeting or canvas (SPARC, 1988). Residence is characterized by extremely small living spaces, minimal access to services and insecure tenure. While such shelter characteristics could be conceived of as inadequate, pavement dwelling often represents a rational choice for low-income urban residents whose work is centrally located (Hardoy and Satterthwaite, 1989). At the same time, it guarantees a source of cheap labour for wealthier urban households and businesses, based on the pavement dwelling population's proximity to work and lack of alternative options (Menon, 2018).

It is difficult to know how many people live in such conditions. Appadurai (2001) suggested that between 5 and 10 per cent of Mumbai's then population of 12 million were pavement dwellers, in other words a total of between 600,000 and 1.2 million people. However, precise figures are not available, as pavement dwellers rarely appear in formal census data. Official unwillingness to acknowledge pavement dwelling has been justified by its apparently temporary nature. In 1985, a groundbreaking initiative by the Mumbai-based non-government organization 'Society for the Promotion of Area Resource Centres' (SPARC) undertook the largest ever survey of pavement dwellings, based on a sample of 6,000 households, in response to large-scale evictions. SPARC (1988) overturned myths about pavement dwelling, finding that despite multiple evictions, households often lived on the same stretch of pavement for decades, rebuilding their housing after demolition due to lack of other options. They also found that most households had at least one individual working, usually in the informal or service sector; and they often paid some form of rent for their space on the pavement, as well as paying cash or in kind for access to water and toilets in nearby shops or factories. Despite advocacy by SPARC and other organizations, large-scale evictions still occur, such as the 2004 destruction of 72,000 dwellings in Mumbai by the State of Maharashtra government, which left 350,000 people homeless (Menon, 2018).

Inner-city informal housing

Informal housing in the inner city is often located in formally built but dilapidated residential or commercial buildings, which contravene building or housing regulations, and may be informally subdivided. Although infrastructure is usually available due to its central location, this type of housing is characterized by poor living conditions, such as small rooms, dense occupation, poor ventilation and insulation, lack of privacy, inadequate lighting and inadequate sanitation facilities (Few et al, 2004). In Latin American cities, tenement-style housing was particularly common during early waves of urbanization in the first half of the 20th century, constituting an important source of housing for low-waged households needing cheap and centrally located accommodation. Known as *vecindades* in Mexico City, *conventillos* in Buenos Aires, *inquilinatos* in Bogota and *tugurios* in Ecuador, these dwellings were often located in old elite residences subdivided for multi-household rent, or purpose-built, privately constructed tenements, with shared facilities in a central patio. Parallels have been drawn between this housing and the 'slums' of 19th-century industrializing cities, discussed in Chapter 2. Tenement-style informal housing has also been observed in the late 20th century in other urban contexts in Africa, and South and South-East Asia (Hardoy and Satterthwaite, 1989).

Much of this older inner-city informal housing has been demolished through regeneration or converted for higher earning uses, due to its location on central and increasingly valuable land; sometimes, such moves are accompanied by efforts to improve living conditions through housing standards and rent control. A contemporary manifestation can be seen in formally built, centrally located residential and commercial buildings which have been abandoned and subsequently informally occupied by low-income residents, often living with provisional or no services. This phenomenon has been observed in São Paulo and Johannesburg (Few et al, 2004), where Ponte Tower, an abandoned city centre tower block, was until recently occupied informally (shown in Figure 3.1). Recent studies have shown how residential occupation of abandoned

Figure 3.1: Ponte Tower, an example of inner-city informal living in Johannesburg

Source: Philipp Horn

inner-city commercial buildings in São Paulo is motivated by both housing need and political objectives, relating to citizenship claims by residents, in response to exclusionary regeneration processes (De Carli and Frediani, 2016). Meanwhile, in highly densely populated cities such as Hong Kong, illegal subdivision of apartments has led to extremely small housing units, including the notorious 'cage' or 'coffin' houses portrayed in a detailed and sensitive ethnographic study by Cheung (2000), which replaced former 'rooftop shacks' built on top of high-rise buildings (Hardoy and Satterthwaite, 1989).

Urban informal neighbourhoods

Informal settlements or neighbourhoods[3] are perhaps the spaces most commonly associated with living informally in the global South, in terms of scale and prevalence. In 2018, it was estimated that more than one billion people worldwide lived in informal neighbourhoods (United Nations, 2021). However, gathering data on this phenomenon is challenging, sometimes due to limited capacity at city or national government level, but also because of its continued under-recognition. Even defining informal neighbourhoods is difficult because of disagreement between researchers, national governments and international agencies over their key characteristics or variables. This issue is neatly demonstrated by Samper et al's (2020) identification of 18 different variables used to define informality in a selection of academic and institutional accounts.

UN-Habitat's (2003) definition of urban informal neighbourhoods is widely used and provides a useful starting point, although it is not uncontested. As shown in Chapter 1, it defines informal neighbourhoods as characterized by inadequate conditions of housing and/or basic services, specifically relating to five characteristics:

- inadequate access to safe water;
- inadequate access to sanitation and infrastructure;
- poor structural quality of housing;
- overcrowding;
- insecure residential status.

These conditions often derive from the neighbourhood's origins, which tend to involve informally acquired land, self-built or self-financed housing, and incrementally obtained services. It is important, however, to note that such a general categorization inevitably obscures a wide range of different housing sub-markets and locations. Additionally, it does not capture the dynamic and interacting nature of these characteristics (Gulyani and Talukdar, 2008). We explore these elements further in what follows, focusing on the processes through which land, housing and services are acquired in informal neighbourhoods.

While the image of informal neighbourhoods is often associated with the iconic morphology of the *favela* (Varley, 2013), there is immense diversity within this category, which includes the well-established neighbourhoods originating as *asentamiento informales* in Latin American cities (such as in Figure 3.2), the 'slums' of South Asian

Figure 3.2: Informal neighbourhood in Xalapa, Mexico

Source: Melanie Lombard

cities, and the rented shacks of Sub-Saharan African cities. More recently, China's 'urban villages' have been recognized as informal neighbourhoods in the context of the country's rapid urbanization over the last 35 years. Urban villages refer to settlements which have rural or peri-urban status, where rural landholding villagers build housing for workers in nearby urban areas or industries, in violation of building regulations (Herrle and Fokdal, 2011). Similar phenomena have been recognized historically in places like Mexico City, where *ejidos* were 'invaded' by the city (Durand, 1983), or in Mumbai, where fishing villages have been incorporated into the urban area (Dovey and King, 2011).

Urban informal neighbourhoods also contain diverse forms of tenure and types of housing, as suggested by the account in Box 3.1. While residents are often characterized as predominantly owner-occupiers, in some older informal neighbourhoods, sub-letting rooms and shacks may be particularly common, with an informal rental sub-market emerging as the neighbourhood becomes consolidated. Particularly common in Sub-Saharan African cities, where incomes are often very low, rental housing may have benefits for both tenant and landlord. Small-scale landlords, usually residents in the same neighbourhood, have traditionally offered affordable rental units for tenants to supplement their income rather than for profiteering (Scheba and Turok, 2020), although this has recently given way to the commercialization of informal rental housing in contexts like South Africa. In some cities, renters may pay a premium for sub-standard but well-located housing, such as Nairobi where rental tenure predominates (Talukdar, 2018). Rental housing is often seen as an interim tenure, offering newcomers to the city easy entry into the housing market, or longer-term tenants the opportunity to save for homeownership; yet research on informal renting in Colombia found that it is frequently a long-term solution, as tenants move from rental to rental, rather than from rental to homeownership, which may have considerably higher entry barriers (Lombard et al, 2021). Despite representing a long-term solution for many people who live informally, informal renting is often ignored by the state, which is frequently fixated on homeownership as the main solution to housing need (Gilbert, 2016). Tenure data is often not collected, or renting is confused with illegal ownership, meaning it can be difficult to establish the scale of informal rental housing in a given context.

Box 3.1: The history of an informal neighbourhood in Cali, Colombia: an account by Alexander López, Asomevid

Charco Azul is a neighbourhood in the Aguablanca District of Cali, Colombia's third largest city. Aguablanca District is a large area of self-built neighbourhoods to the east of the city, which houses around a quarter of Cali's inhabitants. Many of these neighbourhoods were founded by Afro-Colombian migrant communities from the Pacific region, who first started migrating to Cali in around 1950, initially for economic reasons and later due to displacement relating to the country's civil conflict.

Charco Azul was founded through land invasion in 1975, on formerly agricultural land at Cali's periphery, amid millet plantations and next to a pond which gave the neighbourhood its name. As Alex recounted, "[The first settlers] found themselves in a neighbourhood, or rather a millet plantation, which offered the chance to build or acquire housing ... that was the possibility that we found here, to find a home."

The land belonged to a private landowner, but a caretaker allowed the first families to settle. They then alerted other groups of relatives and friends to this opportunity, and the population grew to around 400 households. Initially, Charco Azul lacked basic services, including water, sewerage and public lighting. The neighbourhood flooded frequently, and flies and snakes were commonplace. The threat of eviction was also present, as Alex recalled: "It was complicated because there were evictions, there were confrontations, and there was a struggle by the families, all of us, to remain on the land, and a struggle by the state to remove people from the land. So that was quite a big challenge."

Alex continued: "The other challenge was to do with the [physical] construction of the neighbourhood and accessing basic services, water, electricity, that was basically via collective construction." Household members constructed housing incrementally, starting with shacks (*cambuches*) of bamboo, cardboard and plastic, which were slowly replaced by more permanent materials, such as corrugated iron for roofing, and breezeblocks for walls. Services were initially provisional, with water drawn from the lake, wood fires and candles for cooking and lighting, and sewerage via individual informal connections to nearby irrigation channels. Subsequently the community organized to connect a pipe to the water network in the adjacent Colonia 7 de Agosto, securing informal connections for individual households, although pressure was low and supply unreliable. Electricity was similarly supplied via an informal connection in Colonia 7 de Agosto, with individual households connecting to the supply, generating the characteristic 'spider's web' of cables around informally constructed poles, and causing power cuts and fires.

The community resisted repeated attempts at eviction, and towards the end of the 1990s, leaders organized to negotiate with the local government to legalize land tenure. Assignation of plots was accompanied by reordering of street layouts, which facilitated service provision. Water and electricity arrived formally in the neighbourhood after a long negotiation between residents' work committees (formally known as *Juntas de Accion Comunal*) and local authorities. The installation of electricity meters, poles and transformers, and improvements to the sewerage service, were paid for in instalments by residents. This was accompanied by housing improvements, with support from the local government alongside individual efforts.

Today, the majority of the neighbourhood's plots are legalized, and Charco Azul is a relatively consolidated neighbourhood with around 1,800 households. As Alex highlights: "[It is] totally different, because we basically didn't have water, we didn't have sewerage, decent housing, basic services, we didn't have the infrastructure that exists now, public lighting; the neighbourhood now is totally different." However, some areas of the neighbourhood are still not fully connected to formal services, such as the Sardi area, housing around 400 families, where land tenure is still irregular. Local organizations continue to struggle and negotiate for the extension of services to the whole community, as well as in response to social issues of youth unemployment and violence.

Causal factors

Observers have attempted to account for the causes of informal living from diverse disciplinary perspectives. While most concur that living informally coincides with rapid urban population growth, this factor alone is not sufficient, given that some cities, such as Tokyo, have grown rapidly without large proportions of the population living informally (Hardoy and Satterthwaite, 1989). Indeed, informal living has also been observed in North American and European cities, both recently and historically, an issue which we explore further in the last section of this chapter (see also Chapter 2). Economists have tended to identify causal factors for living informally with barriers to accessing land and housing markets, such as macroeconomic conditions characterized by low incomes and poverty, urban growth without economic growth, regulatory frameworks that slow down land delivery or impede access to land markets, and a lack of investment in infrastructure (Arimah, 2010). Other researchers have emphasized political economic factors, attributing these conditions to the effects of globalization (as highlighted in Chapter 2), particularly the economic crises that resulted from structural adjustment policies imposed on many countries of the global South in return for loans from the World Bank or International Monetary Fund in the 1980s and 1990s, such as economic deregulation, privatization of services, and state withdrawal from the housing sector (Durand-Lasserve and Royston, 2002: 3; see also Davis, 2006).

Other explanations have focused more on planning policy and political factors, such as a lack of accessible or affordable formal housing supply; political clientelism affecting distribution of resources; and a lack of realistic planning, as suggested by Fernandes' (2011) study of Latin American cities. Lack of affordable housing is often attributed less to scarcity than to the difficulties of accessing formal housing markets and programmes, due to the high entry requirements of housing schemes, such as down payments, credit-worthiness or formal employment, which are unrealistic for many low-income households (Mitlin and Satterthwaite, 2013). Here, there are overlaps with planning-focused perspectives highlighted in Chapter 2, such as Harris' (2018) institutionally focused approach which associates informality with non-compliance (by residents) with institutional rules or regulations, along with their non-enforcement (by the state). Critical accounts suggest that non-compliance is caused by the mismatch between legal frameworks and low-income residents' housing needs, meaning that their efforts to house themselves are frequently criminalized (Hardoy and Satterthwaite, 1989).

Mismatching legal and institutional frameworks have been associated with the colonial history of global Southern countries, also highlighted in Chapter 2. Writing on Sub-Saharan African cities, Fox (2014) highlights how colonialism's lasting legacies of underinvestment, weak institutions, and political patronage and rent-seeking by elites, left cities underprepared to respond to high levels of housing demand associated with urbanization, thus producing informal growth. Certainly, the legacies of colonial urbanism have shaped many cities of the global South, leaving their imprint on urban form. This is evident in monumental buildings and urban locations deriving from trade routes and territorial administration, land tenure systems based usually either on English 'common law' or French 'civil law', and social and ethnic segregation, resulting in uneven provision of basic services and inappropriate norms deriving from colonial institutions such as British Town and Country Planning (Hardoy and Satterthwaite, 1989).

These diverse and sometimes conflicting causal explanations demonstrate that informal living is always the result of a complex interaction of diverse factors in any given urban setting, and that the combination and outcome of these factors varies according to context. This suggests that while definitions like UN-Habitat's (presented at the beginning of this section) are a helpful starting point, a more nuanced explanation is required, which accounts for local specificities such as relevant legal and regulatory frameworks, institutions and practices. Connolly (2020) shows how regional and national contextual factors, including legal and cultural norms, combine to shape informality in many possible ways (see Figure 3.3). Her detailed account of informal neighbourhoods in Mexico City, where 62 per cent of metropolitan households live in housing developed informally, highlights factors contributing to this, including: socio-demographic transformations of urban society; national and local housing finance policy; macroeconomic stability, access to mortgages and rising land values; and the differentiated and uneven application of land use and other regulations relating to formal and informal urban development, including changes in the regulation of communal (*ejidal*) property due to the end of the Agrarian Reform.

Determining causal factors for informal living is therefore complex, contingent and contextualized. Nevertheless, in almost all contexts, two critical factors appear to be

Figure 3.3: What do we mean by informal? The branching tree of irregularities in housing

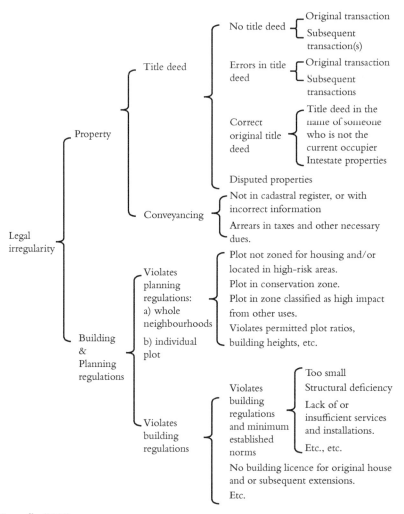

Source: Connolly (2020)

housing need combined with inadequate formal response, underpinned by the twin forces of the state and the market, which structure urban space in most cities (Mitlin and Satterthwaite, 2013). The state provides infrastructure (delivering serviced land) and sets the framework for planning, including housing standards (which the poor are often unable to meet), as well as regulating land markets. Meanwhile, the market plays a role in structuring investment, determining differences between diverse properties and settlements, as well as land values. This leads Mitlin and Satterthwaite (2013: 253) to suggest that '[i]n most cities, the effects of state and market combine with shelter needs to result in a range of low-income neighbourhoods housing a significant proportion of the population on a small fraction of the city's land area'. We explore specific aspects of informal living in the next section, focusing on land, housing and services.

Elements of informal living: land, housing, services

The configuration of land, housing and services depends on external and internal factors, and as suggested earlier, this can affect how an area or neighbourhood develops. While they are often considered in relation to urban informal neighbourhoods, they are also relevant for other forms of informality, including inner-city housing and pavement dwelling.

Land

Land tenure is a key determining element of informal living. Insecure tenure is common in many informal neighbourhoods, as suggested by the inclusion of 'insecure residential status' in UN-Habitat's definition (discussed earlier). Although difficult to estimate due to lack of global data, evidence from the early 2000s suggested that 'between 30 and 50% of urban residents lack security of tenure' (UN-Habitat, 2003: xi), due to urban growth in the context of rising urban land values and increasing demand. Land tenure refers to the relationship between people (whether as individuals or groups) and land (GLTN, 2023). More specifically, it refers to 'the rights of individuals or groups in relation to land' (Durand-Lasserve and Royston, 2002: 7), which may be expressed as a set of rules defining who can do what with a piece of land. Multiple individuals (or groups) can have rights to the same piece of land, and their rights may be different, ranging from access and use, to ownership and transfer rights. The rights of different actors may sometimes overlap, and because of this, tenure is sometimes conceptualized as a 'bundle of rights' (Durand-Lasserve and Royston, 2002: 8), with specific differentiated rights making up an individual or group's bundle.

Secure tenure relates to protection from eviction: 'a person or household can be said to have secure tenure when they are protected from involuntary removal from their land or residence, except in exceptional circumstances, and then only by means of a known and agreed legal procedure' (Durand-Lasserve and Royston, 2002: 8). Conversely, insecure tenure may cause vulnerability to eviction, with potentially devastating social impacts. Evictions, which move the poor away from work, health and education facilities, can reproduce or even cause poverty, creating new settlements populated with displaced residents. Evictions may occur due to legal contestation over ownership of land, or based on the state's designation of a settlement as unsafe, which may overlap with the allocation of the underlying land for infrastructural development. Market evictions are increasingly common, with low-income residents priced out of areas due to rising land values and taxes, as 'residual' land shrinks and peripheral areas become more attractive for middle and high-value development (Everett, 2001). These processes are discussed further in Chapter 6.

The level of tenure (in)security in a given neighbourhood depends on many factors. Residents often lack formal titles to the land on which they are settled, and the absence of formal tenure is often seen as a fundamental characteristic of living informally. Land at the urban periphery tends to be especially viable for informal neighbourhoods, as it may have previously been used for agriculture or other purposes, and consequently be unserviced and therefore cheaper. The land may be formally owned, whether privately (by an individual landowner), publicly (by the state), customarily (by traditional authorities, in some Sub-Saharan African contexts), or collectively (by legally constituted figures such as the Mexican *ejido*). While it is hard to generalize across contexts, levels of tenure security may initially be determined by the process through which land is acquired and settled, although other factors also play a role (discussed further in the next sub-sections). Two distinct processes by which land is informally acquired are land invasion (also sometimes known as squatting) and informal (and/or illegal) subdivision (Durand-Lasserve and Royston, 2002). We briefly discuss these here.

Land invasion

Land invasion, or squatting,[4] was very common in early urbanization processes in Latin America, up to the 1960s in Mexico City and Rio de Janeiro, and the 1970s in Lima, Caracas and Santiago (Hardoy and Satterthwaite, 1989). It usually entails the informal, or illegal, occupation of land, which may be public, or less frequently private, and located centrally or at the urban periphery (Durand-Lasserve and Royston, 2002). Occupation may occur in a sudden, coordinated fashion, or gradually over time. Yet either way, '[a]ccess to squatter settlements is rarely free' (Durand-Lasserve and Royston, 2002: 5). Often, an individual or group controls access to land as part of the informal settlement process, and charges newer settlers for land acquisition and/or use. Such settlements often have extremely insecure tenure: occupants' legal rights are precarious as the occupation is considered illegal, and may be contested by the landowner or other parties, particularly if the land is considered valuable. Construction of dwellings often occurs regardless of local regulations, and services are usually provisional, at least at the outset. As a result, living conditions are often initially poor, although they may improve over time. Globally, invasion appears to have decreased since the end of the 20th century, as the commodification of land delivery systems and the decrease in available public land mean that 'there is no longer free access to land' (Durand-Lasserve and Royston, 2002: 5). Nevertheless, squatting is still found in many cities, observed for example at the margins of existing consolidated informal neighbourhoods in Xalapa, Mexico (Lombard, 2009; see Figure 5.3).

Unauthorized subdivision

The second process of informal land acquisition is known as unauthorized, informal or illegal subdivision. This relates to the unauthorized development of an area of land, based on its subdivision into plots. Occupants buy a plot of land to build housing on, either directly from the landowner, or sometimes via an intermediary or developer. The legal status of these transactions is often unclear, depending on local regulations or national law; in some cases, the land sale itself may be semi-legal, but the development contravenes local building, planning and/or subdivision regulations (Durand-Lasserve and Royston, 2002: 5), as seen in Figure 3.3. However, settlers in these circumstances may have more security than squatters, due to the existence of documentation relating to the (informal) land transaction; and over time, such settlements generally have a higher chance of becoming consolidated and integrated into the urban fabric. Nevertheless, during this process of consolidation, insecure tenure may still prevail, often for many decades, as residents struggle to obtain recognition and basic services (discussed further in the next section).

Housing

Housing is a second determining characteristic of informal living, seen in UN-Habitat's inclusion of 'poor structural quality of housing' and 'overcrowding' in its definition. This may derive from the self-built or self-financed nature of housing, meaning that homes are often constructed 'room-by-room' (Dovey and King, 2011: 27), as suggested in the testimony at the start of this chapter. In general, initial housing development in informal neighbourhoods tends to be characterized by provisional, often temporary materials such as tin, cardboard and wood. Over time, as residents' financial capacity improves, so does housing quality, as more permanent materials such as breezeblock, brick and glass replace earlier materials. Nevertheless, the wide diversity of household capacity means that the pace of housing improvement may be highly variable and is often not linear, as Moser (2009) shows in her 30-year longitudinal study of an informal neighbourhood in Guayaquil, Ecuador.

Moreover, the precise processes by which housing is constructed in informal settings differ between countries, cities and even neighbourhoods, with materials determined by local availability and climate, as well as residents' financial capacity. For example, in Nairobi, Kenya, older informal shack housing is often constructed with mud walls and iron-sheet roofs, while newer tenements may have quarry-stone walls supported by steel and concrete (Mwau and Sverdlik, 2020). In Cali, Colombia, traditional materials such as bamboo (*guadua*) and wood have been superseded by breezeblock and plastic (see Box 3.1). This also suggests that defining 'poor quality' housing can be difficult, as this is not only determined by physical standards, but also by social and cultural norms and processes. Nevertheless, economic circumstances are a significant factor; as Gilbert (2014: 306) argues: 'In general, the poorer the country, the worse the urban housing situation: African and Indian shelter standards are far below those of Latin America.'

In contexts where informal housing prevails, the problem is therefore not a *lack* of housing, but the overcrowded, poorly serviced and flimsy accommodation that often constitutes a home (Gilbert, 2014). In other words, it is housing quality rather than quantity that matters. This suggests that estimates of a given country's 'housing gap', which still dominate official accounts, calculating the number of units required to respond to housing demand, are misplaced. In many contexts, the need is not for new housing – particularly given the mismatch between high housing demand and low national resources or capacity – but for improvement of existing housing, particularly by reducing densities, upgrading and improving services (Gilbert, 2014). These issues are discussed more extensively in Chapter 6. Given the diversity of housing quality between countries and cities (seen in Figure 3.4), standards must

Figure 3.4: Informal housing diversity

Note: Colombia (top left), South Africa (top right), Mexico (top right) and Colombia (bottom right)
Source: Melanie Lombard/Philipp Horn

also be context-sensitive, rather than based on Western standards of housing and overcrowding, which are again often a legacy of colonial histories (Hardoy and Satterthwaite, 1989).

Housing as an asset

For households with low incomes, housing is significant as a physical asset, and a basis for the accumulation of other assets. The asset accumulation framework proposed by Caroline Moser (2009), building on the work of Amartya Sen (2005), defines an asset as a buffer between production, exchange and consumption, for recourse in times of crisis. In other words, assets can be stored, sold or used to generate income when necessary, which is often vitally important for low-income residents, who generally have fewer assets and are thus more vulnerable to crisis. Housing in informal neighbourhoods can act as an asset in several ways. First, as shelter, it reduces household members' physical and socio-economic vulnerability, by protecting them from the elements and providing physical security, as well as giving them a base from which to seek employment in the city. Second, it can support the generation of additional income, providing a space for productive activities such as home-based enterprises (discussed further in Chapter 4), but also potentially a source of rental income, through the subdivision or construction of rooms or additional floors to rent by small-scale landlords, as shown in the opening section of this chapter.[5] Third, it represents an intergenerational asset, to be inherited by the children of the household, and it may be expanded to accommodate a growing household's second generation (Wigle, 2009).

Services

Inadequate access to basic services is a third defining characteristic of informal living, as suggested by the UN-Habitat definition, which highlights 'inadequate access to safe water' and 'inadequate access to sanitation and infrastructure'. The term basic services refers broadly to water and sanitation, electricity and public lighting, waste management, and roads and transport for mobility (see, for example, UN-Habitat, 2020). Infrastructure can be understood as the urban hardware through which services (including transport, energy and waste management) are delivered (UN-Habitat, 2020: 55), such as formal water, sewerage and electricity networks and improved roads and pavement alongside transport systems such as mass transit. While infrastructure is often seen as the responsibility of the government, the reality of deficient infrastructure and services in informal contexts may lead to self-help provision processes. It is also commonly observed that in informal neighbourhoods, the sequence of service provision is often the inverse of formal housing: in informal contexts, inhabitation is followed by construction and then service provision, rather than construction, service provision and inhabitation, which is usually the case in formal settings.

Despite general agreement that inadequate basic services and infrastructure are common factors in informal living, they are again highly variable across countries, cities and neighbourhoods, and can change over time. Global indicators are established by the Sustainable Development Goals, which can help to measure and evaluate provision in a given context. For example, under Goal 6, 'Clean water and sanitation', safe and affordable drinking water is defined as 'located on premises, available when needed and free from contamination'; and safe sanitation and hygiene relates to access to 'safely managed sanitation facilities and at least basic handwashing facilities' (Our World in Data, 2023). Access to electricity is measured at household level (Goal 7, 'Affordable and clean energy'). Waste management and transport infrastructure are covered under Goal 11, 'Sustainable cities and communities'. Waste management is measured by the proportion of urban solid waste regularly collected; and transport defined in terms of accessible, safe, reliable and sustainable public transport systems (Our World in Data, 2023). However, despite these improved indicators for basic service provision, it is frequently still poorly measured, and statistics are unreliable in many contexts. Additionally, there is debate about how to define 'affordability', for example, of drinking water, in contexts where incomes are low (as is frequently the case in informal neighbourhoods). Researchers have criticized measures of affordability which use a proportion of income (for example, 5 per cent of household income) for obscuring whether provision is adequate, measured by the World Health Organization standard of 50 litres per person per day in non-emergency situations (Mitlin and Walnycki, 2020).

Informal neighbourhoods are often established on cheap, unserviced land, as already shown, meaning that residents must initially collaborate to secure some level of service provision, whether formally or informally. Initially, this may include 'pirate' connections to adjacent formal electricity and water networks – often through ingenious use of extension cables and pipes – and individual pit latrines. As a neighbourhood becomes more established, drinking water may be supplied by communal standpipe, or by private water sellers (who may also be involved in illegally tapping water from mains networks, as described by Hackenbroch and Hossain, 2012). For energy, generators or gas bottles may be used, and residents may organize to pay for street lighting and household electricity provision, collectively or individually, installing through self-help processes the basic infrastructure that will allow them to be connected to the main network. Connection to the sewerage network often takes longer, although communities sometimes work together to construct a septic tank, or at household level to install composting toilets (Lombard, 2009). Waste management may initially be via burning solid waste, and later through the participation of informal waste recyclers, before regular formal waste collections are instigated (if at all) by local authorities. Meanwhile, throughout all these processes, residents are often simultaneously involved in petitioning the local authority or other relevant agencies for connection to formal service networks (Moser, 2009).

The level of services in a given settlement is determined by complex context-specific factors including (lack of) resources and capacity at the local level, but also unfair distribution of these resources by local authorities (Mitlin and Satterthwaite, 2013), and local power relationships which give rise to claim-making, negotiation and contestation (Hackenbroch and Hossain, 2012). Nevertheless, the complex configurations of service delivery in informal settings exemplify the 'socio-technical diversity' that characterizes service provision in cities of the global South, which extends beyond standardized conceptions of networked, state-driven infrastructure (Jaglin, 2017). While this relates to 'the creative ways in which people actually succeed, under specific and localised conditions, in devising technical and institutional solutions' to their service needs (Jaglin, 2017: 437), there are also negative implications of infrastructural inadequacies and unregulated service provision. These include health effects, such as the higher prevalence of waterborne diseases from drinking untreated water, or airborne diseases due to lack of paved roads. Unregulated private services may also be much more costly than networked provision, in both financial and environmental terms (Jaglin, 2017).

The significance of consolidation

Through 'consolidation' processes, informal neighbourhoods are considered to improve over time in terms of land tenure, housing and services (Gough and Kellett, 2001). Housing consolidation refers to upgrading building materials, for example, from plastic, wood and laminate, to glass, concrete and cement, as well as extension through additional floors or rooms. Simultaneously, residents may be organizing to petition the local government for services, such as road paving, as outlined earlier. This may result in increased residential density as more residents arrive to take possession of plots and build. All of these changes can be seen in the two sets of photos in Figure 3.5.

The theorized links between land, housing and services that support consolidation processes have been the subject of much debate. They are often understood through the perspective of secure tenure, usually relating to land (although sometimes also to housing). As already suggested, secure tenure is seen as highly significant for

Figure 3.5: Consolidation of a neighbourhood in Xalapa, Mexico, 2006–11

Source: Melanie Lombard

low-income residents living informally, as it apparently enables access to basic services and livelihood opportunities for poor residents, including work, productive activities and rental income deriving from secure housing. Settlement consolidation, through individual improvements leading to services, is often conceptualized as a result of secure land and housing tenure. Moreover, secure tenure is frequently conflated with individual legal titles to land and/or housing; and the relationship between tenure and settlement consolidation is one of the main supporting arguments for tenure legalization or formalization programmes as a response to informality. This and other perspectives are discussed in further detail in Chapter 6.

However, it is worth noting that tenure is more complex than titles alone. Security of tenure depends on 'residents' perceptions of past and present government policy' (Payne, 2004: 173), particularly related to service provision and a lack of eviction (see also van Gelder, 2010). Although there is a relationship between secure tenure and housing quality, it is not one way; in other words, residents' investment in housing can also make an informal neighbourhood more secure. Conversely, some tenure regularization programmes require a certain level of occupancy in order to undertake titling. For example, in the neighbourhood shown in Figure 3.5, residents did not have formal land titles, and this underlines the point that the relationship between tenure security, titles and consolidation is more complex than it might appear.

New developments

Recent debates on urban informality have highlighted the way that living informally is changing in several aspects, often drawing on empirical work in rapidly changing urban environments. Scholars are increasingly interested in elite and middle-class uses of informality, hitherto neglected. New spatial forms are appearing in densely inhabited informal neighbourhoods where vertical development is the only option. Finally, a growing body of literature applies the lens of urban informality to spatial development in the global North.

Elite and middle-class income informality

The uses of informality by middle-income and elite groups have been acknowledged by many authors (for example, Roy, 2005; Varley, 2013), but only recently has emerging research started engaging more systematically with cases of 'elite informality', making up for a previous deficit in this area (Alfaro d'Alencon et al, 2018). Some accounts have identified informal development processes deployed by business elites and 'mafia-like' groups in Mumbai, such as property developers who contravene building regulations, contributing to the 2005 floods that paralysed the city (McFarlane, 2012), as discussed in Chapter 2; or organized criminals, originating as informal service providers, developing schemes such as shopping malls (Weinstein, 2008). These studies show how such groups benefit from a lack of enforcement of regulations, which may be selectively applied, or the circumvention of regulatory frameworks, particularly relating to land development. The local state may supportively neglect such activities if they are aligned with its objectives, such as improving Mumbai's competitive status, and this may be bolstered by 'hefty bribes' from specific powerful groups (Weinstein, 2008: 23).

Recent research has highlighted how elite informality shapes city development. Moatasim's (2019) study of the elite Bani Gala neighbourhood in Islamabad, Pakistan, informally developed in a protected green area, reveals some similarities with low-income informal processes (such as piecemeal development, the role of leaders, and the importance of negotiation), but also highlights significant differences (such as more permanent housing, secure tenure backed by legal challenges, and residents' lived experience of remote locations, with long commutes and lack of services mitigated by access to private vehicles and personal connections to local officials). Others have highlighted the issue of the 'missing middle', namely the lack of research on middle-income groups (Lemanski and Lama-Rewal, 2012), which is especially important given the growing middle class in Africa, and the significance of informal housing as a means of securing homeownership for this social group (Nthambi Jimmy, 2023). Nthambi Jimmy's (2023) study of Kilimani neighbourhood in central Nairobi, where since the 1960s, upper-middle-income Kenyans have replaced White colonial inhabitants, shows how since 2000, low-density housing has been superseded by the development of initially medium- and high-rise buildings of up to 25 floors, despite official zoning regulations permitting no more than eight floors (see Figure 3.6). This in turn has led to the informalization of service provision due to additional demand from increased population density.

Vertical slums

Similarly, in some (low-income) informal neighbourhoods, particularly in Sub-Saharan African and South Asian cities, densification has occurred via informal

Figure 3.6: Informal development in a middle-income neighbourhood, Nairobi, Kenya

Source: Eunice Nthambi Jimmy

construction of multi-storey blocks of flats, which have been termed 'vertical slums' (Mwau, 2019). This has been observed in Nairobi, in low-income neighbourhoods such as Mukuru (discussed in Chapters 5, 6 and 7) as well as the middle-income ones discussed earlier. These tenements, with densely packed single-room units, have replaced shacks, but housing conditions are not much improved. It is estimated that poor-quality tenements house up to 1.5 million low-income tenants in Nairobi in stone, concrete and steel buildings of up to 10 storeys, which are often poorly constructed and at risk of collapse (Mwau and Sverdlik, 2020). While such buildings may be highly lucrative for landlords, whose higher initial investment is followed by greater returns due to their density, residents share bathroom facilities and services are often deficient.

In Cape Town, research has shown that micro-flats, in the form of small freestanding backyard rental units of up to six rooms, are replacing shacks (Scheba and Turok, 2020). Compared to Nairobi, this form of housing represents the densification but also commercialization of vertical informal housing, offering higher-quality but more expensive units in low-income neighbourhoods (Mwau and Sverdlik, 2020). Materials are often more durable than shacks, with better facilities, suggesting a change in informal rental markets towards provision of larger-scale rental properties, often owned by micro-entrepreneurs who may still live on site, but are increasingly professional and may ultimately move out of their dwelling in order to capitalize on space (Scheba and Turok, 2020). This reflects changing contextual conditions in South Africa, including shifting norms towards the acceptance of backyard renting, a growing Black middle class who are potential tenants, and an enduring informal land market, based on the onward sale of formal government-provided housing and plots.

Informality in the global North

Finally, informality is increasingly an object of study for urban researchers focusing on the global North. In some respects this is not new, as discussed in Chapters 1 and 2 when we introduced the Victorian 'slums' of industrializing Britain. Manifestations of informal living have historically been observed in other Northern contexts under conditions of rapid urban growth in the early 20th century, such as the *chabolas* of Madrid, *borgate* in Rome and informal plot development in Athens (Baumgart and Kreibich, 2011). Hardy and Ward's (1984) book *Arcadia for All* revealed the use of plotlands around London as a route to securing seasonal and sometimes permanent housing for working-class families in the UK. Nevertheless, there is a sense that the number of people who live and work informally in the global North is increasing, and that this change is accompanied by new forms of urban informality, often as a response to conditions of crisis, austerity and increasing inequality (Alfaro d'Alencon et al, 2018). For example, Fairbanks (2011) shows how the recovery house movement in Philadelphia, a rehabilitation and housing project which takes advantage of the deregulated environment caused by urban decline, welfare reform and state withdrawal, uses reconfigured abandoned housing to respond to the housing needs of the poorest urban residents.

In the UK, 'beds in sheds' have been studied as a manifestation of informal living, as discussed in Chapter 2. This form of housing is provided through the illegal conversion of sheds, garages and outbuildings for residential use, often in London boroughs or surrounding areas with high levels of housing demand and low-paid jobs. Although no comprehensive data exists, it has been estimated that tens of thousands of such properties may exist, often lacking adequate facilities but commanding market rents. National policy and media accounts have suggested that shed housing is produced and populated by 'illegal migrants', implying that this phenomenon is a 'product of culture', echoing environmentally deterministic accounts of the 'culture of poverty'. In fact, Lombard (2019) found that shed housing in the UK is produced by a confluence of structural factors characteristic of many cities in the North, such as an affordable housing crisis, a growing and deregulated private rental sector, welfare reforms and changes to immigration policy (see also Schiller and Raco, 2021). Similarly, research on informal neighbourhoods at the US–Mexico border has shown how informality is structurally determined, constituted in terms of non-compliance, non-enforcement and deregulation within existing regulatory regimes (Durst and Wegmann, 2017).

These accounts highlight the differentiated character of informal living, depending on the context. They also suggest that there is a need for better dialogue between research across diverse contexts. While there are clear differences between informality in the global North and South, relating to scale, physical aspects, regulatory responses and property ownership, South–North learning may offer theoretical tools to enable better understanding of informality in Northern contexts, such as the insight that 'greater regulation often leads to more rather than less informality' (Durst and Wegmann, 2017: 283), particularly relevant in Northern contexts where regulatory responses tend to predominate. This approach, in line with the postcolonial and Southern urban theory perspectives introduced in Chapter 2, is discussed further in Chapter 8.

Chapter summary

This chapter provided an overview of the multiple dimensions of informal living. We have seen that the experience of living informally varies greatly across different contexts, but there are certain identifiable (although often contested) characteristics, including elements relating to tenure, housing quality and service provision. Establishing causal factors is complex, but observers highlight the significance of colonial (regulatory) legacies, and the role of state and market, in determining outcomes in contexts where high levels of housing need meet low capacity to respond. In particular, it is important to be aware of the heterogeneity of experiences of informal living that exist in all contexts, and the need for a contextualized understanding of power relations that shape these. Land, housing and services are all critical to understand how people live informally. Land tenure in particular can play a determining factor, but the relationship between this and other elements is subject to ongoing debate. New developments include new forms of service and housing provision, elite informality, and informality in the North.

Recommended reading

- Hardoy, J. and Satterthwaite, D. (1989) *Squatter Citizen*, London: Earthscan. We particularly recommend reading chapter 1, 'The legal and the illegal city'.
- Durand-Lasserve, A. and Royston, L. (eds) (2002) *Holding their Ground: Secure Land Tenure for the Urban Poor in Developing Countries*, London: Earthscan. We particularly recommend reading chapter 1, 'International trends and country contexts: from tenure regularization to tenure security'.
- Moser, C. (2009) *Ordinary Families, Extraordinary Lives*, Washington, DC: Brookings Institution Press. We particularly recommend reading chapter 3, 'A home of one's own: squatter housing as a physical asset'.

EXERCISES

Think about examples of living informally you know about (somewhere you have experienced directly, or from sources including those mentioned in this chapter).

- What are their characteristics relating to living informally (think about land, housing, services)?
- What are some of the contextual factors that may have shaped their development?
- Why are they considered informal?
- What are the common factors between the different examples you can think of?
- What differences exist between these examples?

Alternative representations

- We recommend you have a look at *My Home Manantiales* (http://www.mobilitymovilidad.org/home-hogar/manantiales.html) as this website provides some interesting stories from a recently established informal neighbourhood in Colombia.
- To get a better understanding of living informally in the global North, we recommend watching *Spain: Living in a European Slum* (https://www.youtube.com/watch?v=mJTPdOuQDrE).
- In addition to reading Caroline Moser's book (see recommended readings), we also suggest you watch her two documentary films on life in the informal neighbourhood she writes about. These are the 1980 film *People of the Barrio* (https://www.youtube.com/watch?v=cq6hcG18d-g) and the 2020 film *Calle K* (https://vimeo.com/374278445/a62381a630).

4

Working Informally

'In El Alto, economic opportunities don't arise because of your qualifications, but through connections. Many of us have completed our university degrees but all we can do is work in the popular sectors, for example as street vendors or by setting up our own [informal] businesses on the streets, squares, or even in our home. To get a professional [formal] job that matches our qualifications, you need to have the right connections. Corruption is a big problem here and without the right connections you don't get anywhere.'

A young woman in her 20s and graduate in social work at the Public University of El Alto, reflecting on economic challenges among youths in the city of El Alto, Bolivia[1]

Across the globe economic activities – from the conversion of raw materials to the sale of finished products – rely on a combination of formal and informal practices and transactions. A growing proportion of the global workforce can be considered informal, with some operating in what is referred to as the informal sector and others engaging in informal employment in formally registered firms. The informal economy has no physical boundaries and, throughout the last decades, it emerged in new places and in distinct shapes and articulations with close ties to the formal economy.

By following the production chain of specific goods, we can unpack formal and informal economic relations. Take, for example, a T-shirt purchased online from a retailer and delivered by a subcontracted company whose drivers are 'self-employed' gig economy workers, lacking social and legal labour protections (as we will learn later in this chapter, the absence of such protections is a key characteristic of informal employment). The T-shirt might have been designed by a formally registered clothing company, but this company may well make use of subcontracted small-scale informal enterprises that take charge of tailoring and production. This is, of course, a fictitious, stylized and over-simplified illustration, but it demonstrates that, in one way or

Figure 4.1: Examples of informal work in Bolivia and South Africa

Note: Top left: vendors at the Lime and Imphepho market situated below a road junction in inner-city Durban (South Africa); top right: informal welding business in an informal neighbourhood in Johannesburg (South Africa); bottom left: street market scene on the 'Feria 16 de Julio' in El Alto (Bolivia); bottom right: street vendor in El Alto's Ceja neighbourhood (Bolivia).

Source: Philipp Horn

another, all of us are somewhat implicated in the informal economy. For this reason, it is useful to gain a better understanding of this phenomenon.

This chapter provides an historical overview of trends around working informally, reflecting on and deepening the discussion of core conceptual debates introduced in Chapter 2. It traces shifts in understandings of working informally from a focus on the informal sector, which centred predominantly on economic relations of the urban poor in cities of the global South, towards broader understandings around informal employment and the informal economy. The chapter makes use of illustrative case studies from across the globe to examine the diverse articulations of and urban contexts for working informally (see Figure 4.1 for examples of different articulations of informal work in South Africa and Bolivia). Among other issues, it discusses the contribution of the informal economy to economic growth within cities of the global South, in terms of gross domestic product (GDP), employment, income generation and other factors related to socio-economic development. Attention is also paid to the growing informalization of the economy and related workforce in the global North. The chapter sections consider the roles and experiences of different actor groups within the informal economy, emphasizing connections between different places and scales – from the street to the city to the global economy.

The informal sector: historical roots and conceptual approaches

As mentioned in Chapter 2, the concept of the informal sector initially emerged in the early 1970s to make sense of economic realities in cities of the global South where development trends contradicted economic predictions dominant at the time. In this period, it was widely assumed that low-income traditional economies could be transformed into modern economies, mainly through development strategies fostering industrialization, mass production and consumption. Economists like Nobel Prize laureate W. Arthur Lewis (1954) argued that, as part of this process, 'surplus labour', associated with petty trade, small-scale production and casual work, would be integrated into the modern capitalist system. In other words, economic development based around principles of modernization was considered to create new jobs that could absorb people engaged in traditional economic activities into corporate enterprises, providing them with secure wages as well as legal and social protections – characteristics that we associate today with formal work (Chen, 2012). This view of economic change had its roots in European and North American experiences in the 1950s and 1960s, where post-Second World War reform programmes had indeed induced shifts towards mass production, contributing to economic growth and employment generation.

The application of such ideas and reform programmes in the global South was not accompanied by similar results. Despite widespread economic growth, unemployment and underemployment levels remained on the rise in many cities of the global South. The development economist Hans Singer (1970) highlighted that this was because of an imbalance between limited job creation in a context of industrialization driven by the extensive use of technology, and a disproportionate growth of the population – and hence the labour force – due to rapid processes of rural–urban migration alongside improvements in healthcare (leading people to live longer). Singer (1970) therefore warned of an acute risk of job shortages in increasingly overcrowded cities.

Responding to this concern, the International Labour Organization (ILO) involved economists like Singer in employment generation programmes in the urban global South. An observation during the implementation of one of those programmes, the so-called 'Kenya Mission' (previously discussed in Chapter 2), was that the 'traditional' sector – reconceptualized as the informal sector – was in fact quite profitable and provided unskilled urban migrants with income to secure a living.

As discussed in detail already in Chapter 2, the term informal sector, referring to economic relations occurring in unincorporated, small or unregistered enterprises, was further developed by anthropologist Keith Hart (1973) who undertook ethnographic research in Nima district, an area characterized by informal neighbourhoods in Ghana's capital city Accra. Hart's (1973: 81) findings challenged conventional and Northern-centric assumptions in economic theory around employment and unemployment, suggesting instead that unskilled urban migrants can rely on a 'range of opportunities available outside the organised [capitalist] labour market', meaning that 'few of the "unemployed" are totally without some form of income, however irregular'. Hart (1973) mainly associated informal sector work with relatively low-skilled rural–urban migrants who inhabited the growing informal neighbourhoods where they engaged in a range of economic activities, in their homes (for example, selling food, beverages or traditional medicines through their windows, operating hair salons or repair workshops inside their houses) or on the streets (for example, street hawking, waste picking, manually removing nightsoil, construction and infrastructure maintenance work). Work in the informal sector was, hence, considered to be deeply intertwined with living informally.

Hart's (1973) study was largely positive about the informal sector, concluding that rural–urban migrants in Ghana could rely on informal work to make an income and to sustain a living in a context where access to formal employment was limited. In contrast, other scholars such as Caroline Moser (1978) offered more pessimistic accounts, considering informal sector activities to be survival strategies of the urban poor. In addition to observations of the informal sector varying from optimistic to more pessimistic, urban scholars have deployed different conceptual frameworks that led to a distinct analysis of this phenomenon. The most prominent schools of thought are dualism, structuralism, legalism and voluntarism.

We introduced some of these approaches in Chapter 2, and here we discuss them in further detail, with a focus on informal work. A dualist perspective aligns closely with initial observations by Hart (1973) and the ILO's 'Kenya Mission'. It contrasts wage-earning formal workers in capitalist enterprises, who are recruited and employed on a regular or permanent basis, with (often self-employed) informal workers operating in small enterprises which are not incorporated into the wider capitalist system (as suggested in Table 2.1). For dualists, the informal and formal sector are separate entities. Dualist approaches consider the informal economic sector to be made up of marginal activities that provide the urban poor with a basic income and offer people a safety net, particularly in moments of economic crisis. From a dualist perspective, the emergence of the informal sector is a result of people's exclusion from industrialization's opportunities, occurring mainly because of imbalances between population growth rates and job availability, as well as mismatches between people's skills and the modern economy's requirements (Chen, 2012). This binary conception of informal and formal economic sectors builds on wider dualist thinking dominant in economics in the 1970s, for example, around the apparent existence of two systems of production (capitalist versus peasant), economic sectors (high profit versus low profit), labour markets (protected versus unprotected) and accumulation models (capitalist versus vestiges of pre-capitalism) (Moser, 1978; Portes, 1983).

From the late 1970s onwards, a set of different schools emerged which challenged dualist thinking, all sharing the view that informal sector work is associated with a lack of legal and social protections. Structuralist approaches, departing from a heterodox Marxist political economy perspective, do not treat the formal and informal sectors as separate entities but, instead, recognize their interdependencies and overarching contribution to the wider economy. From this perspective, the informal sector is a permanent and subordinate feature of uneven capitalist development (Moser, 1978; Castells and Portes, 1989). According to structuralists, the informal sector emerges first and foremost because of deliberate structural economic changes, and specifically because of growth-oriented practices such as reducing labour costs within formally registered enterprises to increase competitiveness and profit margins. Seen through this lens, outsourcing certain economic activities to the informal sector – where labour costs are lower due to the lack of social and legal protections – enhances profits and competitiveness for capitalist firms.

Unlike structuralists, who view the informal sector as a result of uneven capitalist relations, legalists argue that the informal sector emerges in contexts characterized by a hostile or burdensome legal system that obliges people to operate informally and according to extra-legal norms due to its overly bureaucratic nature. Informal economic practices lead to the generation of 'dead capital', which according to de Soto (1989; 2000) refers to property relations or economic activities that are not legally recognized and that cannot be easily exchanged within formal markets (as discussed in Chapter 2). In other words, de Soto (1989; 2000) considers the informal sector to be an outcome of state over-regulation. Others associate informal sector work with processes of deregulation (that is, efforts to flexibilize markets by reducing market control by states) or a complete lack of regulation (Chen, 2012). Legalists such as de Soto view the informal sector as an exploitative yet simultaneously entrepreneurial system that should ideally be eliminated through the introduction of simplified bureaucratic procedures. This would encourage people to formally register properties and enterprises, so that their productive potential can be unleashed and converted into real capital within the capitalist market system. Seen from this perspective, capitalist market integration does not represent a cause of informal sector work, but a possible solution. De Soto puts this as follows:

> The answer is to change our legal institutions in order to lower the cost of producing and obtaining wealth and to give people access to the system so they can join in economic and social activity and compete on equal footing, the ultimate goal being a modern market economy, which, so far, is the only known way to achieve development based on widespread business activity. (De Soto, 1989: 244)

Similar to legalist accounts, the voluntarist approach also pays attention to how actors in the informal sector often deliberately avoid government regulation and taxation. Yet, contrary to advocates of legalism or structuralism, voluntarists do not pay attention to systemic problems around state over-regulation or capitalist subordination. Instead, they focus on individual agency, treating informal work as a deliberate choice for individuals, while denouncing them as free riders who create unfair competition mechanisms within the wider market system. From this perspective, informal enterprises should be brought into the formal regulatory environment in order to increase taxes and reduce unfair competition (see Levenson and Maloney, 1998; Maloney, 2004).

Amid this heterogeneity of understandings and conceptualizations, 'there is merit to each of these perspectives as each school reflects one ... [yet not all] slices of the (informal) pie' (Chen, 2012: 6). Indeed, a combination of these approaches can better help to unpack the complex and context-specific factors that explain the emergence and continued presence of informal sector work in distinct urban settings. Take, for example, China, where approximately 31 per cent of the urban workforce is estimated to engage in informal sector work (ILO, 2019). Working with 200 informal street vendors in the city of Guangzhou, Huang et al (2018) revealed the heterogeneity of people's motivations for engaging in informal sector activities (see Box 4.1). A key lesson, therefore, is the need to unpack the multiple motivations and structural forces that push and/or pull people to engage in informal economic activities; only by considering this multiplicity is it possible to make sense of the informal sector as a whole.

Box 4.1: Heterogeneous motivations for street vending in Guangzhou, China

Huang et al (2018) highlight a number of different reasons that help explain why people decide to operate as street vendors in the informal sector, including: informal sector work emerges as a response to poor working conditions in the formal sector. Many street vendors in Guangzhou seek to avoid over-exploitation in jobs characterized by low wages, wage arrears, excessive work hours and a lack of opportunities for promotions. Political responses to labour exploitation remain scarce as the Chinese state is considered to support employers and provides very limited union protection. Street vending, in this context, is considered to provide workers with greater flexibility to manage their time, enabling them to balance domestic responsibilities with income generation. The move towards informal sector work can, hence, be understood through a combination of perspectives including voluntarist (people deliberately choose to operate informally) and structuralist (the emergence of the informal sector as a result of capitalist exploitation).

In particular, informal sector work emerges in this context because of rural–urban disparities and rural poverty. Farmers, who represent both permanent and seasonal rural–urban migrants, often engage in street vending activities for at least three reasons. First, and broadly aligning with dualist explanations, some take up street work because they lack the knowledge and technical skills required to find wage-work in industrial firms. Second, other farmers might have relevant skills but struggle to take up formal work in urban settings as they are trapped in the often complicated rural-to-urban *hukou* conversion process (see also Chan and Zhang, 1999). *Hukou* is a system of residency permits that classifies people according to their rural or urban residence, whereby residing in either of these locations is associated with different entitlements to access state-allocated jobs and social services. This scenario – that is, the emergence of the informal sector because of residency regulations – can best be understood through legalist accounts. Third, some farmers engage in street work outside the agricultural season to supplement their income in periods when income generation opportunities are scarce in rural areas and in a context where government social welfare support is in decline.

From informal sector work to informal employment

Research on informal work has advanced considerably over recent decades and, in particular, there is now a recognition that informal work can occur inside and outside the informal sector, both in registered and unregistered enterprises. To account for this reality, key organizations focusing on informal workers, including the ILO, the International Expert Group on Informal Sector Statistics and the global network Women in Informal Employment: Globalizing and Organizing (WIEGO), have developed an expanded definition of informal work conceptualized through the term 'informal employment', which refers to any type of labour without legal and social protection (Chen, 2012).

Types and characteristics of informal employment

Accounts of informal employment suggest that most people do not work informally by choice but because of an absence of opportunities to generate a livelihood elsewhere (Bonnet et al, 2019). Informal employment may take place *within* the informal sector, including employers, employees, own account workers, contributing family workers and members of cooperatives who work in unincorporated and unregistered enterprises (Vanek et al, 2014). But informal employment can also occur *outside* the informal sector, referring to different activities and processes including family or home workers contributing to formal enterprises; domestic workers, in their own or other people's homes; and the increasing informalization of public, private and non-profit sector work (Vanek et al, 2014). As we have already discussed working inside the informal sector in the previous section, we focus here on examples of informal employment *outside* the informal sector.

Let us begin with the example of home-based work. Within the informal sector, home-based work refers to workers who assume all risks and responsibilities as independent operators (that is, from buying raw materials, supplies and equipment to the production and sale of finished goods). In contrast, home-based work outside the informal sector refers to subcontracted activities undertaken by industry workers in their own homes. Home-based work contributes to many industries and sectors, with garment, textile and footwear production being prominent examples (Carr et al, 2000; see also Figure 4.2 and Box 4.2). Home-based workers may be contracted by formally registered factories and firms, or through an intermediary acting on their behalf, to contribute to producing particular goods (Chen et al, 1999; Raju, 2013).

Figure 4.2: Home-based work in a rented home in an informal neighbourhood, Bogota, Colombia

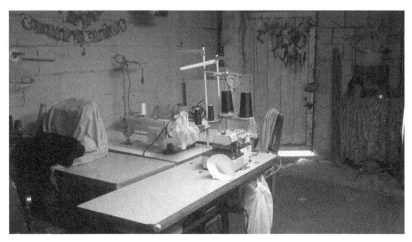

Source: Lorena Guerrero

Home-based workers might be given raw materials and production instructions, but must cover their costs related to production (such as workplace, equipment, electricity and supplies), while not receiving social or legal work protections. They are often paid on a per-unit basis rather than selling the finished product directly. Common challenges of home-workers are that production orders may be subject to rejection, delays and reduced payment. There is often also an intricate connection between home-based work and informal living (see Chapter 3), as workplaces in homes are often located in informal or low-income neighbourhoods, characterized by tenure insecurity, precarious rental arrangements, a lack of working/living space, and poor access to services like water, sanitation and electricity. Poor living conditions, hence, have a direct impact on the wellbeing and productivity of workers (see also Bhan, 2020).

Box 4.2: Home-based informal employment as depicted in the novel *A Fine Balance*

A good illustration of the challenges of home-based work is provided in Rohinton Mistry's 1995 novel *A Fine Balance*. Set in an unidentified large city in India, this novel discusses the coming together of four characters from distinct social backgrounds – Dina Dalal, a middle-aged widow, two tailors called Omprakash (or Om) and Ishvar Darji belonging to India's lower castes who recently migrated and settled in an informal neighbourhood in the city, and an upper-caste student called Maneck Kohlah. To sustain her independence after her husband's death, Dina sublets a room in her apartment to Maneck. Following the recommendation of a friend, she also begins working for a company called Au-Revoir Express which subcontracts tailors to prepare dresses on a piecework basis. Due to health problems and the increasing failure of her eyesight, Dina hires Om and Ishvar to do this work in her flat, with their own sewing machines. This micro-scale tailoring business is increasingly affected by problems and setbacks. For example, as part of a beautification programme the government demolishes informal neighbourhoods in the city, including the one where Om and Ishvar live, leading them to become homeless. Caught in the struggle to find a new place to live, the tailors show up late for work and fail to finish orders to the deadline, leading to increasing tensions with the contractor. In the meantime, Dina, who rents her flat, increasingly struggles to hide her sub-tenant and tailoring business from her landlord, who seeks to evict her based on tenancy rules. *A Fine Balance* unravels the complex challenges home-based workers face to sustain their business in a context of socio-economic hardship and an absence of socio-legal protections. It also beautifully captures challenges related to homes that double as both residential and work spaces, therefore illustrating the interconnections between informal working and living.

Domestic work represents another important economic activity that is associated with informal employment practices. Domestic workers provide services such as cleaning, gardening, shopping, cooking, childcare and care for the elderly and disabled, often within private homes. Some live on the premises of their employer, while others work for multiple employers and often rely on agencies as intermediaries. In a study focusing on the United States, Peggie Smith (2011) argues that domestic work is often characterized by hazardous and abusive working conditions and a lack of health and safety regulations as it takes place in a context of structural isolation, hidden from the public in private homes, and often privileges the interests of clients over those of workers. Similar trends of domestic workers as an exploited, undervalued and yet essential source of labour have been noted also by observers in the global South (du Toit, 2013).

Domestic work is often highly racialized, gendered and structured by class- and caste-relations and immigration status. Women are particularly likely to engage in domestic work, as activities like cleaning, care or cooking are traditionally associated with women's work in many societies (Rojas-García and Toledo González, 2018). In Europe, North America and the Middle East, domestic work is often undertaken by international migrant women of lower-class backgrounds (Anderson, 2000). Migrant domestic workers often lack legal immigration status and, consequently, cannot count on basic worker protections by the state. This further exacerbates workers' vulnerability to abuse, with verbal abuse, physical violence, sexual harassment, and denial of payment and passports some of the most commonly reported challenges (Triandafyllidou, 2013). A good non-academic representation of this topic is Stephen Frear's (2002) movie *Dirty Pretty Things*, which traces the everyday challenges of two international migrants who work in a London hotel and live under constant threat of deportation.

In Latin America, Black and Indigenous women remain over-represented within domestic work arrangements. According to anthropologist Peter Wade (2013), this represents the present-day reproduction of ethno-racial hierarchies established by the Spanish and Portuguese colonizers, who considered these groups as 'backward' and subordinate to the dominant 'White' colonial ruling class (see also Chapter 2). A good non-academic representation of the colonial and ethno-racialized nature of domestic work in Latin America is provided in the Academy-Award winning movie *Roma* (which is the name of an upper-middle-class neighbourhood in Mexico City) that captures the life of live-in cleaner and nanny Cleo, an Indigenous women working for a non-Indigenous family in 1970s Mexico. In South Asian countries such as India, domestic work is structured along caste divides. Work in the home and other urban locations (including 'dirty work' such as cleaning nightsoil) is historically associated with Dalit (the lowest stratum of castes in India); such pre-colonial caste prejudices were reproduced by British colonial rule and continue to structure domestic work (McFarlane, 2008).

Over recent decades, most economic sectors throughout the world have experienced what could be referred to as informalization, notable in the rise of fixed-term, temporary, casual and intermittent work arrangements that blur the boundary between the dependent and socio-legally protected status of employees and wage workers, and independent self-employed workers in the informal sector without social and legal protections (Carré, 2020). Such trends are particularly evident in the rise of the so-called gig economy whereby online web-based or app-based platforms mediate relations between firms, individual customers and a pool of workers who provide services such as private hire transport (for example, taxi service Uber), food delivery (providers like Deliveroo or Just Eat) or postal delivery (such as courier services) (Berg et al, 2018).

The status of these workers is somewhat blurry. On the one hand, gig economy workers work exclusively for a specific company which, in turn, treats them as self-employed and independent workers. Instead of receiving a regular wage, gig economy workers get paid for individual jobs such as delivering food or driving a person from one place to another. They do not have fixed working hours but can control how much they work. However, due to their self-employed status, gig economy workers cannot access basic socio-legal protections such as redundancy payments, a minimum wage, sick pay, paid holidays or pension contributions; they are often also responsible for purchasing and/or leasing as well as maintaining their own equipment (Cherry, 2016). Work in the gig economy and for platforms is not only undertaken by low-skilled workers (a feature traditionally considered to be characteristic of the informal sector), but also increasingly by a more highly qualified labour force who work in call centres or engage in online freelance work (including the provision of transcription, translation, web development, data analysis, sales or marketing services) on digital platforms from their own home (Heeks, 2017; Berg et al, 2018).

Informal employment trends and numbers

Statistical data represents an important tool to highlight the significance of informal employment and to draw the attention of the wider public and of local, national and international policy makers towards this phenomenon. Yet, if a key characteristic of working informally is that it is often unrecorded, how can informal employment be recorded within national and international statistics? Throughout the last four decades statisticians belonging to international organizations such as the ILO, the International Expert Group on Informal Sector Statistics (also referred to as the Delhi Group as they were first convened in this city by the government of India) and WIEGO, as well as national statistics offices, have worked on establishing indicators to capture informal employment (for a detailed discussion on this topic see Vanek et al, 2014; Vanek, 2020). In 1993, the Fifteenth International Conference of Labour Statisticians (ICLS) adopted a standard way of capturing employment in the informal sector. Box 4.3 provides an overview of how informal employment is identified.

Organizations such as WIEGO argue that a focus on the informal sector alone is insufficient as it fails to capture informal wage workers attached to formal firms or working within households. This led to the articulation of a broader statistical definition of informal employment, officially adopted by the seventeenth ICLS in 2003. According to Bonnet et al (2019: 3), 'for a job to be considered as informal, the employment relationship should not be, in law or in practice, subject to national labour legislation, income taxation, social protection or entitlement to certain employment benefits'. Statistically, for employees this can be determined by criteria such as social security contributions by employers (that is, if contributions are made a worker is considered formal and, if not, informal) and entitlements to paid annual leave and/or sick leave (that is, if this is in place the worker is considered to be in

Box 4.3: Capturing informal sector employment

Statisticians tend to follow the definition of the informal sector as comprised of small (single-person, family-run, operated by very few employees) unincorporated enterprises that are not registered by government authorities. Criteria used to identify such enterprises, and workers operating within them, are:

- Registration of the economic unit at the national level (with social security, sales or income tax authorities): If registered, the economic unit is considered part of the formal sector. If not registered, in the process of registering, or the information is missing or not collected, then other criteria are considered to determine whether an economic unit is informal or not (see the following criteria).
- Bookkeeping: This criterion considers whether an economic unit maintains accounts required by law (for example, balance sheets) or keeps some official information. If the unit maintains formal bookkeeping, it is considered formal. If not (or if information is not available), then the following alternative criteria tend to be considered:
  - Employer contribution criterion (for employees): If the employer contributes to social security on behalf of employees, then the unit is formal.
  - Economic unit size and location criteria: if the unit has more than five workers and is located in a fixed visible premise then it is formal; units with five or less workers or not in fixed premises are informal.

Source: Adapted from Bonnet et al (2019)

---

formal employment and, if not, in informal employment). In the case of employers, informal employment is assessed by the nature of the economic unit (see Box 4.3). These statistical definitions have, over recent years, been integrated into the work of national statistics agencies. In addition, since 2002 organizations such as the ILO have been publishing international compilations of statistics on informal employment (see ILO, 2019).

Based on global statistical estimates, approximately 61 per cent of people employed aged 15 and above can be considered informal workers (ILO, 2019). Of this, 51.9 per cent of employment takes place in the informal sector, 6.7 per cent in the formal sector and 2.5 per cent in households (ILO, 2019). In addition, of the 44 per cent of workers worldwide who are self-employed, 60 per cent represent informal workers (Vanek, 2020). Informal employment is particularly prevalent within the job sectors discussed in the previous section. A total of 260 million people worldwide, including 35 million in high-income countries in the global North, engage in home-based work (for a detailed overview and statistical breakdown, see Bonnet et al, 2019). Approximately 67 million people worldwide work as domestic workers, with a majority (80 per cent) of these women (ILO, 2019). There remains limited evidence on the precise number of people operating in the gig economy. Recent attempts to estimate the size of the online gig economy in Europe estimate that one in five people have engaged in work in this sector. It is estimated that out of 45 million registered online freelance workers linked to Western platforms, approximately 36 million are from low- and middle-income countries in the global South with particularly high concentrations in India, Philippines, Pakistan and Bangladesh (Heeks, 2017). In addition, approximately 25 million gig workers are registered on Chinese platforms (To and Lai, 2015).

There exist important regional variations (see Figure 1.4 in Chapter 1) as well as gender, class and intergenerational differences around informal employment. For example, in low-income countries (situated predominantly in the global South) 90 per cent of employment is informal. This number is slightly lower (67 per cent) for lower-middle and upper-middle-income countries situated in the global South and North-East and even lower (18 per cent), although still significant, in high-income countries situated in the global North (ILO, 2019). When accounting only for urban areas (by excluding agricultural activities conventionally associated with rural places) these figures reduce slightly, with 73 per cent of employment being informal in low-income countries, 59 per cent for lower-middle to higher-middle-income countries, and 17 per cent for high-income countries (ILO, 2019). As suggested earlier, across the globe, most people who work informally tend to do so in the informal sector. However, in Europe and North America there exists a significant proportion (7.9 per cent) of people who are employed informally within the formal sector. This is likely to relate to the recent informalization of formal sector jobs, especially noted with the rise of the gig economy, discussed in the previous section.

At a global scale, men tend to have higher rates of informal employment than women. However, patterns are different in low-income countries where the percentage of women employed informally (92 per cent) is higher than for men (87 per cent) (Vanek et al, 2014). Women are also more likely to work in more precarious and low-paid informal jobs than men. Women's share of informal employment must be understood in relation to women's share in total employment, which tends to be lower in certain world regions (that is, the Middle East, Sub-Saharan Africa and China) than others (Vanek et al, 2014).

ILO (2019) estimates offer important insights on the interconnections between poverty and informal employment. While by no means all people who work informally can be considered poor (see, for example, the case study from Bolivia in Box 4.4), statistical evidence suggests that working members of low-income households are much more likely to be employed informally than those belonging to higher-income groups. For example, in low-income countries less than half of workers belonging to wealthier households are informally employed, while anywhere between 50 to 100 per cent of workers from low-income households work informally (ILO, 2019).

Levels of informal employment are also disproportionately high among younger and older people, especially in low-income and middle-income countries. According to the ILO (2019), globally, 77.1 per cent of young people aged 15–24 and 77.9 per cent of people older than 65 are working informally. Youth populations tend to confront a growing unemployment crisis, as suggested by the testimony at the start of the chapter. This is particularly evident in Sub-Saharan Africa where, according to Banks (2016b: 440), 'young people are particularly hard hit by [formal sector] unemployment', with 14 million formal sector jobs required to meet the needs of Africa's growing population which is predominantly young, urban and making a living by working informally. Informal employment among the elderly is also particularly evident in low-income and middle-income countries, where people aged 65 and above often lack income security through pensions, making it impossible to retire and forcing people to work throughout old age (Alfers et al, 2021).

Box 4.4: Informal workers in El Alto, Bolivia: many are young and some are rich

Figure 4.3: Informal market scenes in El Alto, Bolivia

Note: Top right: street vendor in El Alto; top left: aerial shot of the Feria 16 de Julio; bottom: cholet with El Alto's 'statue of liberty' behind a popular market.
Source: Philipp Horn

El Alto is situated on the Andean plateau bordering the city of La Paz, seat of Bolivia's national government. Only existing as autonomous municipality since 1988, El Alto is a city of rural–urban migrants predominantly of Indigenous descent (Arbona and Kohl, 2004), thereby countering colonial ethno-spatial hierarchies that associate Indigenous people with the countryside rather than the 'white city' (Horn, 2019; see also Chapter 2). It is estimated that approximately two-thirds of the city's population works informally. Informal work is perhaps most visible in the city's large street markets. Out of these, the Feria 16 de Julio, a bi-weekly street market bringing together more than 10,000 traders, represents the largest in the city and possibly in Latin America.

Levels of poverty remain high in the city, with most people earning lower than average wages. More than half of the city's population can be classified as young, aged 27 and below (Escobar de

Pabón et al, 2015). Young people in El Alto are increasingly highly qualified, with university degrees; yet professional qualifications often do not translate into formal sector jobs. Instead, nine out of 10 youths are likely to be engaged in precarious work, often juggling multiple jobs, mainly in the informal sector where they lack social and legal protections.

Informal work should, however, not be conflated with urban poverty. Some informal business owners in El Alto have acquired substantial wealth over time and now make up a new Aymara 'non-bourgeois upper-middle class' (Tassi 2017: 26). Material wealth is displayed by wearing expensive *chola* (a term referring to Andean market women) fashion, as well as architecturally through the construction of expensive residential *cholets* (a neologism combining the term *cholo* – referring to rural-to-urban Indigenous migrants – with chalet) that stand out in the urban landscapes with their colourful designs (Tassi 2017).

It is also widely recognized that employment in the informal sector increases in times of economic crisis (Tokman, 1984; ILO, 2019). In contexts in which formally registered enterprises reduce staff, workers often cannot find alternative forms of formal employment and, especially in contexts characterized by insufficient social protection schemes such as unemployment contributions, they start searching for work in the informal economy. This was evident in Latin America, Asia and Africa during periods of structural adjustment and economic crisis in the 1980s and 1990s (mentioned in previous chapters), in former Soviet states affected by economic transition, and during the global economic crisis of 2008 (Chen, 2012). At the time of writing, our world continues to be affected by the legacies of the COVID-19 crisis, and many countries have experienced inflation as well as economic crisis due to wars in different parts of the globe, including Ethiopia, Israel/Palestine, Myanmar, Syria and Ukraine. While it is too early to reflect on the implications of these wars, interconnections between COVID-19 and informal employment can already be noted. Considering the financial collapse and closure of many businesses throughout the pandemic, and the lack of social and economic protections available to workers especially in low-income and middle-income countries, informal employment expanded significantly (ILO, 2020). At the same time, working conditions in different forms of informal employment significantly deteriorated in the light of a global health crisis accompanied by social distancing and lockdown regulations but insufficient socio-economic protections (see Box 4.5).

Towards a comprehensive approach on the urban informal economy

At this stage, it should be clear that informal work comprises a range of activities beyond the informal sector and describes a day-to-day reality for a significant proportion of the global workforce. Moving beyond a focus on informal sector and employment, current scholarship puts emphasis on the need to study the informal economy, a concept that refers to 'all units, activities and workers so defined and

Box 4.5: Economic informality and COVID-19

The COVID-19 pandemic came with negative economic consequences for many workers, forcing some to lose their formal sector jobs and search for alternative work in the informal sector (Alvarez and Pizzinelli, 2021). COVID-19 had a particularly negative effect on those working in informal jobs who lack social and legal protections. Lockdowns or calls to 'work from home' were simply not feasible for most informal workers, especially those who make a living in other people's homes or on the streets. Where strict lockdowns were introduced, informal workers lost crucial earnings, with many falling into poverty and struggling with hunger or even starvation. A testimony by a street vendor in Mexico City published in a WIEGO blog post underlines this point: 'People say, if I don't go out and work, I'll die of hunger, so I go out and work. The risk is that I get sick and die, but if I don't die of one thing, I'll die of another.' Fears hence varied from abstaining from work to the health risks associated with the virus. There now exists a rich repertoire of studies on links between the COVID-19 pandemic and economic informality. Here are some useful entry points:

- WIEGO website on the COVID-19 crisis and the informal economy: https://www.wiego.org/covid-19-crisis-and-informal-economy-study-0
- ILO resource base on COVID-19 and the informal economy: https://www.ilo.org/global/topics/employment-promotion/informal-economy/publications/WCMS_743546/lang--en/index.htm
- A position piece on the pandemic and Southern urbanisms by Bhan et al (2020).

---

the output from them' (Chen, 2012: 8). Crucially, the informal economy comprises both the informal sector and informal employment, and it is closely connected to the formal economy, as well as national and global patterns of growth, poverty and inequality. The informal economy is studied by multiple disciplines, ranging from economics, anthropology, global politics and development, to urban planning. Among other issues, and as discussed in detail earlier in this chapter, existing research focuses predominantly, though not exclusively, on those engaged in informal employment. Others focus on the legal and/or illegal nature of informal economic activities, the contribution of the informal economy to the overall economy, formal/informal economy interactions, and the underlying causes of the informal economy. We discuss these topics next.

Legal and illegal informal economic activities

Informality should not be equated with illegality. While some informal economic activities might indeed be considered illegal, many others are legal. Economic activities often referred to as informal are conventionally defined as 'market-based production of goods and services, whether legal or illegal, that escapes detection in the official estimates of GDP', by circumventing or avoiding 'government regulation, taxation or observation' (Smith, 1994: 18). Schneider (2012: 6) further expands this

Table 4.1: A taxonomy of informal economic activities

Type of Activity	Monetary transactions		Non-monetary transactions	
Illegal activities	Trade with stolen goods; drug dealing and manufacturing; prostitution; gambling; fraud; human trafficking; and weapon trafficking		Barter of drugs; stolen goods; smuggling, and so on. Produce or growing of drugs for own use. Theft for own use	
	Tax evasion	Tax avoidance	Tax evasion	Tax avoidance
Legal activities	Unreported income from self-employment; wages; salaries and assets from unreported work related to legal services and goods	Employee discounts; fringe benefits	Barter of legal services and goods	All do-it-yourself work and neighbour help

Source: Schneider (2012)

definition by highlighting that such economic activities not only avoid taxation and government regulation but also a 'payment of income ... payment of social security contribution ... having to meet certain legal labor market standards ... complying with certain administrative obligations'. Some of these activities may indeed be legal as they may refer to everyday exchanges such as do-it-yourself work or neighbourly support. Others, such as drug or human trafficking, are illegal as they violate the law of local, national and supranational jurisdictions. Table 4.1 provides an overview of different legal and illegal economic practices that are often considered to form part of the informal economy.

Estimating the informal economy's contribution to the overall economy

The informal economy is considered difficult to measure for a variety of reasons, including purposefully not reporting activities or avoiding paying tax or social service contributions (see previous sections), or because informal economic activities are so small-scale in nature that they fall below official thresholds for business or tax registration (Quiros-Romero et al, 2021). Nevertheless, in recent decades different approaches have emerged to measure the contribution of the informal economy, ranging from direct measures such as labour force, household or business opinion surveys, and indirect approaches that measure informal economic activities via proxies such as electricity consumption, cash in circulation or satellite data on economic activities in public spaces such as street markets (Ohnsorge and Yu, 2022).

While measures of the contribution vary by approach (see previous discussion), Ohnsorge and Yu (2022) estimate that the informal economy accounts for approximately 32 to 33 per cent of GDP at the global level. Similar to informal employment, there exist widespread regional variations among high-, middle- and low-income countries, with Latin America and Sub-Saharan Africa having the comparatively highest levels and Europe and East Asia the lowest (see Figure 4.4).

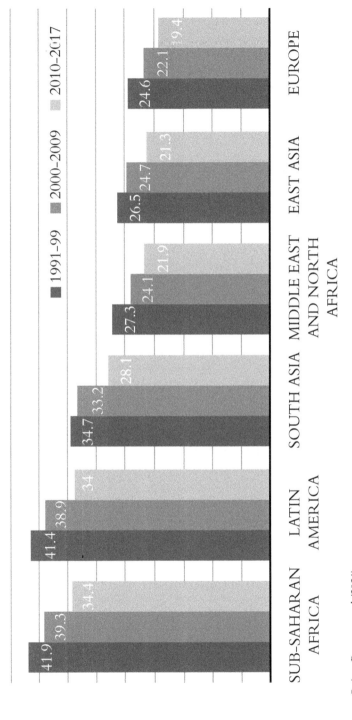

Figure 4.4: The informal economy by region measured by percentage of gross domestic product contribution

Source: Quiros-Romero et al (2021)

Connections between the formal and informal economy

Another body of scholarship focuses on connections between the formal and informal economy, for example, by paying attention to employment relationships between informal workers and their firms, with the latter often belonging to the formal economy as highlighted, for example, in the case of the gig economy. Chen (2012) also explores connections between informal and formal enterprises, distinguishing between individual transactions, sub-sector relations and value chains. Individual transactions refer to scenarios whereby informal enterprises 'exchange goods and services with formal firms in what might be characterised as open or pure market exchange', an exchange that is mainly – though not exclusively – controlled by the formal firm (Chen, 2012: 12). An example of individual transactions can be found in the city of El Alto, discussed in Box 4.4, where Indigenous Aymara traders have developed close trading relations with Chinese family-run firms in places such as the Chinese International Trade City of Yiwu. The Aymara traders' ability to produce such articulations was not based on conventional marketing principles but on kinship alliances and family networks. For example, Tassi (2017: 97) highlights how Bolivian and Chinese traders arrange business agreements through informal verbal agreements and 'social investments' (that is, gifts, formation of personal relations between families, and participation in cultural events). This enabled Aymara traders to negotiate competitive prices and request the production of culturally-appropriate products catering to Bolivian tastes that can be sold on informal markets at home (Tassi et al, 2012; Tassi, 2017).

Formal–informal relations in economic sub-sectors, defined as 'networks of independent units involved in the production of a particular product or commodity', occur when different 'individual units are involved in a series of transactions with suppliers and customers', with these transactions often 'governed largely by the dominant [and often formally registered] firm' (Chen, 2012: 12). The fictitious example from the novel *A Fine Balance* outlined in detail in Box 4.2 represents a good illustration of sub-sector relations. Here, an informal home-operated enterprise undertakes subcontracted piecemeal tailoring to supply 'Au Revoir Express', a firm that represents an intermediary supplying finished clothing products to retailers and customers.

Finally, formal–informal interactions are also often visible in domestic or global value chains, defined as activities that are required to bring a product or service from conception through the different phases of production (involving a combination of physical transformation and the input of various producer services), delivery to final consumers and final disposal after use (Gereffi et al, 2001). Activities in each element of a value chain may be undertaken by different (formal or informal) firms, though terms and conditions are often set by a lead firm (Chen, 2012). Figure 4.5 provides an example of a hybrid informal–formal value chain for ready-to-eat chickens in the South African city of Tshwane.

More recent research by scholars such as Gago (2018) and Simone (2019; 2021) highlights the need to move beyond economic perspectives on formal–informal connections. Instead, closer attention should be paid to the complex needs and everyday practices of the world's urban majority who, in an age of technological advances and despite increasingly high levels of education, confront a lack of job

Figure 4.5: Value chain of ready-to-eat chickens in informal markets in Tshwane, South Africa

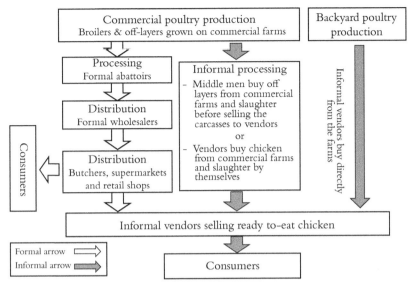

Source: Oguttu et al (2014)

opportunities, declining wages, and deteriorating levels of social protection and social care. In this context, the urban majority has to engage in what these scholars have termed 'popular economies' to generate a livelihood. Popular economies refer to the 'variegated, promiscuous forms of organising the production of things, their repair, distribution, use, as well as the provision of social reproduction services that simultaneously fall inside and outside the ambit of formal capitalist production' (Simone, 2019: 618). Crucially, popular economies are more than just jobs and move beyond the realm of economic relations, capturing instead the different social, economic, cultural and political practices required by people to stay put, ranging for example from earning a living through wage labour supplemented by informal trading, to arranging childcare, and repairing and maintaining basic infrastructure in one's neighbourhood. Such activities are, hence, not reducible to the informal–formal divide but capture a lived multi-activity reality whereby people participate in diverse socio-economic, political and cultural practices. Paying attention to such complex realities requires considering but simultaneously moving beyond the realm of the economic and the informal to capture human activities in all their diversity. We discuss popular economies and other alternative representations of working informally in further detail in Chapter 8.

Chapter summary

This chapter introduced the topic of working informally, paying attention in particular to different articulations, namely those related to the informal sector, informal employment and the informal economy. Focusing on this topic matters, as a significant contribution towards GDP derives from the informal economy, and a large proportion of the global workforce works informally, without legal and social protections. While some manage to make a decent living by doing such work, the majority – 85 per cent of informal workers (Quiros-Romero et al, 2021) – are working in precarious conditions and continue to do so mainly because they lack other economic opportunities. Working informally must be understood in relation to wider multi-scalar processes, starting from the street level, to the city, national and all the way to the level of global governance and economic relations. Working informally must also be understood in relation to issues such as poverty, inequality, urban coloniality, race, gender and intergenerational divisions. Understanding its causes and consequences is crucial for anyone interested in providing solutions to more sustainable and inclusive cities across the global North and South.

In subsequent chapters, we will further explore what is being done by different actors – from the informal workers themselves to policy makers operating at different levels – to address the issue of informality. However, for now, you may want to go deeper into the literature and alternative representations on working informally. To help you with this, we provide a list of alternative representations and further recommended reading.

Recommended reading

- Chen, M. (2012) 'The informal economy: definitions, theories and policies', WIEGO Working Paper No. 1. Cambridge, MA.
- Hart, K. (1973) 'Informal economic opportunities and urban employment in Ghana', *The Journal of Modern African Studies*, 11(1): 61–89.
- Chen, M. and Carré, F. (2020) *The Informal Economy Revisited: Examining the Past, Envisioning the Future*, Abingdon: Taylor & Francis.

EXERCISES

- Please look at some of the alternative representations listed here and, reflecting on these representations, write down how you would define the key characteristics of working informally.
- The informal economy is the result of a variety of multi-scalar processes, shaped by distinct actor groups, and can be understood best through the combination of multiple conceptual lenses. Here, we want you to test your understanding of these different perspectives. Box 4.6 provides you with a number of scenarios about the informal economy. Please read them and identify which conceptual approach (for example, dualism, legalism, structuralism, voluntarism or maybe even the popular economy) would be the best to make sense of these scenarios.
- You may also want to think about an articulation of working informally in your hometown, the place in which you currently live, or a city you are interested in. Ask yourself, what type of working informally is this? Does it relate to the informal sector, informal employment or to the wider informal economy? What are the underlying causes for this phenomenon and what approach would you deploy to make sense of it?

Box 4.6: Different causal explanations for the informal economy

- The informal economy is an integral element of our advanced profit-oriented global capitalist system characterized by technological advances, increasing flexibilization and ever-increasing demand for cheaper goods and services.
- The informal economy is the result of policy and planning practices such as over-regulation (for example, excessive regulation that creates barriers to working formally), deregulation (for example, flexibilization and liberalization of markets) and lack of regulation (for example, ignoring certain economic practices).
- The informal economy is largely separate from the formal economy and provides certain population groups, such as the urban poor, and international as well as rural–urban migrants, with economic opportunities.
- The informal economy is comprised by free riders – including the rich and the poor – who seek to evade taxes and business regulations.
- The informal economy is just one of many realms which ordinary people rely on to make a living.

Alternative representations

- For a fictional perspective on informal markets in Latin America, you might want to watch the film *7 Cajas* (2012, https://pragda.com/film/7-boxes/).
- The movie *Sorry We Missed You* (2019, https://www.sorrywemissedyou.co.uk/) provides an excellent account of the rise of the gig economy in the United Kingdom.
- The online photo exhibition *Waste and Recycling in an Urban Slumscape: A Window into Slum Lives and Spaces* by Tatiana Thieme (https://www.geog.cam.ac.uk/library/exhibitions/thieme/) provides an interesting account on informal waste and recycling practices in urban settings in Kenya.
- The *Photo Essay on Sanitation Workers in India* by Shara Prasad (2020, https://www.susana.org/en/knowledge-hub/resources-and-publications/library/details/388) explores the situation of informal sanitation workers in India.
- *WIEGO Worker Stories* (https://www.wiego.org/informal-economy/worker-stories) provide accounts from informal workers around the world.

5

Governing Informally

'I am a resident of Mukuru and also a community mobilizer that brings people together to improve living conditions. My method as a community mobilizer is very simple. I make friendships with people that I live with. Through those friendships, I have brought together many here in our area of Mukuru and it has given me the capacity to be like a leader in the lives of other people. People I speak to want successes and they want services to trickle down to this area. To show the need for services we collect data from each household. We ask people questions like: Who owns the land? Do you rent or own the house? How many people live here? Where and how do you access services? We use the data that we have collected to defend ourselves and demand better services from our government. But collecting data and speaking to the government is not enough to bring change in this area of ours. So, what am I waiting for? I am expecting to see services delivered to our area. I want those of us who live here, and not some tycoons, to receive title deeds. I want to say that Mukuru is ours and that this is a place to be proud of.'

Resident and community mobilizer in the informal neighbourhood of Mukuru in Nairobi, Kenya, reflecting on processes of community mobilization to raise awareness of poor services and infrastructure[1]

Existing debates on urban informality tend to focus mainly on the dimensions of living and working informally, with less attention paid towards political elements. This chapter addresses this gap. It offers a conceptualization of governing informally and advances debates on urban informality as a tripartite concept associated with living, working and governing informally. Governing informally can be loosely defined as practices that stand in contrast to formal politics (Lombard and Meth, 2016), or as efforts to shape 'rules of the game ... outside of officially sanctioned channels' (Helmke and Levitsky, 2004: 725). Governing informally is not new, and it can be observed across the global South and North. Occurring at multiple scales, and in rural and urban settings, a variety of institutions and actors engage in informal governance practices or are affected by them (Goodfellow, 2022). The interrelations between politics and informality have initially been observed in political sciences literature. These debates emphasize how informal institutions and practices such as bargaining, clientelism, favouritism and corruption shape formal institutional outcomes such as selection of political candidates, legislative and judicial politics, party organization, government–business relations, and campaign finance (Helmke and Levitsky, 2004). From this perspective, discussed further in the first substantive section of the chapter, governing informally is inherent in the structure of state and state–society relations (Hilbrandt et al, 2017).

More recent debates in urban and development studies focus on how governing informally is particularly prevalent in global Southern contexts affected by governance transitions associated with (post)colonial development and rapid urbanization. We explore these debates in further detail in the second section, where we highlight how (post)colonial governments often imposed formal governance regimes grounded in 'modern' legal and planning traditions that foster differentiated citizenship dynamics, leading to some segments of society being granted citizenship rights and others remaining excluded (Holston, 2009). As a result, formal governance regimes may lack legitimacy (especially among excluded groups) and are further undermined by the co-existence of informal institutions, political and regulatory practices grounded in 'familiar', 'indigenous' or 'tribal' traditions (Alfasi, 2014). This situation is often referred to as dualist polity or legal pluralism (Griffiths, 1986; Holzinger et al, 2016). We also demonstrate that governing informally requires particular attention in urban(izing) settings as this is where state institutions associated with formal governance are concentrated and where they may be confronted and undermined by a variety of informal institutions and practices (Goodfellow, 2022).

Diverse studies have focused on how governing informally unfolds in practice in urban settings. We bring together different perspectives in the third section where we emphasize how governing informally shapes or is shaped by informal living and working. We discuss the informal politics of ordinary urban residents, paying attention to political tactics[2] deployed by people who live in informal neighbourhoods and/or work in informal jobs to engage the state and improve their conditions. We then explore the informal politics of state actors who may deliberately design regulations to create legal ambiguity and parallel governance systems to foster informal practices, or who are unable or unwilling to implement formal rules. The informal governance practices of ordinary urban residents and state actors cannot be analysed in isolation and close attention is paid to their interrelation, and to how informal practices interact with formal modes of governance, planning and regulation. Throughout, we draw on a variety of case study illustrations.

Politics and informality

Let us begin by defining politics and its relationship with informality. According to the *Cambridge Dictionary*, politics refers to 'activities of the government, members of law-making organizations, or people who try to influence the way a country is governed'. Such activities normally occur through elections, demonstrations, community mobilization or engagement in different government bodies (executive, legislative, judicial) operating at distinct levels such as the local, national or international scale – each characterized by their own formal regulations, norms and rules (Goodfellow, 2020). Although informality is often conceived of as the antithesis of formal political systems, as activities that 'lie beyond or circumvent state regulation' (Lindell, 2010: 5), the informal is closely related to politics.

Scholars of political sciences have for decades explored the patterns characterizing informal politics and pointed out its close relationship with formal politics. Foundational work by Mills (1956), for example, illustrates how informal political relations among members of powerful elites in the United States often blend with, inform and shape formal politics. Mills considers political and business elites in the United States as forming part of a quasi-hereditary system through which they, either consciously or unconsciously, access influential positions via involvement in informal institutions such as family networks, member-based associations in Ivy League universities, or social clubs. Similarly, focusing on Mexico, Langston (2003) notes that presidents are often not selected based on rules set out in this country's constitution but through an unwritten rule whereby the current president reserves the right to nominate a possible successor.

Patterns in which informal institutions and practices shape formal politics have been observed in many other geopolitical settings. Such patterns include, among others, decision-making processes via unofficial factions in political parties; lobbying and pressure group activities occurring outside of formal structures; financial transfers to authorities that take place outside or evade formal channels; and informal negotiations between distinct social groups to shape policy reform (Goodfellow, 2020; for further examples, see also Helmke and Levitsky, 2004; Ledeneva, 2018a). Some country-specific examples include 'cash for access' – a phenomenon reported in the United Kingdom referring to an 'exchange of money between two or more parties, with the donor seeking to gain access to an office holder and the recipient facilitating access in exchange for money' (Webb, 2018: 184); *blat* – a colloquial term used in Russia to 'denote ways of getting things done through personal contacts' and not via formal institutional channels (Ledeneva, 2018b: 40); and *Vetterliwirtschaft* – a Swiss-German term referring to the 'favouring of friends or family by those in position of power' (Koechlin, 2018: 267).

Political science literature broadly distinguishes between informal institutions and practices that contribute to and/or undermine democratic life and formal governance. For example, in regard to contributing practices, research on consociationalism – defined as agreements of social elites to ensure stability and power sharing in societies that are divided along ethnic, religious or linguistic lines (Lijphart, 1975) – highlights how this often occurs through informal channels such as private deliberations or unwritten laws and practices (see, for example, Bogaards [2019] on Lebanon or Dodge [2020] on Iraq). An often-mentioned example of an informal practice that undermines democratic life is corruption, defined as the abuse of political power for private gain.[3] Other examples such as clientelism – defined as an asymmetric political exchange occurring between someone in a position of political power (a patron) and recipients with limited resources and power (clients), whereby the former supplies benefits and services to the latter in exchange for political support – can have both positive and negative implications. As highlighted by Mitlin (2014), and discussed via different examples in subsequent sections, patron–client relations can, on the one hand, be conceived of as highly stratified social relations that serve to maintain and deepen socio-political inequalities while, on the other hand, they can provide genuine resource transfers and lead to empowerment.

This overview of the relationships between politics and informality starts to flesh out what we refer to here as governing informally, namely informal institutions (for example, alliances or social networks) and practices (for example, exercising power, developing influence, advancing particular goals) that stand in contrast to and may take place outside the realm of formal politics while nonetheless seeking to influence and shape formal politics, socio-economic relations and public life. We elaborate this concept further in the next section through a focus on governing informally in (post) colonial urban settings.

Governing informally, (post)colonial development and the urban

Governing informally is often understood as associated with 'developing' and urban(izing) and (post)colonial settings situated mainly, though not exclusively, in the global South (Harris, 2018; Goodfellow, 2020). In addition to shifts towards socio-economic progress and wellbeing, development also refers to incremental improvements in the organizational and institutional capacities of states and to enhancing the effectiveness of formal governance (Brett, 2009; Acemoglu and Robinson, 2012). In the global South – a contested term referring predominantly to countries in Africa, Asia and Latin America (see Chapter 1) – but also in settler colonial societies of the global North such as Australia, New Zealand, Canada or the United States, formal governance channels have not evolved organically through internal political struggles. Instead, they have been (or in some cases, are still) superimposed by colonial forces, postcolonial regimes or external actors including foreign governments, international organizations and donor bodies (Goodfellow, 2022). In such contexts, particular segments of society are often included and recognized more than others via formal governance channels, leading to situations in which formal state institutions may lack popular legitimacy.

Unpacking this trend requires engaging with the ongoing legacies of colonial governance and planning cultures. Here, we briefly return to discussions introduced in earlier chapters, to make sense of the link between informal politics and (post)colonial development. The work of James Holston (2009) on 'differentiated citizenship' provides a useful entry point. Writing on the development of the state and citizenship in Brazil, Holston (2009: 255) outlines how Portuguese colonizers and subsequent (post)colonial republican governments 'formulated a regime of citizenship using social differences that were not the basis of national membership – differences of education, property, race, gender and occupation – to distribute different treatment to different categories of citizens'. For example, prior to independence, citizenship rights were restricted to landed elites of Portuguese descent while native populations and slaves, often of African descent, were denied citizenship rights and involvement in formal governance. 'Differentiated citizenship' has been maintained after independence, for example by postcolonial governments restricting electoral suffrage as part of constitutional reforms in 1881 to literate Brazilians (for example, White landed elites of Portuguese descent), while excluding others (for example, Indigenous peoples and former slaves) from rights to education, thereby denying them the possibility of exercising citizenship (Holston, 2009).

'Differentiated citizenship' patterns occur in diverse (post)colonial states, but how they unfold varies according to geopolitical context. For example, writing on Sub-Saharan Africa, Myers (2003) uses the 'House of Wonders' – a prominent building in Stone Town in Zanzibar, a historical centre of colonial administration characterized by three verandahs that encircle above each other – as a metaphor to describe racial hierarchies imposed by the colonial state in four urban settings in Africa: Nairobi, Lusaka, Lilongwe and Zanzibar. According to Myers (2003), the bottom verandah is inhabited by the 'governed' and 'colonized' Black Africans, the middle verandah by Indian and African bureaucrats (referred to as the 'colonized middle'), and the top by the British colonizers. According to Myers (2003), it was the top verandah that introduced policies and planning regulations, the middle verandah that implemented them and the bottom verandah that was excluded from policies, denied from citizenship rights, and – as a response – challenged, undermined or imposed their own informal practices of how cities should be governed and used (for further examples from Sub-Saharan African countries see Watson [2009]; see also Porter [2010] on settler colonial societies in the global North and Yiftachel [2009] on contemporary formal/informal governance relations in Israel/Palestine).

Those excluded from formal governance and citizenship in (post)colonial societies should not be conceived of as passive victims. They may undertake politics autonomously according to their own principles and norms, for example, through preserving and relying on 'traditional' governance and justice – often grounded in Indigenous, tribal, and kinship cultures and practices – that operate outside of and are deemed 'illegal' or 'informal' by formal state institutions (Goldstein, 2005; Meagher, 2007; Alfasi, 2014). Holzinger et al (2016) refer to such a scenario as a 'dualist polity' – a situation where people are governed to varying degrees by formal modern governance while at the same time organizing themselves collectively according to their own rules and principles. Others have highlighted how those excluded contest oppression and – with varying degrees of success – demand inclusion within formal governance and claim citizenship rights by deploying a variety of informal tactics including, for example, protest, quiet rebellion, political negotiation or alliance building with state authorities (Scott, 1998; Bayat, 2000; Holston 2008; 2009). We discuss urban examples of autonomous practices and other informal tactics in the next section.

Others pay closer attention to how formal governance systems in (post)colonial societies create patterns of exclusion. Holston's (2008) work on differentiated citizenship, discussed earlier, is an illustrative example. Scholars like Chatterjee (2004; 2008), meanwhile, examine how state engagements with wider citizenry are often characterized by both formal and informal practices. Taking the case of India, Chatterjee (2004; 2008) denotes how the state engages differently with distinct segments of society as the co-existence of civil society and political society. The

Indian state is considered to restrict civil society – referring to modern associational life originating in Western institutions – to a small body of the citizenry such as the urban middle classes. In contrast, political society is composed of large sections of the country's population living in rural areas or living and working informally in cities. These groups 'are governed, not within the framework of stable constitutionally defined rights and laws', or what we could consider to be formal politics, 'but rather through temporary, contextual and unstable arrangements arrived at through direct political negotiations', or what we refer to here as governing informally (Chatterjee, 2008: 57). In a similar vein to Chatterjee, Pritchett et al (2018: 14) focus on what actually happens in state–society relations in 'developing' countries. Focusing less on state–citizen relations but more on state–business interactions, they highlight that such relations tend to be dominated not so much by formal rules but by deals – defined as interactions rooted in informal, personalized relations that deviate from formal rules. An example of an informal deal is provided by Goldstein (2016) in his book *Owners of the Sidewalk* that traces practices of governing informally linked to informal sector work in Cochabamba, Bolivia. He highlights how municipal authorities in Cochabamba settled a land conflict with a neighbouring town called Tiquipaya by allowing 'flower vendors from that town to sell on certain street corners during specific hours of the morning', thereby tolerating informal trade that otherwise stands in 'direct violation of municipal law' (Goldstein, 2016: 76).

Moving beyond a focus on (post)colonial politics at the regional or national level, more recent research by Goodfellow (2020; 2022) and Harris (2018) offers an explicitly urban perspective. Goodfellow articulates this as follows:

> In urban areas, constellations of institutions such as laws, ordinances, plans, and regulatory frameworks are particularly dense and complex, being the spaces in which colonisation and formal authority generally establishes itself. Cities in the global South are thus thick with formal institutions, but are also places in which such institutions are widely undermined by informal institutions and practices. (Goodfellow, 2022: 42)

This perspective suggests that closer attention needs to be paid to governing informally in Southern cities because of the density and co-existence of, as well as possible clashes between, formal and informal political institutions and practices. Moving beyond a place- and region-specific focus on cities in the global South, Harris (2018) offers a more processual perspective by arguing that governing informally emerges particularly during urbanization processes such as urban expansion and peri-urban development (see Figure 5.1 for an example from Bogota). Harris (2018) highlights that prior to urbanization rural land uses tend to be guided by traditional/communal property regimes and, in such settings, amateur construction on land is often acceptable. In contrast, urban areas tend to be guided by Western/individual property regimes and by a competitive real estate sector that ideally requires formal regulation. These different regulatory logics tend to enter into juxtaposition and conflict during urban expansion, a process characterized by rural–urban land use changes and real estate developments that lead to increases in land and property

Figure 5.1: Ciudad Bolivar, Bogota, Colombia

Source: Lorena Guerrero

values in suburban or peri-urban settings (for a more detailed review on literature on rural–urban land transformations see also Lombard and Rakodi [2016] and also Chapter 3). As part of urban expansion, 'land is dragged, sometimes kicking and screaming, into the urban fold' (Harris, 2018: 268), leading to a situation whereby previously accepted rural building practices or traditional/communal property rights regimes are now considered 'unacceptable' and not compliant with urban land use regulations and building standards. In other words, what was previously acceptable is now considered illegal and may co-exist, challenge and undermine formal urban governance regimes (for an example, see our discussion on hyperregulation in La Paz, Bolivia, in Box 5.1).

What is clear from this is that governing informally seems to be particularly associated with cities and urbanization processes in the global South, in terms of their shared histories of colonialism, although it is also prevalent in other places with settler colonial histories and beyond. The next section explores how governing informally unfolds in practice in Southern and other urban contexts, paying close attention to the relationship with articulations of living and working informally discussed in previous chapters.

Articulations of governing informally

A key feature that distinguishes cities and places affected by urbanization in the global South is, to paraphrase Pritchett et al (2018: 24), 'the gap between the official formal laws and regulations and what actually happens'. Making sense of what actually happens requires moving beyond legal texts and recognizing that politics is undertaken by heterogeneous actors. For the purpose of this book, which focuses on the interplay between governing, living and working informally, particular attention is paid to the role of and relationships between state actors and ordinary urban residents who live and work informally. As we demonstrate in what follows, in addition to being guided by formal regulations, the practices undertaken by these actors might be influenced by individual agency,[4] involvement in specific actor coalitions (for example, formal or informal institutions) or the wider structural context[5] characterizing a particular urban place (Watson, 2009; 2012). Hence, a combination of factors might help explain why ordinary people and/or state authorities 'may be unable or unwilling to conform to [formal] regulations' (Harris, 2018: 273), contributing to what we refer to here as governing informally. In what follows, and building on the distinction between bottom-up (citizen-led) and top-down (state-led) practices presented in the introductory chapter and in previous sections, we offer a discussion of different articulations of governing informally, as initiated by ordinary people who live and work informally and by state authorities, always paying close attention to the interrelationship between these actors (Banks et al, 2020).

Governing informally from below

Informal governance is often undertaken by those unable, unwilling or denied opportunities to engage in formal politics. In urban contexts, it is particularly those living and working informally who represent such informal political actors as they are often excluded from formal politics and are unable to access or denied tenure rights, secure housing, services, and socio-economic and legal protections through formal channels, as discussed earlier and in Chapters 3 and 4.

This suggests that factors contributing to the emergence of different forms of living and working informally are themselves political in nature. In particular, urban informality may emerge because of exclusionary (post)colonial governance regimes and differentiated citizenship dynamics, as argued earlier, or because weak, under-resourced and underprepared state actors and institutions are unable or unwilling to respond to urbanization and informal growth, as seen in previous chapters. As we outline in what follows, in such situations governing informally may emerge from below, involving those who are excluded, disenfranchised and confined to the margins of urban society. In our discussion, we distinguish between autonomous informal political tactics and those that, implicitly or more explicitly, engage with or confront the state through quiet encroachment, collective organization and insurgent politics.

Autonomous political organization

Earlier accounts considered those living and working informally to be politically passive victims of exclusion who found themselves trapped in a 'culture of poverty', incapable of improving their living conditions (Lewis, 1967b; see also Chapter 2). This perspective has been challenged in subsequent decades by academics who foreground the agency of the urban poor. An early advocate of such a perspective is Manuel Castells (1983), who highlighted that those living and working informally in cities such as Lima (Peru), Mexico City and Santiago (Chile) sought to occupy land, construct their own homes and organize their own services autonomously. John Turner (1967), writing on Lima, also demonstrated patterns of self-help housing whereby informal owner-occupiers constructed parts or all their accommodation. Such trends were common across the global South in the 1970s and 1980s (see also Chapter 3). For example, according to Caroline Moser's (2009: 48) longitudinal study on the informal neighbourhood Indio Guayas in Guayaquil (Ecuador), land invasions and self-help housing 'were the principal manner in which the low-income population … obtained housing' in the 1970s, a period where 'most of the urban poor were effectively excluded from the conventional public and private housing markets'. Self-help housing is not confined to the global South and has been observed in the global North, often apparently associated with international migrants whose status is either transient and/or illegal. For example, Breeze (2023) noted how migrants on their route to the UK remained stuck in the French port town of Calais where they lacked shelter support from the French or British authorities. Instead, they relied on self-help – sometimes aided by volunteers and non-government organizations (NGOs) – to construct temporary shelter, as in the 'Campe du Lande', an informal camp situated on a toxic former industrial waste area in Calais. However, informal housing practices are undertaken by diverse actors beyond migrant communities in the global North, and care must be taken to properly examine the actors and structures involved, as argued in Chapter 8.

Autonomous organization often goes beyond the remit of informal housing, encompassing activities that seek to address a multiplicity of absences. For example, when people cannot access formal finance, they often engage in informal institutions such as savings groups or access informal service providers such as loan sharks (see Chapters 6 and 7 for examples). In a context in which people residing in informal settlements are unable to connect to formal water and electricity networks, they may rely on informal service providers (see Chapters 3 and 7 for examples). When businesses and trading activities are neither registered nor monitored by the state, or when security is not provided by the police, those living and working informally often take regulation, monitoring and justice into their own hands. For example, Agbiboa (2018) highlights how so-called *agberos* (area boys) control the flow of goods and services and help to maintain peace in informal neighbourhoods in Lagos (Nigeria), although this may be at a cost to residents who are required to make financial contributions, and may be at risk of arbitrary 'justice' procedures. A similar trend has been noted for informal neighbourhoods in Bolivian cities such as Cochabamba, El Alto and La Paz. Here, marginalized communities exercise lynch-mob justice to protect their homes and businesses from criminal activities in a context of police absence (Goldstein, 2005; 2012; Risør, 2010). To alert the public that lynch-mob justice is exercised, organized communities display warning signs on walls or light-posts that illustrate what punishments await those who do not obey the laws of the street (see Figure 5.2).

Such autonomous political practices represent articulations of what we call here governing informally, in the sense that they occur outside official channels and regulatory frameworks. But, as highlighted by Castells (1983), they should not be looked at in isolation from formal urban politics. Instead, autonomous political action represents a direct response to a lack of effective political support. It also only emerges in a context of relative state permissiveness, although not necessarily state absence,

Figure 5.2: Signs evidencing community and lynch mob justice in El Alto, Bolivia

Note: Left: informal street access barrier to control traffic; right: doll hanging on a street light indicating that criminals will be hanged and wall graffiti stating, '*Ladron pillado sera quemado*' ['Thieves who are caught will be burned']

Source: Philipp Horn

which is a contested narrative sometimes associated with informality. In other words, while squatting, self-construction or exercising lynch-mob justice may not be legal, such practices occur because state authorities tolerate them, often because they are unable or unwilling to provide such services themselves.

Quiet encroachment, collective organization and insurgent politics

Governing informally from below also refers to those everyday political tactics of marginalized individuals and collectives that seek to reshape cities and urban politics. Bayat's (2000: 545) work on quiet encroachment – referring to the 'silent, protracted but pervasive advancement of ordinary people on the propertied and powerful in order to survive and improve their lives' – provides a helpful entry point to make sense of individual political tactics. Quiet encroachment may, among other examples, include urban poor individuals living and working informally who engage in a series of practices already discussed in previous chapters, such as illegally tapping into municipal electricity networks to access energy (see, for example, McFarlane, 2010a), encroaching on public or privately owned land to construct shelter or set up a street vending businesses (see, for example, Moser, 2009; Goldstein, 2016; Vargas Falla and Valencia, 2019), refusing to pay rent or utility bills (Park, 2019), or illegally redesigning, rearranging, partitioning or expanding public housing (see, for example, Lemanski, 2009). Quiet encroachment is often undertaken by highly marginalized individuals who engage in such practices to meet basic needs for survival. It occurs especially in urban contexts such as Egypt and the Middle East where state governance is repressive and where overt contestation is therefore less feasible.

Individuals engaged in quiet encroachment do not necessarily attach political meaning to such acts themselves, but Bayat (2000: 247) nevertheless refers to them as a 'politics of redress', defined as 'a struggle for an immediate outcome through individual direct action'. From this perspective, quiet encroachment can be conceived of as political tactic in the sense that it contests, albeit perhaps not consciously or overtly, 'many fundamental aspects of the state prerogatives, including the meaning of order, control of public space, of public and private goods' (Bayat, 2000: 546). It can also be seen as an example of governing informally, because related practices tend to occur outside officially sanctioned channels and implicitly challenge or violate existing urban regulations.

Individual acts of quiet encroachment can turn into more overt, and collective, political action during moments of external threat, for example, when state authorities no longer tolerate the cumulative growth of informal neighbourhoods or street vending in public spaces, and propose to evict individuals associated with these phenomena (for discussions on evictions, see Chapters 6 and 7). It is in such moments that previously 'atomized individuals' actively communicate with others who share a common identity. Bayat (2000: 552) illustrates this as follows: 'When a threat occurs ... [affected people] are likely to get together even if they do not know each other or have not planned to do so in advance.' This may lead to collective struggles such as 'episodic moments of open protest, collective mobilisation, and violence' to defend encroachment practices (Banks et al, 2020: 233).

In some cases, episodic collective action may lead to the formation and subsequent consolidation of collective organizations (for example, trade unions representing street workers or neighbourhood associations representing those living informally) that defend the rights of marginalized individuals over a longer period of time. This is the case, for example, in El Alto (Bolivia) where residents established informal neighbourhood organizations in the 1980s to collectively protect their rights to occupy land, self-construct housing and access services. These neighbourhood associations were later formally recognized as civil society organizations following the 1994 Law of Popular Participation. Currently, they serve as an interface between state and citizens in channelling public services for infrastructural improvements into informal neighbourhoods (Kohl, 2003; Lazar, 2008).

Similar trends can also be observed in informal neighbourhoods situated in Beirut's southern suburbs – known as Dahiye – that are home to a majority of Shia Muslim residents, a group that has historically been marginalized and positioned at the bottom of Lebanon's social hierarchy (Nazha, 2018). Writing on the informal urbanization of Dahiye, Nazha (2018: 46) emphasizes how collective organization among Shia residents helped to consolidate the neighbourhoods, as well as residents' right to the city, in political periods in which the Lebanese state was initially 'unequipped to face the massive influx of newcomers to Beirut' in the 1950s to the 1970s, then 'collapsed as a functioning body in the midst of the civil war' between 1975 and 1990, and finally 'progressively lost authority, control and physical presence within Dahiye' from 1990 until the present day. During early urbanization processes in the 1950s and 1960s, Shia rural–urban migrants engaged in illegal land subdivisions by purchasing land from Druze and Christian landowners, officially zoned for agricultural use, for the construction of urban homes. These new urban informal residents subsequently formed collective organizations ranging 'from the Islamic Institution of the Arts to the Mabarrat Association and the Islamic Centre of Haret Hreik, with the main intent to provide basic services in the fields of education, healthcare and charity' in a context where state-led planning was either absent or hostile towards new settlers; they also formed political movements such as the 'Movement of the Disinherited' and later Hezbollah that, among other issues, contested for the 'need for presence', by demanding better political representation in city governance and fairer distribution of services across urban districts and national regions (Nazha, 2018: 48). Collective action and political mobilization helped to consolidate Dahiye and, over time, organizations such as Hezbollah, which are associated with the area's predominantly Shia population, gained in national political importance and entered formal politics, for example through representation in parliament.

Collective struggles uniting previously 'atomised individuals' provide only one example of what could be referred to more broadly as insurgent politics, 'purposeful actions that aim to disrupt domineering relationships of oppressors to the oppressed, and to destabilise such a status quo through consciousness of the past and imagination of an alternative future' (Miraftab, 2009: 44). Insurgent political tactics 'do not constrain themselves to the spaces for citizen participation sanctioned by authorities (invited spaces)',[6] but often 'invent new spaces or re-appropriate old ones' with the aim of advancing counter-hegemonic interests (Miraftab, 2009: 35). As such, insurgent politics are examples of governing informally in the sense that they are carried out by citizen organizations and collectives that are not formally recognized. The overall aim of insurgent politics is to challenge socio-spatial exclusion, articulate different ideas of urban citizenship and promote alternative models of city-making, and this may be done through engaging in illegal activities such as violence, in active non-compliance with the law, or through inventing practices that are not recognized within formal governance and planning procedures (Frediani et al, 2018). Examples include, among others, efforts by gangs to obtain political control in Brazil's urban peripheries (Holston, 2008), building occupation practices in central São Paulo (Brazil) by the Housing for All Movement (Frediani et al, 2018), anti-eviction campaigns by collectives of slum dwellers in South Africa (Miraftab, 2009), and violent uprisings against neoliberal reform packages by a loose coalition of informal traders, informal neighbourhood residents, peasant organizations, Indigenous movements and miners' unions during El Alto's gas war in 2003 (Zibechi, 2010).

Insurgent political tactics can also refer to efforts to claim invited spaces of participation and engagement in formal institutional channels. What initiates as informal/illegal political action may over time transform into attempts to obtain formalization/legalization. It is also possible for informal/illegal actions, like violent protest, to occur simultaneously alongside more formalized political actions such as lobbying. The previously discussed case of the emergence, consolidation and formalization of neighbourhood associations in El Alto offers one example of such transformations. Another more recent example is the case of political mobilization in the informal neighbourhoods of Mukuru in Nairobi, Kenya (Horn et al, 2020). In 2009, local residents from these neighbourhoods approached professionals working for the NGO Muungano wa Wanavijiji – Kenya's affiliate of the international network Shack/Slum Dwellers International (see Chapter 7 for a more detailed discussion of this organization and its approach towards addressing living informally) – to ask for advice and support around eviction threats. This led to a collaboration between local residents and the NGO, and ultimately to the deployment of a series of political tactics to confront eviction threats, including resistance (for example, organizing protests), self-organization (for example, community mobilization via door-knocking campaigns, citizen-led enumerations and formation of savings groups), research, lobbying, media campaigns and dialogue with state authorities. It was precisely because of this combination of individual and collective action, insurgent planning, autonomous practices, alliance building and political negotiation that evictions could be avoided. This combination of political tactics, realized via informal and formal institutional channels, helped to convince government authorities in Nairobi to recognize and address problems faced by Mukuru residents, through Mukuru's declaration as a Special Planning Area (see also Chapters 6 and 7).

Governing informally from above

We now focus on state institutions and related top-down practices of governing informally. It should be clear by now that urban informality exists in relation to the state, which ultimately 'has the power … to determine what is informal and what is not' (Roy, 2005: 149). From this perspective, states have the capacity to deliberately engineer urban informality, something we discuss through a focus on what Roy (2003; 2009; 2011) refers to as calculated informality. In addition, through examining urban clientelistic practices, we also discuss how engagements between government authorities and those living and working informally often do not follow formally recognized procedures but occur through unofficial channels.

Calculated informality

Ananya Roy (2009: 83) defines calculated informality as a political practice that 'involves purposive planning and action, and one where the seeming withdrawal of regulatory power creates a logic of resource allocation, accumulation, and authority'.[7] From this perspective, informality 'sits at the heart of the state and is an integral part of the territorial practices of state power' (Roy, 2009: 84). State actors may consciously create a situation of informality to enhance their sovereignty and/or to reward and discipline others, but how this unfolds varies according to context. For the example of Calcutta in India, Roy (2003; 2009) describes how planners deliberately violate or suspend laws, leading to deregulation which is defined as a situation where 'the ownership, use, and purpose of land' can no longer be clearly 'fixed and mapped according to any prescribed set of regulations or the law' (Roy, 2009: 80). Deregulation enables state actors to legitimize and undertake certain urban developments, such as the construction of real estate for wealthy population groups on risk-prone or environmentally protected lands, while deeming other developments such as informal neighbourhoods illegal and worthy of demolition (Roy, 2003; 2009).

Elsewhere similar conditions are established through distinct political strategies by the state and other elite groups. Writing on Israel/Palestine, Oren Yiftachel (2009) shows how planning authorities use land regulation as a strategic tool to generate 'gray spaces' by selectively including or excluding specific individuals and groups from inhabiting urban space. Yiftachel (2009), for example, illustrates how Israeli planning authorities 'darken' the nomadic and collective land-use patterns of Indigenous Bedouin Arabs by declaring them as illegal. Meanwhile, the land occupation processes of Jewish settlers are being 'whitened' and declared legal. For Beirut, Lebanon, Mona Fawaz (2017: 1943) notes how local authorities issue exceptions – defined as 'an assemblage of concessions, facilities, and temporary measures' – to manage speculative urban development. In Istanbul, Turkey, local authorities make use of 'the strategic utilisation and manipulation of ambiguous forces and laws' to create private property regimes within informal neighbourhoods (Kuyucu, 2014: 611).

Calculated informality perspectives have also been deployed to make sense of the governance of informal workers. Writing on Bolivia, Daniel Goldstein (2016) notes deliberate state neglect of informal market traders, and especially street vendors, operating in Cochabamba's informal market 'La Cancha'. Goldstein (2016: 7) identifies a dynamic of state-organized disorder which he refers to as *dis*regulation – a scenario whereby the 'market's chaos (like that of other neglected spaces, including poor urban neighbourhoods) is to a large degree engineered' by the state, which 'administers its own preferred forms of regulation while ignoring others'. The previously discussed example of a political deal to settle a land dispute in another town by allowing flower traders from this town to sell on street corners in Cochabamba, where informal trade is otherwise prohibited by municipal law, is an illustration of such selective practices linked to *dis*regulation.

Jaffe and Koster (2019) note that *dis*regulation should not only be associated with 'shady power moves and "less-than" modes of governance' in places like Cochabamba and other cities in the global South. Instead, they argue that such practices also occur in the global North, but here *dis*regulation practices are often celebrated as laudable policy innovations. To illustrate this point, they reflect on the case study of Amsterdam's (Netherlands) Red Light District, where government authorities operated a toleration policy from the 1960s until the 1980s, with activities such as sex work and selling drugs – elsewhere declared illegal – spatially contained and tolerated within certain areas. As toleration led to criminal excess (for example, a rise in human trafficking activities and emergence of other illicit activities such as informal banking), local authorities in Amsterdam shifted towards a 'clean up' strategy in the 1990s, whereby the municipality bought or expropriated properties in the Red Light District and introduced zoning regulations that promoted more 'desirable' businesses such as boutiques, cafes and bars. In line with the *dis*regulation observed by Goldstein in Cochabamba, toleration and 'clean up' initiatives in Amsterdam involved a 'highly flexible use of legality in its application of administrative law', but rather than associating this with corrupt practices or a violation of the rule of law, local authorities defended these 'measures as necessarily creative solutions to an intractable governance problem' (Jaffe and Koster, 2019: 566).

The state-led creation of organized disorder does not only emerge because of deliberate state withdrawal, deregulation, exceptionalism or *dis*regulation. It can also emerge in a context where state authorities deliberately enable the overlap and co-existence of distinct jurisdictions and regulatory regimes – a situation also referred to as legal pluralism (Griffiths, 1986; von Benda-Beckmann, 2002), overlapping territorialities (Agnew and Oslender, 2010) or hyperregulation (Horn, 2022). Such a situation can be short-term and transitional, occurring when new legal regimes are introduced – for example, when urban land regimes are introduced in rural settings or when colonial regimes introduce new rules on colonized territory – while others disappear (Harris, 2018: 271). In other contexts, such a situation can prevail as a more long-term phenomenon, as seen in Box 5.1.

Box 5.1: Hyperregulation in Bolivia

Writing on peri-urban land and real estate developments in La Paz, Bolivia, Horn (2022) demonstrates how legislative reforms by Bolivia's national government on decentralization and municipal delineation deliberately fail to establish clear jurisdictional boundaries. This leads to a situation of hyperregulation, whereby multiple local authorities claim political control over the same territory by deploying distinct, and at times conflicting, legal and planning frameworks. While hyperregulation serves to enable a loose coalition of elite actors – including government authorities, resident leaders of peri-urban neighbourhoods and private sector representatives – to advance specific political and socio-economic interests, it puts ordinary residents in a situation of permanent uncertainty. The deliberate nature of long-term hyperregulation is perhaps articulated most clearly by a government representative working in Bolivia's Ministry of Autonomies:

> Places affected by boundary conflicts are lucrative sites. Here, most of our country's urban development happens. Our cities no longer have room for more people. For this reason, urbanization occurs beyond their limits. A situation with unclear municipal boundaries provides you with flexibility for urban development to happen. For this reason, we face a lot of resistance to resolve boundary conflicts, including by people within our own national government. Basically, if you have boundary conflicts, you have different municipalities who are active in the same area and this is of benefit for some influential people. You see, what one local authority declares illegal is declared legal by the next as all compete over resources and political control. Such a situation creates winners and losers. Most people lose out because they do not know how the system works and they lack influential contacts. But some, especially, *loteadores* [a term used in Bolivia to refer to urban informal developers], know the laws and different procedures by distinct government authorities. This legal know-how provides them with opportunities, for example to undertake land conversions. The people involved in such transactions have political weight, and they have an interest in the continuation of boundary conflicts. For this reason, there is no serious attempt to resolve these conflicts anytime soon. (Testimony from an interview conducted on 22 November 2016, in Horn 2022: 2495)

The top-down creation of informality tends to enable state authorities, but also other elite actors, to exploit ambiguity in order to meet specific ends. The role of non-state elite groups in such practices has further been highlighted in research on transport

Figure 5.3: Land invasion at the edge of an established informal neighbourhood in Xalapa, Mexico

Source: Melanie Lombard

agberos in Lagos (Agbiboa, 2018), Mumbai's 'development mafia' (Weinstein, 2008), the 'water mafia' in Bangalore (Ranganathan, 2014) and land brokers in Mexico (Lombard [2016] associated with the type of development seen in Figure 5.3), as well as for big property developers in Mumbai (McFarlane, 2012), as discussed earlier.

While often designed to serve elite interests, it must also be recognized that calculated informality may support disadvantaged groups in resolving challenges associated with living and working informally. This is the case, for example, in informal neighbourhoods in Mukuru, Nairobi (see Figure 5.4), which were declared a Special Planning Area (see previous section). As a consequence, development and planning interventions were suspended in the area. This suspension (a result of deregulation) helped to establish a space for innovation around inclusive informal settlement upgrading in an otherwise politically hostile context where conventional governance and planning practices had failed to address local needs (Horn et al, 2020; Horn, 2021; see also Chapter 7 and Banks et al, 2020: 233).

Urban clientelist politics

Clientelism emerges as another core feature characterizing political relations between state authorities and those living and working informally in the global South. As outlined previously, clientelism refers to the granting of public goods and services (by politicians to ordinary people) in exchange for political favours such as votes. Clientelist relations normally occur based on personal connections rather than on established formal rules and principles. Mitlin (2014: 6) argues that clientelist relations are 'particularly prevalent in informal settlements, due to the lack of services and the need to negotiate with politicians and sometimes officials to secure such investments'. Patron–client relations tend to emerge in contexts where states are unable to guarantee universal access to rights and services. In such contexts, 'politicians use personalised relations to manage protest as they buy off, co-opt and absorb pressure and protest from the urban poor' (Mitlin, 2014: 6). For example, Özdemirli (2018) illustrates how the emergence and consolidation of *gecekondus* (informal neighbourhoods) in Ankara in Turkey should be understood

Figure 5.4: Mukuru informal neighbourhoods in Nairobi, Kenya, a street view

Source: Philipp Horn

in relation to evolving patron–client relations. Reflecting on the period from the 1950s until the present context, Özdemirli (2018: 29) demonstrates that distinct governments, who were unable to fill housing gaps and therefore tolerated informal neighbourhoods, initially bought 'votes in exchange for amnesties and legal titles, then with the provision of infrastructure, later by offering citizens the right to expand dwellings vertically, and lastly offering new units by redevelopment in exchange for land'. *Gecekondu* dwellers reacted to this by 'agreeing to support a political party – irrespective of their ideological preference [outlined by a discussion in historical shifts in support towards centrist, right and left-leaning, and Islamic political parties] – which promised title deeds, additional development rights or upgrades in city services' (Özdemirli, 2018: 29).

Existing literature highlights both benefits and pitfalls of urban clientelist politics (see Box 5.2). Those highlighting the benefits of clientelism argue that such relations are often the only avenues for urban poor communities to obtain access to services and to engage with political elites. Benjamin (2004; 2008), for example, illustrates this for slum dwellers in urban India. While lacking formal input into political decision-making processes – something that is confined to the state and civil society – the urban poor form part of what Chatterjee (2004; 2008) refers to as 'political society', as discussed previously. The urban poor exert their claims for, among other issues, tenure security, business permits and prevention of evictions by approaching elected municipal representatives or lower-tier government officials. The latter often respond positively to such requests in exchange for votes or by charging small bribes. According to Benjamin (2004), 50 to 75 per cent of India's urban population – especially those living and working informally – use such clientelist channels to meet their needs. A similar perspective is put forward by Auyero (2000) on informal political relations in informal neighbourhoods in Buenos Aires in Argentina. In this context characterized by 'hyper-unemployment' and state neglect, residents of informal neighbourhoods have no other option than to resort to personalized relations with local representatives from the Peronist party to obtain food, medicine, jobs and other basic services.

While providing an important route for the urban poor to access benefits and services, clientelist politics may also have negative effects. Clientelism tends to reinforce vertical authority, socio-economic inequality and political exclusion, leading to situations in which the most disadvantaged groups remain unable to access vital services and rights (Mitlin, 2014). Such critiques are acknowledged even by those who highlight clientelism's benefits. For example, in the same study on Buenos Aires, Auyero (2000) demonstrates that, especially in a context of severe economic crisis, political patrons are incapable of addressing the needs of everyone. Instead, patrons tend to engage with local community leaders – referred to as brokers – who provide a small inner circle (that is, neighbours, friends, political allies) with essential favours while others remain excluded.

This situation of internal power relations in informal neighbourhoods has also been well explained in fictionalized accounts, including Mistry's *A Fine Balance*, in which the protagonists are dependent on the goodwill of the local 'slum lord' to find adequate housing. Similarly, in Boo's fictionalized account *Behind the Beautiful Forevers*, Asha is an aspiring female slum lord who uses her political connections to rise to power in Annawardi, the slum at the centre of the narrative (see also alternative representations list at the end of the chapter).

It should be clear by now that the benefits of clientelist relations are unequal and often restricted to a small fraction of those living and working informally. But even for those who benefit, patron–client channels may narrow over time. This may be because of shifts in political leadership (for example, a patron being forced out of office) or through other reconfigurations within the local state. The latter is illustrated by Ghertner (2011) in a study on Dehli's Bhagidari scheme that led to the rise of Resident Welfare Associations, composed of urban middle- and upper-class groups, as new players in participatory and citywide urban governance (see also Chapter 2). As a consequence, 'elected councillors who have historically had the closest ties with the urban poor – have increasingly had to cater to the demands of Resident Welfare Associations in order to maintain their political relevance and visibility' (Ghertner,

> **Box 5.2: Unequal clientelist politics in Dhaka, Bangladesh**
>
> Writing on urban poor politics in three informal neighbourhoods in Dhaka (Bangladesh), Banks (2016a) illustrates the hierarchical and unequal character of clientelist politics (see also Hackenbroch and Hossain, 2012). Banks (2016a) reveals how benefits from clientelist relations are often restricted to community leaders who represent the top of the social hierarchy within informal neighbourhoods. Leaders maintain direct personal ties with local politicians and distribute rewards among a group of 'supporters (including their strongmen and other large landlords in the neighbourhood) and family or kinship networks' (Banks, 2016a: 280). The latter group represents the second layer of the social hierarchy. This group may lack direct political connections but has established networks with local community leaders, something that is 'associated with active political support or kinship and family lines' (Banks, 2016a: 284). Finally, the bottom of the social hierarchy is composed of 'between 66 and 83 per cent of households' across the informal settlements studied by Banks (2016a: 285). This group lacks political, family and kinship ties with upper tiers of the social hierarchy. To make ends meet, these households might rely on their own survival networks (for example, savings groups or family networks that enable access to small-scale loans) but they also depend on members of the higher and middle tier of the social hierarchy to access services and loans, often at extortionate costs and with threats of violence and retribution if they are unable to return payment.

2011: 526). In other words, the emergence of formal participatory governance channels that benefit wealthier social groups was accompanied by a decline in patron–client engagements that benefit those living and working informally.

In sum, while clientelist relations clearly represent an important channel to transfer resources and some level of political power to those living and working informally, they are nevertheless highly stratified, reproduce inequalities and exclusion dynamics, and rarely (if ever) lead to substantive improvements in living conditions and political representation.

Chapter summary

This chapter introduced the topic of governing informally, paying close attention to how this intersects with living and working informally. We began by tracing the roots of the concept of governing informally within political science debates, highlighting that informal politics is an inherent feature of socio-political relations everywhere. We then examined why governing informally is particularly prevalent in (post)colonial development settings, especially in Southern cities and places affected by urbanization, although also beyond them. It is in urban(izing) places where formal institutions and governance practices are particularly dense, and where informal institutions seek to undermine, engage with and influence formal politics. The remainder of the chapter discussed different articulations of governing informally, with particular attention paid to efforts from below such as autonomous political organization, quiet encroachment, collective organization and insurgent politics, as well as efforts from above such as calculated informality and clientelism. The outcomes of such different informal political articulations vary significantly, with some helping those living and working informally to meet their basic needs and contributing to wider democratic life in cities, and others reinforcing social hierarchies and political exclusion, while also undermining formal governance.

Recommended reading

- Goodfellow, T. (2020) 'Political informality: deals, trust networks, and the negotiation of value in the urban realm', *The Journal of Development Studies*, 56(2): 278–94.
- Harris, R. (2018) 'Modes of informal urban development: a global phenomenon', *Journal of Planning Literature*, 33(3): 267–86.
- Helmke, G. and Levitsky, S. (2004) 'Informal institutions and comparative politics: a research agenda', *Perspectives on Politics*, 2(4): 725–40.

EXERCISES

- Can you think about an example of governing informally that is unique to the place you are from or currently live in? To do so, you might want to engage again with the *Global Encyclopedia of Informality* (Ledeneva, 2018a, see also exercise in Chapter 1) as it provides many examples on informal politics from across the world.
- In the first substantive section of this chapter we discussed how political science literature broadly distinguishes between informal institutions and practices that contribute to and/or undermine democratic life and formal governance. Building on this body of research, Goodfellow (2020; 2022) developed a typology to capture variations in how informal politics relates to formal urban governance and institutions. He distinguishes between four types of informal politics: (1) a-formal (defined as informal practices that broadly support formal political institutions or help to build them); (2) anti-formal (political activities that deliberately challenge or weaken formal institutions and processes); (3) para-formal (informally institutionalized political practices that exist in parallel with formal institutions without either supporting or intentionally undermining them); and (4) a-formal (grey spaces where no clear rules – whether formal or informal – apply). To gain a deeper understanding of this typology, please read Goodfellow's (2020) article (see recommended readings). Afterwards, please revisit the different articulations of governing informally discussed in this chapter (that is, autonomous practices, quiet encroachment, collective organization, insurgent politics, calculated informality and clientelism) and discuss to what extent and how each of them represents an example of one or more components of Goodfellow's typology.

Alternative representations
- The novel *Americanah* (2013) by Chimamanda Ngozi Adichie provides a captivating account of informal politics in Lagos, Nigeria (see especially Chapter 2).[8]

- We again recommend engaging specifically with Chapter 6 of Rohinton Mistry's (1996) *A Fine Balance* to get a fictional perspective on governing informally.
- Set in the city of Mumbai, Katherine Boo's (2012) book *Behind the Beautiful Forevers: Life, Death and Hope in a Mumbai Slum* also provides an evocative account of living, working and governing informally in the Indian context.

6

Responses to Living Informally

'The planning consultations were okay. Most of us agreed with the experts about the issues of better sanitation infrastructure. People were so happy because you know when we have toilets on our plots, it improves sanitation in the ghetto. But constructing toilets, housing and other infrastructure can also be problematic. Some people believe their land will be taken away. Someone says, "Eeh!" Now when it comes to the issues of roads and drainages, when you tell someone: "The drainage will pass here through your plot"; they calculate and say: "Two of my houses will be demolished to pave way for drainage!" This is when upgrading becomes a problem, especially for structure owners who make their money from renting out houses. These people then start telling other residents: "Don't accept. Whatever you are signing, your houses will be taken away."'

Resident and community mobilizer in the informal neighbourhood of Mukuru in Nairobi, Kenya, reflecting on planning consultations, implications of upgrading interventions and conflicting perspectives among local residents[1]

Prior to the 1960s, provision of affordable housing and services was low priority for urban policy makers (Kiddle, 2010). In the context of the rapid urbanization outlined in Chapters 1, 2 and 3, observed initially in mid-20th-century Latin America, limited provision of privately rented housing could not meet the massive demand for low-cost housing. Some national governments attempted to provide housing for the families establishing themselves in the city, who were often employed in low wage and/or informal jobs. Policy responses usually focused on state-subsidized housing for sale to formal workers, excluding informally employed workers, who would anyway have been unable to afford even the low-cost housing produced by public programmes (Murray and Clapham, 2015). By the 1970s, this type of state-provided formal housing constituted up to 15 per cent of housing stock in cities like Mexico City, Bogota, Santiago and Caracas, but it remained inaccessible for most low-income households (Balchin and Stewart, 2001).

The limited availability and accessibility of formal housing options led to the establishment of informal neighbourhoods, often on cheap unserviced land at the edge of the city, as described in Chapter 3. This boosted levels of homeownership through informal processes of land acquisition and housebuilding (Gilbert, 2016). Initial responses to the growth of informal housing were characterized by eviction, demolition and clearance. By the late 1960s, the proliferation of informal neighbourhoods had forced states and agencies to consider how to respond to the need for land, housing and services for urban residents with the lowest incomes (Kiddle, 2010). In this way, early approaches which sought to clear and eradicate informal settlements gave way to more tolerant and supportive approaches which recognized (to a greater or lesser degree) the existence of these neighbourhoods and the effort that had gone into constructing them. This trajectory of responses to living informally, from punitive to supportive, was both shaped by and contributed to shaping the conceptual and policy debates outlined in Chapter 2.

In this chapter, we explore in more detail diverse approaches to providing or improving the provision of land, housing and services in contexts characterized by informal living. First, by way of context, we briefly explore the role of international agencies, focusing on the United Nations' (UN) shelter agency, UN-Habitat, and the emergence of a global urban agenda. Next, we explore state-led responses such as eviction, sites and services, formalization and regularization, showing how these have evolved over time, from eradication to aided self-help and enabling approaches. We then outline citizen-led responses, drawing on examples of civil society organizations that take a multi-scalar, pro-poor approach which seeks to centre the needs and interests of residents who live informally. Finally, we briefly address how these approaches might be combined, drawing on recent debates around co-production. Throughout, we reflect on regional, national and intra-urban variations of these responses, drawing on examples from Latin America, Asia and Sub-Saharan Africa.

The emergence of a global urban agenda

As the introduction suggests, responses to the informal provision of land, housing and services have been informed by global agendas, and particularly the evolution of a global *urban* agenda. This, in turn, has been framed in relation to the emergence of development agendas, led by international organizations such as the World Bank and the UN, at which national governments are represented. The era of global governance established after the Second World War saw, on the one hand, the creation of international organizations such as the World Bank and the International Monetary Fund in pursuit of economic development through global economic cooperation, trade and investment; and on the other hand, the creation of the UN to foster social development through a human rights agenda (Huchzermeyer, 2011). The UN, understood as 'a forum for discussion and norm creation' (Giovannini, 2008: 259), has played an important role in supporting the formulation of policy positions to address urban issues, including a focus on the needs and interests of those who live informally.

Particularly significant have been the Habitat conferences I, II and III, organized by the UN. They emerged from a series of UN events drawing attention to development and urban issues, on human environments (1972), population (1974) and human settlements (1976) (Environment and Urbanization, 1990). The last of these, known as the Habitat I conference, took place in Vancouver in 1976, and represented the 'first real push for a global debate on urban policy' (Parnell, 2016: 531) in a development context which had been previously dominated by the World Bank's concern with poverty alleviation in rural and urban settings. The conference enabled national governments to come together to discuss recommended actions on human settlements in urban areas, and included a dedicated side event, the Habitat Forum, attended by 20,000 civil society representatives (Satterthwaite, 2016). Its inclusive approach was expressive of more progressive attitudes towards urban informality, through its focus on housing and basic services for the urban poor (Parnell, 2016). The ensuing Vancouver Declaration on Human Settlements, which was discussed and endorsed by participants, recommended 64 actions, such as universal provision of adequate water and sanitation, and resulted in commitments from national governments (Satterthwaite, 2016).

One of the major outcomes of Habitat I was the creation of the UN Centre for Human Settlements (UNCHS) in 1978, later renamed UN-Habitat. UN-Habitat has arguably played a significant role in shaping global urban policy and influencing national urban policy, through its position in setting 'the normative base [and] systems of implementation for urban change' (Parnell, 2016: 533), for example, through the formulation of National Urban Strategies and City Development Strategies for subsequent adoption by national governments. The Habitat II conference, held in Istanbul in 1996, extended stakeholder participation to include private companies, donors and development planning academics, leading to 'a universal commitment to the right to adequate housing' (Parnell, 2016: 532). This reflected the global emergence and spread of neoliberal economic policies, among international agencies and national governments, accompanied by a concern for good governance which manifested as urban governance at the city level.[2] Reflective of this environment, Habitat II included a strong focus on land tenure and associated titling initiatives, captured by the inclusion of 'legal security of tenure and access to land to all people' in the Habitat Agenda adopted by the conference, and the ensuing UN-Habitat Global Campaign for Security of Tenure, launched in 1999.

Although critics are sceptical about the post-conference commitments made by national governments, most of which remain unfulfilled (Satterthwaite, 2018), the historical evolution of the global urban agenda promoted by the Habitat conferences and UN-Habitat is understood to have influenced two 'seasons' of policy approaches with relevance for urban informality (Kiddle, 2010; Chiodelli, 2016). First, the Habitat I conference is associated with the recognition of the self-help approach outlined in Chapters 2 and 3, and the promotion of policies to support these processes, which can be termed 'aided self-help'. From around 1972 to 1982, in recognition of widespread state failure to meet low-income housing demand, international agencies, particularly the World Bank, financed policies which supported self-help, through sites and services and upgrading of informal neighbourhoods (Kiddle, 2010). These approaches are discussed in detail later.

Second, the Habitat II conference has been associated with the enabling approach, which saw the state taking a lesser role in order to facilitate market processes, more in keeping with legalist conceptions of informality (see also Chapters 2 and 3). This 'enabling' era, which focused on legalization and regularization of informal land, housing and services (Chiodelli, 2016), saw the alignment of the UN with World Bank policy in the era of New Public Management[3] (Huchzermeyer, 2011). The World Bank's policy shift from around 1983, to a more general urban policy with a programmatic framework, promoted housing finance systems in pursuit of social and economic development.

We discuss these policy approaches in the next section, exploring state-led responses targeting informal living, from eradication to enablement. At the same time, this emerging agenda has been influenced by and has in turn influenced civil society movements, which we discuss in the section that follows, on citizen-led responses. Finally, a third key moment associated with the 2016 Habitat III conference (Quito), which ratified the New Urban Agenda with an explicit focus on informal urban development, is still unfolding, and we discuss this in Chapter 8.

State-led responses

Responses that address the situation of people living informally may focus on land, housing or service provision. As already suggested, policy responses often fall under housing or shelter policy, although in practice they may also include provision of household services. Such policy is usually determined by the national government in a given country, although regional and local (usually urban) governments, particularly in federal systems, play an increasingly significant role. They may be influenced to a greater or lesser extent by international agencies' approaches, sometimes bolstered by finance, as already mentioned.

Here, we take an approach which broadly follows the chronology in which these approaches emerged, to explore the most common state-led responses. We draw on the framework identified in the last section, relating to two main 'seasons' of policy approaches, aided self-help and enablement, to explore sites and services, upgrading, legalization and regularization. Prior to these approaches, attempts at eradication were more commonplace, in the form of evictions and demolition, which we explore first of all.

Eradication

Initial responses sought to eradicate informal living, with evictions representing one of the earliest state responses. In Latin American cities in the 1950s, they often characterized approaches to irregular settlements that were formed through land occupation or informal subdivision, underpinned by an assumption of their illegality and illegitimacy. Eviction often goes beyond simply moving residents out of an area, as it involves demolition of informally built houses and destruction of residents' belongings, using heavy machinery such as bulldozers. The state is frequently involved due to its regulatory and enforcement role, meaning it has the power to mobilize these arrangements, although private landowners (whether individual or corporate) may also be the instigators of eviction, sometimes in conjunction with the state. In other words, '[l]ocal governments play a central role in evictions, along with landowners, developers, police and armed forces' (Everett, 2001: 455).

In some cases, evictions may be legally justified and follow due process, as outlined in Chapter 3. However, attempts to eradicate informal neighbourhoods usually result in forced eviction, defined as 'the involuntary removal of persons from their homes or land' (Gupte et al, 2019: 1), with little consideration of compensation or relocation for residents. Evictions may be justified by the state, based on infrastructural development or environmental risk. For example, in Bogota, local governments have used the threat of landslides to justify evicting marginalized urban residents on the city's eastern slopes, although lack of evidence for this risk suggests underlying political and economic motivations (Everett, 2001; see also Zeiderman, 2016). In other cases, the threat of eviction may hang over a neighbourhood even while 'governments and policy-makers quietly [ignore] the growth of irregular settlements' (Ward, 2012 in Chiodelli, 2016: 761), suggesting the ineffectiveness of this response in preventing informal development.

Eviction and displacement can have devastating social impacts for residents, breaking up families, destroying social networks, and disrupting education and livelihoods. The experience of demolition has been shown to affect individuals' wellbeing for years after the event (Gupte et al, 2019). Even where it does not occur, the perception of insecurity can be highly damaging for individuals and communities (van Gelder, 2010). The insecurity deriving from eviction processes or threats of displacement may overlap or resonate with power relations deriving from historical forms of colonization, as they target specific racialized, gendered and otherwise marginalized groups (Yiftachel, 2020), as discussed in Chapter 5.

A well-known example of eviction by the state is Zimbabwe's Operation Murambatsvina (translated into English as Operation Clean Up Rubbish) in 2005. This process, driven by the central state, involved mass evictions from informal neighbourhoods, costing at least 700,000 Zimbabweans their homes and/or livelihoods, and indirectly affecting around 2.4 million people, a fifth of the country's overall population (Tibaijuka, 2005). While the policy was justified as a crackdown on illegal housing, black market trading and insanitary conditions, some observers argue that it was politically motivated, targeting urban dwellers supporting opposition to the then-ruling Zanu-PF party. For example, in Porta Farm settlement, 850 structures were destroyed.

While evictions appear to have decreased since the 1960s, they have not disappeared as a policy response. Although reliable data can be difficult to obtain, it was estimated that from 2004 to 2006, 150,000 people were evicted in Latin America (Fernandes, 2011). Moreover, a resurgence in eradication policies has been noted in recent decades. In South Africa, the Slums Act of 2007 in KwaZulu-Natal Province, mentioned in Chapter 2, led to the demolition of 'slum' neighbourhoods and displacement of their mostly Black populations, despite fierce resistance by grassroots organizations (Abahlali baseMjondolo, 2009). As discussed earlier, Huchzermeyer (2011) traces this policy of

Figure 6.1: Evictions in Cape Town, South Africa

Source: Daneel Knoetzee/Groundup

slum eradication to the 'Cities without Slums' campaign spearheaded by the Cities Alliance (a multilateral organization founded by the World Bank and UN-Habitat), which promoted this well-meaning but misguided slogan to accompany Millennium Development Goals Target 7.D, 'By 2020, to have achieved a significant improvement in the lives of at least 100 million slum dwellers'. The interpretation of this campaign to mean 'slum free cities' resulted in the implementation of local policies which saw the resurgence of eradication by stealth. Other more recent examples of forced eviction, demolition and displacement can be seen in Nigeria (Cerf, 2021) and China (Ren, 2018), as well as in other areas of South Africa (see Figure 6.1).

Meanwhile, it is also important to be aware of more insidious forms of eviction. Small-scale market eviction, where individual households are unable to meet increased market rents following urban regeneration and gentrification, and are consequently pushed out of their homes, is increasingly common. For example, Linz (2021) discusses how these processes constitute an everyday crisis for urban residents in Mexico City, which may be as catastrophic as high-profile episodic events such as the 2017 earthquake. Nevertheless, market eviction, which is sometimes seen as 'soft' eviction, can often be hard to detect, as it affects individual households over a longer time-scale.

At a global scale, the dominance of eradication policies in the mid-20th century gave way in the 1970s to more supportive approaches. As aid and funding agencies (especially the World Bank) recognized the failure of formal state provision and structural issues faced by low-income urban residents (Chiodelli, 2016), they simultaneously attempted to support and formalize self-help processes, increasingly recognized due to their prominence in research on the provision and consolidation of informal land, housing and services. These approaches, termed 'aided self-help', are explored in the next section.

Aided self-help approaches

Broadly speaking, these approaches saw the potential of informal living as a 'solution' rather than a 'problem', in keeping with Turner's theory of self-help housing (discussed in Chapter 2). This occurred through financing of two main complementary approaches, sites and services and in-situ settlement upgrading. Both of these components have a strong focus on service provision alongside housing and land, although the precise emphasis depends on specific programmes and their contexts. In both cases, financing by the World Bank since the 1970s has been a significant element in their uptake by national governments.

Sites and services

Sites and services schemes aimed at providing new housing through a process which sought to 'repeat the success of the incremental house building and improvement process of the informal settlements' (Keivani and Werna, 2001: 86). Under this approach, local or central governments provided low-cost, developable lots, often in large areas of (newly available) land, already equipped with basic facilities (such as latrines and community water sources), and sometimes public services (such as electricity and roads) (UN-Habitat, 1992). Such schemes sometimes also provided a core housing unit which could be occupied initially and extended according to household capacity and income. While the configuration of facilities, plots and other elements varied according to distinctive programmes and the contexts in which they developed (Chiodelli, 2016), building or completing the house was left to residents. In other words, an underlying principle of the sites and services approach was that the residents would undertake self-help processes to provide their own housing through their own labour, although ultimately this often resulted in self-financed processes as (usually small-scale and local) building contractors were bought in, intersecting with informal economic activities. In this way, costs could be kept down in this form of 'indirect housing provision' (Keivani and Werna, 2001: 86).

Many sites and services schemes were financed by international agencies, although in some cases national governments were responsible (Keivani and Werna, 2001). Villa El Salvador in Lima, Peru, is an example of a sites and services project initiated by the Peruvian government (see Figure 6.2). Following the 1971 invasion of land outside Lima by 4,000 homeless families, in 1975 the government relocated them to a piece of vacant land south of the city, additionally offering plots to other families in Lima in need of housing. Lots were organized into 'residential units', groups of several blocks with a central plaza, a scale which supported community organization.

Figure 6.2: Villa El Salvador in Lima, Peru, past and present

Source: Institute of Housing and Development Studies/Alamy

By 1980, the community had organized to demand infrastructure improvements and service provision, including underground electricity lines. The government supported these requests, providing water, electricity, street lighting and schools. On this basis, the area grew to 70,000 inhabitants, and by 2015 it contained 600,000 inhabitants. Today it is a consolidated low-income neighbourhood.

Upgrading

In-situ upgrading programmes mainly focused on rehabilitating and improving the condition of the existing informal neighbourhood fabric, rather than constructing new units, although some programmes demolished housing to make way for improved shelter or infrastructure, as the testimony at the start of the chapter suggests. At its most basic, upgrading refers to provision of basic services in informal neighbourhoods, through addressing infrastructural deficiencies, particularly relating to water and sanitation, electricity, waste collection and street lighting (Devkar et al, 2019). Such programmes normally focus, first, on basic infrastructure provision (for example, sanitation, plumbing, wiring); second, on providing security of land tenure for inhabitants to guard against future risk of eviction; and third, on providing access to credit for low-income households (Chiodelli, 2016: 792). Ultimately, many upgrading programmes have succeeded in improving material conditions but have had less success in guaranteeing secure tenure and credit (Chiodelli, 2016). However, upgrading often implies some degree of tenure security through the implicit acknowledgement of the settlement's legitimacy via service provision (Satterthwaite, 2012).

Similar to sites and services, financing has often been via international agencies, although occasionally by national governments. Upgrading is undertaken on a project basis, usually with a degree of government involvement, due to its infrastructural component with cost recovery through household payments (Keivani and Werna, 2001). It may be undertaken via processes that are more or less participatory, involving residents and the organizations that represent them. For example, at the less participatory end of the scale, in South Africa 'upgrading' of informal neighbourhoods can refer to a process where 'such settlements are replanned and cleared shacks are replaced by newly built subsidised houses complete with services and legal tenure' (Patel, 2016: 2741).

Aided self-help has attracted criticism. During its heyday, some observers such as Moser and Peake (1987) challenged these approaches on ideological grounds, based on the double exploitation of marginalized populations' labour, both at work (where wages were low and often unregulated) and in housing construction (through their involvement in self-help or self-build processes), discussed in Chapter 2. The so-called 'freedom to build' was actually the only option for many (Burgess, 1978), and therefore represented more necessity than free choice, while often involving suffering and appalling living conditions for many years. Perhaps most problematically, it seemed to absolve the state of its housing provision role, 'as self-help releases government from its responsibility to provide adequate housing as a basic need for its low-income population' (Moser and Peake, 1987: 5; see also Chapter 2).

Additionally, evaluation of aided self-help approaches over time has shown that they raise multiple issues, including infrequent cost recovery, poorly located housing, weak institutional capacity, and persistently insecure land tenure during upgrading. Keivani and Werna (2001) summarize the problems with aided self-help approaches. First, low output has not matched demand; in the decade from 1972 to 1981, nine million families had received housing provision from either sites and services or upgrading programmes, compared to an average *annual* demand of 8.7 million units. Second, programmes are costly in terms of the bureaucracy, land costs and charges required to set them up and maintain them, meaning they are inaccessible to the lowest income households. Continued failure to meet demand has resulted in 'inflated land and housing costs – making quality shelter a very expensive item for the urban poor' (Beall, 2000 in Kiddle, 2010: 885). Third, sites and services schemes are often located in peripheral areas due to the need to purchase cheap land. Meanwhile, they can lead to speculation as they are a sign of the area's development potential. Finally, they have failed to recreate the informal processes that they are designed to emulate, undermining both these processes' collective impulse and also their economic advantage in terms of low costs, while also failing to provide sufficient technical support for residents.

Aided self-help was significant in representing a shift in government attitudes from punitive to supportive responses to informal living (Chiodelli, 2016). Nevertheless, while upgrading remains prevalent in some contexts today (Satterthwaite, 2012), the scale of these approaches has been limited by the challenges that accompanied them. From 1983, World Bank policy shifted to a more general urban programme approach, fostering housing finance and seeking socio-economic development through 'enablement', which we discuss in the next section.

Enabling approaches
Titling

The shift to enabling housing policy can be clearly seen in the widespread adoption of titling programmes as a response to informal living, towards the later decades of the 20th century. Titling essentially seeks to legalize or formalize informally held property in support of secure tenure (discussed in Chapter 3), through 'the allocation of real property rights on land … that can be transferred, inherited and mortgaged' (Payne et al, 2009). The approach is often associated with the work of Hernando de Soto, a Peruvian economist who popularized titling as the 'solution' to poverty, introduced in Chapters 3 and 4. In his well-known book *The Mystery of Capital* (de Soto, 2000), he suggested that the condition of the poor in the global South relates to the fact that the property that they own, whether land, housing or business assets, is 'dead capital' as it is acquired informally, meaning its owners don't have titles. Without these documents, he suggests, their owners cannot sell or transfer this property in the formal market, or use it to raise loans, meaning they are unable to invest in developing their businesses or improving their homes. De Soto suggested that formalizing or legalizing assets allows people to gain access to formal credit, enabling them to invest in homes and businesses, and therefore reinvigorating the wider economy. In other words, '[i]f low-income residents can gain formal ownership of their informal property, they will be in a much better position to reap the benefits of the market' (McGranahan et al, 2008: 86). The solution to poverty, de Soto (2000) suggests, is therefore to allow citizens of the global South to participate in formal property systems like those in the global North, which allow assets to be converted into capital.

The link between titling and poverty reduction, explicitly articulated in de Soto's work, has been reinforced by international agencies (Payne et al, 2009). Its influence can be seen in the international campaigns mentioned here, such as the 1999 UN-Habitat Global Campaign for Security of Tenure. Indeed, secure tenure has been used as an indicator for both the Millennium Development Goals Target 7.D, formulated in 2000, and the Sustainable Development Goals Target 11.1, formulated in 2016, which by 2030 seeks to 'ensure adequate access for all to adequate, safe and affordable housing and basic services and upgrade slums'. Reinforcing the proposed connection between legal titles and poverty reduction, titling programmes have been promoted by international agencies and national governments. De Soto's influence can be seen in the work of his think tank, the Institute for Liberty and Democracy, which has applied its diagnostic formula in countries including Ghana, South Africa, Thailand and India. However, other titling programmes pre-date de Soto's ideas, including in Mexico (discussed further in Box 6.1) and Peru, where a legalization programme was established in 1996, and had issued one million title deeds by 2000 (McGranahan et al, 2008: 86).

The attractiveness of titling programmes to governments relates to their perceived benefits. In socio-economic terms, they integrate low-income residents into the formal sector, through the provision of formal titles for their property (Monkkonen, 2011). This, in turn, is perceived to stimulate investment in individual property and neighbourhoods. They may also improve the efficiency of local land markets, through the privatization and individualization of property rights. This results in simplified and more legible tenure regimes (Scott, 1998), helping to avoid land conflict (Appendini, 2001) and increase revenue from property taxation. Political benefits may include increased legitimacy for the state, as individuals are brought into a direct relationship with the local and national state (Ward, 1989).

Nevertheless, the approach has been subject to intense debate. Critics argue that despite its prevalence, titling has not resulted in the expected wealth creation or poverty reduction, particularly for the urban poor (Fernandes, 2007; Musembi, 2007). Contrary to de Soto's arguments, it appears that titles are not a guarantee of credit: for example, in Peru, only 1.3 per cent of title deeds allocated to families resulted in mortgage loans by 2002 (McGranahan et al, 2008: 86). Moreover, as the state's role shifts from welfare provider to market facilitator, titles may justify withdrawal of government support to low-income households (Davis, 2006: 71–2). Increased costs due to land taxes and formal services may lead to a heavier financial burden for residents, with certain groups more vulnerable after titling, including women if title is assigned to the male head of household (Varley, 2007). Land titles may also directly conflict with customary or other local forms of tenure (Musembi, 2007), as most titling programmes conceive of land tenure as closely related to private property (de Souza, 2001), an individualized, Western understanding of tenure which obscures its complexities.

Box 6.1: Titling in Mexico, the case of the Commission for the Regularisation of Land Tenure

Mexico's 43-year titling programme has been the subject of extensive evaluation. In Mexico, informal urban development accompanied rapid urbanization from the mid-20th century, with the rural *ejido* landholding system acting as a low-cost, illegal land market allowing land acquisition by the poor (Austin, 1994). An *ejido* is land owned communally by farmers, established by the 1917 post-Revolution constitution, which was legally inalienable until 1992, meaning it could not be bought, sold or transferred outside of the community. However, pressure from urban growth led to *ejidal* land becoming one of the main sources of land for informal urban neighbourhoods, known as *colonias populares*.

In response, titling has become a routine form of state intervention to address informal living in Mexico. A national titling body, the Comisión para la Regularización de la Tenencia de la Tierra (CORETT), was established in 1974, and by 2000, it had issued 2.2 million land titles. The legalization of informally held land occurred through presidential decree, expropriating the land from the *ejido* in favour of CORETT, which then sold the land to residents. On this basis, residents of informal neighbourhoods paid twice for their land, once at the point of (informal) acquisition, and once when it was legalized. Despite reforms to the *ejido* system in 1992, enabling formal sale through the conversion of *ejidal* land to private property, the complicated nature of this conversion process means the informal market endured, and remains an important source of land for housing for low-income populations (Salazar, 2019).

Given its longevity, Mexico's titling programme has been subject to much scrutiny. Instigated during the one-party state era of the Institutional Revolutionary Party, there were concerns about the exploitation of titling for populist political ends, particularly the manipulation of urban poor populations' voting patterns. Its systematic use from the 1970s was seen as a strategy for social and political integration of the urban poor (Varley, 1998), thus offering a 'safety valve' supporting peaceful urban development, but also a tool for co-opting opposition movements (Azuela and Duhau, 1998). Moreover, it had the contradictory effect of protecting and promoting illegality at the same time as removing it. While CORETT was replaced by the National Institute for Sustainable Land in 2016, its legacy remains significant. In the 'twilight legal terrain' of Mexico's enduring informal land market, disputes and dispossession are common, with negative effects often disproportionately felt by the low-income urban communities who hold land informally (Lombard, 2016; Salazar, 2019).

In sum, critics suggest that contrary to expectations, titling may generate further insecurity and displacement, due to increased land speculation, 'downward raiding' by middle-income groups, and market evictions (Payne, 2001). This suggests that the link between titling and settlement consolidation is less strong than its promoters argue. Certainly, research has shown that investment in housing by low-income families may be based on other *de facto* indicators of tenure security, such as service provision (Payne et al, 2009). Conversely, others suggest that there is little evidence for displacement due to titling, for example, Varley's (2016) more recent research in Mexico. While debates contesting the merits of titling continue, it is increasingly acknowledged that individual freehold titles should not be the only response to tenure insecurity in the context of living informally.

Regularization

While titling has been applied in diverse contexts around the world, there is a growing recognition that alternative approaches are equally valid. These approaches acknowledge that while titles may help to promote tenure security and protect against eviction, they are usually not sufficient for socio-spatial integration. Some suggest that titling 'should be part of a package of measures' that widen access to serviced land and housing, rather than a stand-alone programme (Payne, 2004). In this sense, different forms of rights may also be appropriate, beyond individual freehold titles, such as leasehold (or use rights), specific types of rental contract, community land trusts, cooperatives and temporary permits. An alternative approach known as regularization has been developed in some contexts. The regularization approach emphasizes that security of tenure and socio-spatial integration should be pursued jointly to guarantee the permanence of communities, with better living and housing conditions on the land they have long occupied.

This approach has been applied in Rio de Janeiro, Brazil, through the Favela Bairro programme (1994), replaced by the Morar Carioca programme (2010), a participatory upgrading programme with a strong social integration component. The programme, which targeted 253,000 residents in 73 neighbourhoods, involved large public investment in infrastructure, services, public spaces and community facilities, combined with continuous housing consolidation carried out by residents, to be followed by legalization in some areas (Fernandes, 2011). In this way, Brazilian regularization policies linked legalization through titling with upgrading policies – as well as socio-economic programmes – while emphasizing effective popular participation in all stages of the process.

However, critics have highlighted the high costs associated with regularization. Costs vary between settlements, depending on topography, location and so on, but in general, retrofitting services is two or three times more expensive than providing services at the construction stage (see Figure 6.3). Paving, sewerage and drainage accounted for 50 to 60 per cent of expenditure, due to having to dig up and replace existing pavements and roads for installation. Moreover, observers suggest that regularization may also lead to gentrification (Abramo, 2010), similar to fears about titling. Even after regularization, 'the residents of informal settlements are still perceived – and see themselves – as favela dwellers and, as such, they are discriminated against by the labour market' (Payne et al, 2009: 455).

Nevertheless, given the limitations of titling, regularization seems to offer a more contextualized approach, which addresses some of the risks of titling for vulnerable communities, acknowledging power and political dynamics, as well as existing tenure arrangements. Clear progress in responses to informal living can be seen in the shift

Figure 6.3: Costs of regularization

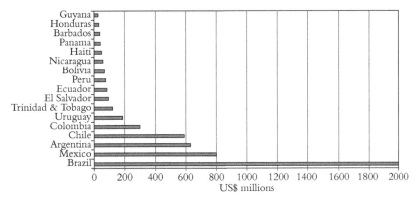

Source: © 2011. Lincoln Institute of Land Policy. From Regularization of Informal Settlements in Latin America/E. Fernandes

from eradication as a predominant approach, to its general substitution by more progressive aided self-help and enabling responses. Box 6.2 discusses the evolution of approaches to informal neighbourhoods in Karachi, Pakistan, and how to support such processes, in conversation with Arif Hasan of the Urban Resource Centre.

However, for many informal neighbourhoods, state-led processes have failed to keep pace. For example, we could recall that the reduction in the overall proportion of 'slum' populations globally has been accompanied by an increase in their absolute numbers, as discussed in Chapter 1. Moreover, as Arif Hasan suggests, the experience of state-led responses has often been negative for residents involved, who are recipients of rather than participants in these processes. As Mitlin and Satterthwaite (2004: 270) point out, '[m]any agencies turned to supporting self-help, but not to the increased community participation and control that was meant to go with it'. As an alternative to state-led responses, the next section of the chapter turns to what we call citizen-led responses to living informally. We use this term to capture responses that can be clearly distinguished from those led by the state, outlined in this section, as they seek to centre the interests of people living informally.

Citizen-led responses

Citizen-led responses are often particularly concerned with the interests of residents of informal neighbourhoods, and therefore incorporate a higher degree of community participation and control. They may be led by residents themselves, or organizations which include or represent them. There is overlap between citizen-led approaches and civil society, a term which refers to 'those social organisations, associations and institutions that exist beyond the sphere of direct supervision and control by the state' (Friedmann, 1998: 21). Citizen-led responses to informal living often place particular emphasis on the local scale, where community-based organizations (CBOs; sometimes also known as grassroots organizations) operate, with a high degree of local resident involvement and limited access to external resources (Mercer, 2006). In order to

Box 6.2: Supporting communities in Karachi, Pakistan: a conversation with Arif Hasan, Urban Resource Centre

Arif Hasan is an architect, researcher and writer who directs the Urban Resource Centre (URC) in Karachi, Pakistan. His work on the Orangi Pilot Project, a groundbreaking sanitation scheme connecting self-built provision with a formal trunk system in low-income areas in Karachi, has been recognized globally. We spoke to Arif about evolving responses to informal neighbourhoods in Pakistan, known as *katchi abadis*, where economic activity has shifted away from small-scale local enterprise towards supplying formal industry (such as gaskets for the automobile sector), in a context marked by higher levels of education, greater female labour participation and changing voting patterns.

Physical changes have also occurred, notably densification through vertical informal development (as discussed in Chapter 3). Arif described the consequences for overcrowding and basic services as follows:

'Those *katchi abadis* which were originally single or double storey, are now becoming three, four, five, six, seven, eight storeys high. … This is how many settlements that are near the city centre are being converted into high rises for low-income groups, or for low- and middle-income groups. So these new apartments are either being rented out or they are being purchased on instalments, by people, many of whom are coming in from the periphery of the city, to live here. So that is changing the demography, and … the densities are high. The number of toilets as a result have decreased, so you might have settlements where in one building you have one toilet seat for maybe 20 persons.'

In response, Pakistan's authorities have attempted to eradicate the newer high-rise settlements, with limited success: "There is a Supreme Court that … passes a judgement that all these illegal high rises should be demolished. So they demolish a few buildings and after that the demolition stops because the state cannot demolish these buildings without creating a major law and order problem." This shift reflects an increasingly punitive response by the state:

'The state today considers everything that has been created, in an unplanned manner, as an encroachment, which was not so 20 years ago. And the courts of law also consider anything that is not a part of the planning process or the result of bylaws and zoning regulations, as an encroachment. … There are court judgements today that actually state that everything that has not been planned, quote unquote "planned", should be demolished. It should be removed. And of course, you can't do that because there'll be no city left. So they begin the demolition process, then they stop it because they cannot continue, which has happened in Karachi many times in the past four or five years.'

The consequences of this shifting approach have included increased displacement:

'All this has led to a process of gentrification, especially within the inner cities of Pakistan and Karachi, certainly. Especially in heritage zones, where you chuck out the existing residents and turn them into cafes, bookshops, museums, etc. So there's a lot of opposition to this as well from citizens groups, that this heritage belongs to the people, and it should be left with the people. That issue is very much alive.'

Meanwhile, public opinion has become more sympathetic to informal neighbourhoods, led by organizations such as the URC who seek a dialogical approach with the state, as Arif highlighted:

'Much of my work over the last few years has been with the Urban Resource Centre ... giving physical space in its premises, in its hall, to various affected communities ... who are being affected or are to be affected by the anti-encroachment drive. So you give them that space, you develop the literature, on the Internet, regarding the issues and problems, which we do regularly. You monitor what is happening to them, and you write a critical analysis of the situation. And you try and bring these communities and the government authorities closer to each other, so that they can have a dialogue. ... And that has made a difference in the sense that a sizeable number of the middle class, which would never have supported informality, today do support the informal neighbourhoods, and are against these demolitions. This was not possible, let's say 20 years ago, support to informal neighbourhoods.'

This has been enabled through organized collaboration, but preparing for this is challenging:

'I think what has worked well ... is when the media, academia, and an organized community come together, and have facts and figures and receipts and research to back their claims. ... But that requires an organized community as well. Now, where do you get that organized community from? In the case of Karachi, in our work, we got that organized community from the Orangi Pilot Project Sanitation System, where communities came together to build their sanitation system. We also got that community from organizing to resist development projects through demonstrations, through court cases, through protests of various types, in which the media became supportive of them.'

This suggests the importance of civil society organizations, academics and communities cohering around an issue, supported by the experience of collective processes of resistance and self-help, which have much in common with citizen-led approaches.

---

support their activities, CBOs may sometimes work with and receive support from non-government organizations (NGOs), which tend to have a greater presence at national, regional or international level.

Citizen-led responses to living informally can be understood within the context of the historical trajectory of the global urban agenda outlined earlier in this chapter. The Habitat conferences signalled the growing need for civil society to challenge state-led responses to informal urbanization. Here, we explore two approaches emerging from these origins, which are particularly significant in the sphere of living informally, associated respectively with two movements which aim to engage with 'collective forms of spatial production' (Frediani and Cociña, 2019: 150): first, the social production of housing, associated with the Habitat International Coalition (HIC);

and second, the model of community-led development associated with Shack/Slum Dwellers International (SDI). These movements represent articulations of citizen-led responses that have developed over several decades, achieving significant national and regional coverage, based on pro-poor and highly participatory models which tend to prioritize the local scale while negotiating with national states and international agencies when necessary. These approaches rest (implicitly or explicitly) on asset-based approaches to urban issues (outlined in Chapter 3), seeking to recognize what is already there and build on it rather than starting anew. Finally, they offer a set of experiences which can help us to understand responses to informality differently, through their 'grassroots-led processes of social mobilization, production and management of space in the city' (Frediani and Cociña, 2019: 150).

Habitat International Coalition and the social production of habitat

The origins of HIC derive from the Habitat Forum at the Habitat I conference in Vancouver in 1976 (discussed earlier in this chapter), at which NGOs recognized the need for permanent pressure from civil society on national governments and international agencies in the area of shelter. Following the creation of the UN Centre on Human Settlements (later UN-Habitat), the Habitat International Council initially brought together a membership of NGOs based largely in the global North, widened in 1985 to encompass a more global scope. In 1987, a conference in Limuru, Kenya was organized as part of the UN International Year of Shelter for the Homeless, resulting in the organization's reconfiguration to include representation from Asia, Africa and Latin America. The Limuru Declaration, which was signed by 45 NGOs from the global South, and 12 international NGOs, committed signatories to 'reversing current trends toward ever increasing homelessness, over-crowding, lack of basic services and other forms of social and economic deprivation' (HIC, 1987: 1).

HIC's current agenda focuses on 'the defense, promotion and realization of human rights related to habitat and a safe place to live in peace and with dignity, both in urban and rural areas', working with a network of 354 member organizations globally.[4] Its working processes link networks of NGOs and CBOs in different regions and countries, supporting them through articulation with international agencies and frameworks. These NGOs and CBOs, in turn, support communities to engage in shelter production and improvement, and act as intermediaries between them and the state where appropriate. HIC has developed different theoretical approaches to support action on diverse issues including land and housing rights, gender equality and sustainable environments, including most notably its promotion of the social production of habitat (SPH).

SPH is a citizen-led approach to living informally developed and promoted by HIC, 'as a key concept and strategy to focus and reap the greatest potential from the efforts undertaken by the inhabitants' (Romero, 2003: 13), reflecting and building on grassroots organizations' work in supporting the self-help housing practices of the urban poor in Latin America. Beyond its analytical value, this concept and approach aims to support and strengthen processes of accessing and providing land and shelter by low-income communities. Simply put, SPH is understood as 'the evolutionary development process of habitat, spontaneous or planned, to achieve satisfaction of the tangible and intangible needs of the traditionally excluded social sectors' (Enet et al, 2001 in Romero, 2003: 13). It suggests seeing housing as part of broader structural conditions, requiring improved economic, social and political capacities among marginalized urban populations to improve housing conditions (Romero, 2003).

The level of organization involved ranges from self-production to individual or collective participation, and even organization of communities by government institutions (HIC, 2003). While community participation and control in housing production are key components of the process, SPH recognizes that they require a facilitating framework of policies, instruments and finance. Although similar to self-help in its view of housing as a process rather than a product, its range is wider (at the neighbourhood rather than individual housing scale), including questions of social justice in the built environment (Schütz, 2003). The success of the movement and concept can be seen in its insertion into Mexico's 2006 Housing Law, which enabled CBOs to receive housing subsidies directly from the central government. However, this initiative was ultimately limited by political changes which led to the majority of the designated subsidies being distributed to developers. More generally, HIC's presence remains most significant in Latin American countries and cities.

Shack/Slum Dwellers International and community-led development

SDI is a transnational network of grassroots organizations and federations' in over 18 countries in Africa, Asia and Latin America, founded in 1996. Its origins lie with the foundation and evolution of diverse groups of organizations, representing or made up of low-income groups, and their interaction and exchange over time. The experience of the Indian Alliance – formed in the 1980s through the partnership of the National Slum Dwellers Federation of India (founded in Mumbai in 1976 to contest local evictions), the Society for the Promotion of Area Resource Centres (an Indian NGO working with pavement dwellers, as discussed in Chapter 3) and Mahila Milan, the first pavement women's organization – was foundational for SDI. A visit from the National Slum Dwellers Federation of India to South Africa led to the formation of the South African Homeless People's Federation in 1994. Further exchanges between groups from Asia and Africa in the 1990s led to the launch of SDI as an international network (D'Cruz and Mitlin, 2005).

SDI's membership is made up of bottom-up, often women-led groups, which aim to address insecure tenure, basic services, housing and livelihoods in informal neighbourhoods. These groups are usually set up around the practice of daily savings, encompassing an estimated 1.1 million savers worldwide (Chitekwe-Biti et al, 2014). SDI seeks to respond to the needs of people living informally through a multi-scalar approach, at the settlement, city and global level. At the neighbourhood level, it undertakes practical activities to address local needs, particularly related to housing affordability, through housing interventions that enable participation of the lowest-income households. On this basis, it also pursues collective efforts to negotiate political alternatives, blending local action with global support to secure political commitment to pro-poor changes.[5]

SDI's processes rest on a set of practices for change, including the participation of women as savers and leaders in pursuit of a bottom-up change agenda, as women are frequently among the most vulnerable groups in informal neighbourhoods. The practice of daily savings provides a financial base for groups and their members, and an outwardly apolitical basis for regular local meetings. Learning exchanges are key to SDI, among savings groups within and between neighbourhoods, and between cities and countries, in order to develop capacities through peer support. Indeed, SDI has been characterized as 'a learning movement based around a structure of exchanges, involving small groups of the urban poor travelling from one urban settlement to another to share knowledge in what amounts to an informal learning process' (McFarlane, 2009: 563). SDI also deploys data collection approaches such as enumerations which are undertaken by residents to gather and compile settlement information on land use, access to services (water and sanitation, electricity, health, education, and so on), livelihood opportunities, and demand for planning and housing. This information is often the basis for negotiating with local authorities about neighbourhood improvements and upgrading. These data-collection and profiling tools also serve advocacy and awareness-raising purposes within informal neighbourhoods, allowing data collectors and community mobilizers to organize local residents and inform them about pressing issues and possible solutions.

The multiple potentials of community-led enumerations are evident, for example, in Nairobi's informal neighbourhood Mukuru where, as part of a participatory planning process occurring between 2018 and 2021 (discussed also in Chapters 5 and 7), data collectors linked to Kenya's SDI affiliate enumerated local households.[6] A total of 100,561 households were identified within the informal neighbourhood and the enumeration estimated a housing density of 2,400 households per acre. During the enumerations each housing unit received a physical address and data collectors also gathered mobile phone numbers from each household representative, which could later be used to mobilize residents to attend planning meetings and other community activities. The enumerations not only helped to organize local residents and identify problem issues (for example, data collected highlighted that on average, 234 households share access to only one water tap). They also uncovered aspects that could subsequently be used to convince political authorities to promote better public services in the area. For example, the enumerations revealed that there is a poverty penalty exacted on low-income residents in Mukuru who tend to rely on informal service providers and are charged on average 142 per cent more for electricity fees and 300 per cent more for potable water than middle- to high-income residents living in formal housing serviced by Nairobi County government. This information was used by community mobilizers in negotiations with local government authorities in Nairobi to highlight that residents in Mukuru are capable of paying public service charges and that formal electricity and water provision should therefore be extended into the neighbourhood.

In contexts where government support is rare, SDI supports communities working together to secure shelter improvements. Savings schemes enable members to access loan funds and start incremental housing development based on collective effort; however, the state's involvement via financial subsidies is critical, particularly for whole settlement upgrading, where the resources required are often beyond the community's means. Because of this, financing upgrading projects often involve combining community contributions with leveraged resources based on dialogue with the state, through subsidy or match funding. Given the extremely low incomes of many residents of informal neighbourhoods, affordability is a major challenge; nevertheless, SDI aims to ensure that 'all members who choose to be included can afford to make the savings contribution and sometimes loan repayments that are required' (Chitekwe-Biti et al, 2014: 118).

While SDI promotes a network model which aims to 'encourage autonomy and change as knowledge travels', the dominance of certain organizations within the network has generated tensions. As McFarlane (2009: 567) suggests, this may be related to the uneven power distribution across diverse nodes and individuals, including well-connected professionals and also better established organizations. This points to the difficulty of constructing sustainable and authentic citizen-led responses to living informally, discussed further in Box 6.3 and the next section.

Alongside the attributes outlined at the start of this section, what these citizen-led approaches have in common are their federated approach, which allows collaboration between different scales and types of (civil society) organizations (Mitlin and Satterthwaite, 2004: 267). This approach addresses some of the limitations of local scale processes, where CBOs may be heavily entangled in political processes, and therefore reproduce local patterns of inequality, while also struggling to extend beyond the neighbourhood scale. Meanwhile, NGOs are often reliant on externally formulated processes or practices which are less context sensitive and therefore not sustainable. Through federation processes, involving both types of organization (CBOs and NGOs), citizen-led approaches can strengthen community processes while also improving accountability, amplifying their voice and enabling power for local communities to negotiate with authorities at different scales (Mitlin and Satterthwaite, 2004: 273). At the same time, critical voices have suggested that these processes may risk reproducing existing inequalities, particularly if membership is restricted to groups that are already relatively powerful (Frediani and Cociña, 2019). While the organizations mentioned here attempt to address the needs of the poorest, this is often an issue where incomes are very low (Mitlin and Satterthwaite, 2004).

In sum, this section suggests that although local communities may set the agenda, engaging the state is a critical element of responding to informal living through neighbourhood improvements (Chitekwe-Biti et al, 2014). State intervention or cooperation is necessary in order to offer development opportunities to all through settlement- and city-level housing responses, and this may be secured through co-production – something we discuss further in the next section.

The importance of co-production

At its simplest, co-production has been described as the 'co-operation between the government and NGOs/CBOs in providing urban services' (Devkar et al, 2019: 333). Orthodox definitions of co-production define it as 'the process through which inputs used to produce a good or service are contributed by individuals who are not "in" the

Box 6.3: Supporting affordable housing in Mumbai, India

The example of affordable housing provision in Mumbai shows how the SDI Federation in India sought land and access to basic services for informal neighbourhood residents. Sixty per cent of Mumbai's population lives in informal neighbourhoods, while formal housing often consists of single-room tenements housing five to eight people. In the context of rapid growth and geographical limits to expansion (due to Mumbai's coastal location), access to affordable land and housing has become ever more limited, and evictions are a regular occurrence, as the government attempts to clear land for infrastructure improvements to support economic growth. Resettlement of evicted communities has often been far away from their original location and hence from their livelihood opportunities.

Recognizing the challenge of providing affordable housing in the context of high land values, in 1998 the Indian government introduced the Slum Rehabilitation Act, a landmark piece of legislation which introduced the practice of land-sharing, a poverty reduction policy that has been criticized for its entrepreneurial approach to housing provision (McFarlane, 2004). The Act allowed community NGOs to use land occupied by informal neighbourhoods to construct middle- and low-income housing at increased density. The Act enabled higher-density construction via an increase in the floor space index, which allowed formal developers and, crucially, NGOs to build smaller units than had previously been permitted. This enabled organized groups of slum dwellers to undertake their own construction projects on the land which they occupied, supported by NGOs. Reordering the existing dwellings, they worked with an organization established by the Society for the Promotion of Area Resource Centres, of the Indian Alliance (introduced in Chapter 3), to finance, build and sell new middle-income housing stock on this land at market rates. The profit from these sales was then used to subsidize the construction of smaller, high-rise dwellings for the original residents, to enable them to continue living in the neighbourhood.

This process has not been without difficulties, including the cost of transition from informal to formal services, and the need for a high degree of community organizing. Additionally, the legislation and accompanying institutional frameworks have generated some controversy, including critiques that the approach prioritized the interests of housing developers over NGOs and communities, who were poorly represented in the overall process. Nevertheless, it has been argued that '[t]he history of shelter in Mumbai reflects the success of collective agency to prevent eviction and secure relocation where required and *in situ* upgrading elsewhere' (Chitekwe-Biti et al, 2014: 124).

---

same organisation' (Ostrom, 1996: 1073). This is often viewed through the prism of state-provided services such as health, education and infrastructure (even if these are contracted out to private providers). As Ostrom (1996: 1073) says, '[c]o-production implies that citizens can play an active role in producing public goods and services of consequence to them', which is often important in both the quality and outcomes of the service (for example, think about the importance of your own active participation in your education!).

Nevertheless, the technical expertise and financial capital required for the provision of large-scale services in cities, particularly in areas like sanitation, suggests that state involvement is usually necessary. However, as seen throughout this book, state provision of basic urban services often cannot keep pace with demand, particularly for low-income urban communities. Ostrom (1996) outlines two examples of co-production, from Brazil and Nigeria, where residents successfully worked with governments to provide sanitation and education, respectively. In both cases, she suggests, the attitude of government officials was a key factor in determining whether co-production was successful. Co-production requires commitment from both sides but can pay dividends for both citizens and providers in terms of more effective and equitable service provision and higher levels of engagement on both sides.

Mitlin (2008) provides an alternative view of co-production as a political process, exploring examples of interaction between the local state and pro-poor organizations and movements in Pakistan, Namibia, India and Brazil that seek to address urban poverty through the provision of basic services, a key deficiency in informal contexts. She highlights the importance of contributing resources on both sides, but also the role of co-production in 'a broader struggle for choice, self-determination and meso [city] level political relations' (Mitlin, 2008: 347). In other words, the value of co-production lies not just in making services more affordable, efficient and accessible for low-income urban residents, but also in shifting relationships between these residents as citizens and local government, in order to address issues of voicelessness and powerlessness that are often characteristic of urban poverty (Mitlin and Satterthwaite, 2013). This is based on a process of 'self-organized co-production, with grassroots organizations engaging the state while at the same time maintaining a degree of autonomy within the delivery process' (Mitlin, 2008: 347), allowing improved civic and political engagement as the basis for ongoing negotiation with the state around wider issues. It also implies that such movements draw on the long-standing processes of citizen-led collective action and self-help outlined earlier.

Therefore, as Chitekwe-Biti et al (2014: 129–30) suggest, while self-help is critical to responses to informality, 'self-help does not mean that the state is excluded, government redistribution is ignored and government regulations are disregarded', but rather that communities are meaningfully involved in developing such responses. This position acknowledges that due to its scale and cost, city-wide infrastructure such as water and sanitation must be the responsibility of the state; however, it insists on the involvement of communities where there is the capacity and willingness to participate, in order to improve and supplement the state's offer through a process of self-organized co-production.

Chapter summary

This chapter presented diverse approaches responding to living informally, focusing on state-led responses from punitive eradication attempts to more supportive approaches of aided self-help and enablement. It discussed how these approaches have been influenced by the evolution of a global urban agenda, which has involved the participation of international agencies, national governments, urban authorities and civil society. Nevertheless, it has shown that state-led approaches may suffer from a lack of beneficiary participation, which results in weak ownership and maintenance of the housing and infrastructure provided. A higher degree of resident participation, often a characteristic of citizen-led approaches, may lead to greater ownership of housing and infrastructure, resulting in better maintenance and durability. But a major limitation of such approaches is their restricted scope for scaling up, as well as the time and resources required from those who participate. The limitations of both approaches may be overcome through a synergistic partnership where government, community and alternative service providers work together, such as co-production between the government and NGOs/CBOs to provide urban services.

Recommended reading

- Frediani, A. and Cociña, C. (2019) ' "Participation as planning": strategies from the south to challenge the limits of planning', *Built Environment*, 45(2): 143–61.
- Keivani, R. and Werna, E. (2001) 'Refocusing the housing debate in developing countries from a pluralist perspective', *Habitat International*, 25: 191–208.
- Kiddle, G. (2010) 'Key theory and evolving debates in international housing policy: from legalisation to perceived security of tenure approaches', *Geography Compass*, 4(7): 881–92.
- Parnell, S. (2016) 'Defining a global urban development agenda', *World Development*, 78: 529–40.

EXERCISES

- Thinking about examples of living informally that you know, consider the following questions:
  - In this context, why might legalization or titling present an attractive policy option for governments?
  - What might some of the challenges of legalization be, specific to this context and more generally?
- Have a look at the 'Alternative representations' section and consider the following questions:
  - What can you learn about living informally and other forms of informality in these different contexts?
  - What kinds of responses to living informally are in evidence?
  - Are these responses supportive, punitive or something else?
- Think of an example of state-led OR citizen-led responses to living informally:
  - What are the advantages of this type of response?
  - What are the disadvantages?

Alternative representations

- For a different angle on responses to living informally, including upgrading processes and COVID-19 response, have a look at Know Your City TV (https://www.youtube.com/c/KnowYourCityTV/featured), a YouTube channel showcasing the work of an international collective of young people living and working informally.
- Read the article 'Everything dey scatta' by Mathew Cerf (2021) in *Otherwise Magazine* (https://www.otherwisemag.com/everything) on the devasting consequences of evictions for the residents of informal neighbourhoods in Lagos, Nigeria.
- Linked to this, watch *Our World Apart* (https://youtu.be/WUUhHU8m0OY), a short film directed by Nasu Adbulaziz, an evictee of Otodo Gbame, one of the evicted neighbourhoods. It tells the story of a family torn apart by the eviction, and the enduring hope to reunite in a return to their community.

7

Responses to Working Informally

'We are talking more or less about 80 or 85 per cent of residents working in informal jobs. By informal jobs I mean informal selling. Another percentage also do domestic work, in basic jobs. That covers the vast majority of people. And there are some other people who do have the possibility of setting up a small business, or accessing public space [to do this]. ... The problem with entrepreneurial activities like these is that there is not much institutional accompaniment, or substantive programmes that help. So some sort of initiative or support [such as micro-credits] is set up to generate entrepreneurship in the neighbourhood, for up to 1,000 people. This means [the support] is very limited, but it's the best option that people have to make a living, with the small businesses that people have at home, such as a hairdressers, selling things, food, etc. These are the most common, but there is no direct support for this except for these micro credits, which are a one in a thousand possibility.'

Community leader reflecting on informal working
as entrepreneurial activity, and the limited support
for this, in Cali, Colombia[1]

Informal work is often conceived as an urban policy problem that stands in tensions with 'world class city' aspirations by city authorities and efforts to promote 'cleaner', more 'orderly' and 'competitive' cities that attract domestic and foreign investment (Skinner and Watson, 2020). As a consequence, policy responses often include the eviction of informal workers from streets and public spaces, relocation to formalized vending spaces such as indoor markets and shopping centres, or formalization efforts such as worker registration, licensing and taxation reforms (Chen, 2012). Despite eradication and formalization efforts, informal work prevails across the global South and North, as is evident in figures around informal sector work and in informalization trends discussed in Chapter 2. Recognizing such trends, some policy makers, activists and informal worker representatives are increasingly calling to embrace the informal economy within urban policies and planning interventions and to better address the interests and priorities of informal workers.

This chapter discusses distinct responses to informal work, from more punitive to supportive approaches. We begin by returning to core conceptual debates (dualism, legalism, structuralism and voluntarism) introduced in previous chapters and discuss their implications for policy and planning practice focusing on informal work (when reading this you may also ask yourself how these conceptual debates would inform responses to living informally, discussed in Chapter 6). The chapter then examines interventions that treat working informally as a 'problem' for urban development. These include evictions and revanchist responses that seek to exclude and displace informal workers from urban public spaces as well as efforts to formalize the informal workforce. We then focus on a series of top-down, bottom-up and co-productive responses that consider working informally not as an urban 'problem' but as an irreversible trend that must be embraced. We structure our discussion of responses that embrace working informally along a series of interrelated themes, including governance and informal worker representation, place-specific planning, financial solutions, legal and social protection, and educational reform. We recognize that, in practice, none of these responses occur in isolation but instead represent a portfolio of responses that often coincide and co-exist. Throughout the chapter, we draw on case studies from across the globe to critically examine the effectiveness of different responses. While the review presented here is selective – as it is impossible to cover all responses to informal work in a book like this – we hope to provide an overview of general trends and share critical perspectives on relevant intervention strategies.

Responses as seen through different conceptual lenses

Any response is influenced by the way we understand and think about a certain issue. Let us therefore begin by returning to core conceptual approaches to urban informality introduced in previous chapters and explore their implications for responses to informal work.

As you may recall, earlier conceptualizations of urban informality deployed a dualist perspective, considering this phenomenon as marginal and separate from formality. From a dualist perspective, informality is associated with specific places (for example, street markets, or home-based work in informal neighbourhoods) or types of economic relations (for example, unincorporated enterprises forming part of the informal sector) that provide marginalized groups such as the urban poor with a safety net (Hart, 1973). From this perspective, governments should respond to problems associated with informality by absorbing marginalized groups into the formal economy. As we will see in the next section, similar to the responses discussed in the previous chapter, efforts to pursue formalization still represent a common approach to addressing different aspects of informal work in the current juncture.

Unlike dualists, structuralists believe that informality is not separate or isolated from formality, nor is it considered to be marginal or temporary in nature. Instead, formal and informal economic arrangements are considered to exist along a continuum and show some degree of interdependence. For example, workers living in informal neighbourhoods may contribute their manual labour to the construction of formally registered houses for the urban upper and middle classes (Roy, 2009). Registered enterprises may outsource work to the informal sector to reduce operational costs (Castells and Portes, 1989). Structuralist accounts, especially those departing from a heterodox Marxist perspective, consider working informally to be a permanent feature of the wider global capitalist system (Moser, 1978). Postcolonial accounts further highlight how capitalist labour relations are often structured along ethnospatial hierarchies introduced by colonizers; they also demonstrate that such trends prevail to some degree until the present, with historically marginalized Indigenous, Black and native populations disproportionately accounting for the labour force in the informal economy (Myers, 2003; Wade, 2009; Yiftachel, 2009; Porter, 2010; Dorries et al, 2022).

From a structuralist perspective, responses to working informally can vary significantly. To make sense of these variations, we apply Erik Olin Wright's (2019) work on distinct forms of anti-capitalist struggles, characterized by 'smashing', 'taming', 'dismantling', 'resisting' and 'escaping', to classify responses to working informally. Approaches that follow the logic of 'smashing' call for complete system change through revolutionary struggle that destroys capitalism, promotes decolonization and introduces alternatives. As highlighted by Moser (1978: 1056), however, such calls for revolutionary change, while analytically useful, are often 'political statements' that rarely translate into action and are hence of 'little help to those committed to the amelioration of poverty'. In reality, policy responses that build on structuralist and postcolonial paradigms tend to be more moderate and reformist in nature. They may seek to 'tame' or 'dismantle' capitalist or colonial structures from within, for example through democratic reforms that gradually break down socio-economic and racial inequalities to improve the livelihoods of those living and working informally. This can be achieved by governments playing a stronger regulatory role, for example, by granting specific labour rights and introducing social protection policies for historically marginalized groups (for example, better access to education and work programmes), or by addressing systemic inequalities between capitalist enterprises and informal sector workers (for example, stricter business regulations and worker protections). While 'taming' and 'dismantling' require sustained political action and efforts to exercise state power (something associated mainly, though not exclusively, with 'top-down' responses), endeavours to 'resist' capitalism and colonial power tend to be more 'bottom-up' in nature as they are often driven by social movements, workers' collectives and citizens' groups who seek to change the behaviour of those in power (Wright, 2019). Finally, 'escapist' responses attempt detachment from dominant structural forces, without necessarily achieving revolutionary or systemic change, through the establishment of self-sufficient micro-alternatives (Wright, 2019). Practical examples of 'escapist' responses include efforts to create workplaces that are structured around principles of cooperation, the commons, or fairer trading practices (see, for example, Gibson-Graham et al, 2013).

Legalists consider informality to be the result of excessive regulations that create barriers to accessing formal work (over-regulation), efforts to flexibilize and 'informalize' markets to reduce labour costs (deregulation), or the lack of a regulatory environment that overlooks informal economic practices altogether (lack of regulation) (Chen, 2012). Depending on the specific circumstances, governments should therefore undertake legal and bureaucratic reforms so that those living and working informally are encouraged to register and unleash the economic potential emerging from their businesses (de Soto, 1989). As we will see, past and contemporary efforts around legalization, whether related to the granting of tenure rights (as discussed in Chapter 6) or business permits, depart from this conceptual perspective.

Finally, voluntarists hold the assumption that people who work informally do so to avoid taxation or other costs associated with operating formally. Responses, from this perspective, could therefore include efforts to encourage people to enter formal regulatory environments. This may be through providing tax and investment incentives or offering people space and services required to set up a formal business. More punitive interventions, however, would call for the erasure of informality altogether. In practice, such mechanisms tend to be evictions or forced removal. We discussed this in the previous chapter as a response to living informally and, as we will demonstrate in the next section, such punitive interventions also represent one of the most dominant top-down responses to address informal work.

So far, we have explored what could be done to respond to working informally from the perspective of different theoretical lenses. The remainder of this chapter critically examines in further detail existing responses to working informally. When reading through these sections, think back about what was discussed here and in previous chapters and ask yourself to what extent these responses are inspired by dualist, structuralist, voluntarist or legalist perspectives, or by a combination of these different conceptual approaches.

Conventional top-down responses

Governments across the globe often continue to perceive informal work as an urban problem that should either be eradicated through revanchist interventions such as evictions, or absorbed via formalization efforts. Next, we discuss these two top-down responses and factors that contribute to their prevalence.

Revanchism and evictions

Responses to informal work (and also informal living, as discussed in the previous chapter) are still dominated by eviction, criminalization and sanitizing efforts. Specific planning and city imaginaries by local governments play a key role in the prevalence of such responses. To paraphrase Robinson (2006: 13), city authorities often remain guided by the 'fantasy of Western urban modernity'. From this perspective, the 'modern' city is associated with 'order', 'cleanliness', 'regulation' and formal economic relations, in contrast to the 'backwardness', 'unruliness' and 'traditional practices' associated with the informal economy. As discussed in detail in previous chapters, colonial regimes in the global South and North often followed such understandings when establishing urban settlements. They used planning tools such as regulation, design and zoning to control population flows and socio-economic activities, prioritizing the needs of White settler communities while excluding native populations. Such population divisions were unsustainable, and in most cases were dismantled after independence, especially since the second half of the 20th century, when cities grew rapidly through 'illegal and extra-legal occupation and use of urban space' (Kamete and Lindell, 2010: 890).

Even though cities experienced new occupation and socio-economic dynamics, including an increase in people living and working informally, post-colonial planning laws and practices remained largely unchanged, and are still in force today, in many geopolitical settings. They draw on dominant Western understandings of the 'modern' city and reproduce colonial cultures of planning. Consequently, conventional planning arguments such as 'the need to "restore order", "modernise" and "clean up the city"', continue to be used to justify the eviction of informal vendors (Skinner and Watson, 2020: 125). Efforts to evict street vendors have been widely documented, with notable examples including the 'Malecón 2000' development in Guayaquil, Ecuador (Swanson, 2007; see also Box 7.1), 'Operation Clean Sweep' in Johannesburg and Durban, South Africa (Bénit-Gbaffou, 2016; see also Figure 7.1), and the 'Reclaiming Pavements for Pedestrians' initiative in Bangkok, Thailand (Boonjubun, 2017).

Other factors explaining evictions, criminalization and sanitizing efforts, according to UN-Habitat (2016: 9), relate to the key role of 'the corporate private sector, including property developers, formal retailers, and waste management companies, among others, whose relative power grants them access to decision-makers and whose interests are served by commercial property development and approaches that exclude the urban poor'. City officials are also often guided by 'world class city' imaginaries and aspirations, which leads them to compete for domestic and foreign investment and prestige projects that mimic planning and redevelopment processes in other places like New York, Dubai and Shanghai (Sassen, 2018). For instance, this has been noted in research on urban renewal, revitalization and touristification processes in Guayaquil (Swanson, 2007; see also Box 7.1), evictions in the informal economy of Lagos (Omoegun et al, 2019) as well as in developments linked to the Olympic games in Rio de Janeiro (Müller, 2017). While such efforts may be beneficial for business elites, they often come with negative consequences for street vendors, beggars and other informal workers who are pushed out of inner-city spaces. Neil Smith (1996) has referred to this approach as revanchism, an attempt by the dominant elites to bring the city under their control. Others like Caroline Skinner and Vanessa Watson (2020: 125) consider such projects as 'new versions of urban colonial modernisation' that serve 'to marginalise and exclude even further those working and living informally'.

Regardless of the underlying justification, research consistently shows that evictions have detrimental and often devastating consequences for those working informally, including psychological trauma, loss of livelihoods, deterioration of social and

Figure 7.1: Banner promoting cleanliness in the inner-city streets of Durban, South Africa

Source: Philipp Horn

economic support networks, and deepening of poverty (for a helpful review, see Omoegun et al, 2019). Some of these negative effects may be mitigated in contexts where governments have accompanied evictions with relocation efforts. For example, research on Singapore and Belo Horizonte highlights how traders were relocated to purpose-built indoor markets, which led to improvements in their physical working environment (Yeoh and Kong, 1994; Carrieri and Murta, 2011). At the same time, relocation entailed significant disadvantages for traders in both cities as many lost socio-economic networks and their customer base. Recognizing these adverse effects, UN-Habitat (2016: 46) argues that evictions 'should always be avoided or be a strategy of last resort', and that, 'if relocations are necessary, those should be planned with the participation of those being relocated'.

Box 7.1: Malecón 2000: promoting Guayaquil to tourists while reproducing urban colonialism

Geographer Kate Swanson (2007) provides a compelling case study on the multiple logics that serve to justify the eviction and criminalization of informal workers. Focusing on the Ecuadorian city of Guayaquil, Swanson examines urban revitalization efforts linked to the development of a new coastal promenade called Malecón 2000, a leisure space designed for use by international tourists and wealthy urban elites (see Figure 7.2). While aiming to attract these social groups, municipal authorities sought to keep away informal vendors and beggars who are conceived of as 'urban undesirables'. For this reason, the city of Guayaquil contracted William Bratton – former New York City Police Commissioner, renowned for the urban revanchist strategy implemented under Mayor Rudolph Giuliani – to overhaul the city's security strategy. His recommendations, later referred to in Guayaquil as 'Plan Bratton', included harsh punishments for informal workers trading in inner-city public spaces, with penalties including sanctions of up to US$500 or prison sentences. City authorities implemented 'Plan Bratton' through an inner-city securitization strategy whereby areas like Malecón 2000 were equipped with video cameras and monitored by armed police that decided who could enter this area and who could not, with particular focus on the punitive exclusion of informal workers.

Figure 7.2: Malecón 2000 in Guayaquil, Ecuador

Source: Diego Grani/Alamy

Swanson (2007) demonstrates how this strategy offers a clear example of revanchist urban revitalization policies travelling from cities like New York to the global South for purposes of 'world class city' image-making and touristification. She also discusses the unique local features of such revanchist strategies. In Guayaquil, as in many other Latin American cities (see also Wade, 2013; Horn, 2019), informal vendors are predominantly of Indigenous descent. Yet, as Swanson's (2007) empirical analysis shows, among urban elites, who are predominantly non-Indigenous, Indigenous people are considered to be 'backward peasants', 'inferior' and 'unhygienic ... urban invaders'. She puts such racist representations into historical context, emphasizing the colonial roots of ethno-spatial rural–urban divisions, and highlighting how city authorities rely on what she refers to as 'hygienic racism' to displace and exclude Indigenous people from the urban core. From this perspective, revanchist practices simply represent a contemporary version of urban colonial practices.

Formalization

Another common top-down response towards informality is formalization, defined as 'shifting informal workers to formal wage jobs' (Chen, 2012: 15). Similar to evictions, advocates of this approach depart from the assumption that informal work represents a problem that requires resolving. Chen (2012) highlights that formalization efforts can be categorized into responses targeting self-employed people operating in unregistered enterprises (something we would associate with the informal sector, discussed in Chapter 4), and wage workers in jobs that lack social and legal protections (something we would associate with informal employment, also discussed in Chapter 4). She offers an overview of formalization responses and related benefits, focusing on processes associated with registration and licensing reforms, and efforts to expand worker social and legal protections (see Box 7.2). Formalization should, however, not be considered a one-size-fits-all approach; rather, it is context-specific, requiring adaptation for different jurisdictions characterized by specific governance and regulatory environments. Specific approaches are also likely to address different types of informal work, leading to distinct interventions that generate varying degrees of formality.

Efforts to formalize the informal economy continue to be part of global, regional, national and local development agendas. At the global level this is evident in the United Nations Sustainable Development Goals, particularly in Goal 8 on decent work and economic growth, which emphasizes the aim, in Target 8.3, to 'encourage the formalisation and growth of micro-, small- and medium-sized enterprises' (UN, 2015: 23). At the regional level, the International Labour Organization's Program for the Promotion of Formalization in Latin America and the Caribbean (FORLAC) conducted studies to identify whether specific policies and regulatory changes implemented in different Latin American countries reduced informal working, such as the provision of insurance, healthcare, pension and maternity leave support for workers, or incentives for enterprise registration. Results show that formalization trends vary within the Latin American region, with countries like Uruguay and Brazil – who already had high levels of social security and labour protections prior to formalization reforms – performing better than countries like Mexico or Paraguay, where state contributions to social security remain low for the overall population (see also Staab, 2020).

In addition to noting differences between countries, Staab (2020: 217) also highlights that formalization efforts work better for 'informal wage workers, such as temporary agricultural workers, domestic workers or workers in informal enterprises where employers can be incentivised to contribute their share'. Formalization tends to be

Box 7.2: Formalization of the informal economy: a comprehensive approach

Formalization of informal sector enterprises:

- Registration and taxation:
  - simplified registration procedures
  - progressive registration fees.
- Appropriate legal and regulatory frameworks, including:
  - enforceable commercial contracts
  - private property rights
  - use of public space
  - occupational health and safety regulation.
- Benefits of operating formally:
  - access to finance and market information
  - access to public infrastructure and services
  - enforceable commercial contracts
  - limited liability
  - clear bankruptcy and default rules
  - access to government subsidies and incentives, including procurement bids and export promotion packages
  - membership in formal business associations
  - access to a formal system of social security.

Formalization of informally employed workers:

- Legal recognition and protection as workers.
- Rights and benefits of being formally employed:
  - freedom from discrimination
  - minimum wage
  - occupational health and safety measures
  - employer contributions to health and pensions
  - right to organize and bargain collectively – membership of formal trade unions.

Source: Chen (2012)

less, or not at all, feasible or desirable for informal enterprises and self-employed individuals, especially those with very low earnings such as street vendors or waste pickers, who are unable to afford costs such as social security contributions or business registration fees (see also Austin, 1993; Slocum et al, 2011). Thus, despite widespread efforts around formalization, and positive results such as the reduction of worker vulnerability in some contexts, informal work persists in cities across the globe. This suggests the need for responses that accept and even embrace this phenomenon.

Embracing informal work

Despite eviction threats, informal workers often have no choice other than to stay put in contexts where formalization is not a possibility. This was particularly evident during the COVID-19 pandemic, when governments across the world introduced lockdown restrictions to reduce infection rates. In this context, informal workers, especially those operating as street vendors in public spaces, tended to continue as normal, as 'social distancing' and 'working from home' regulations were simply not an option for people who 'move, every day, both alone but also in concert with others' to earn a living in contexts where social and legal protections remain absent (Bhan et al, 2020; see also Chapter 4).

It is evident, then, that informal work is a phenomenon that is here to stay. International organizations, governments, non-government organizations (NGOs) and community-based organizations increasingly recognize this trend and promote interventions that do not penalize but, instead, embrace informal work by aiming to better respond to worker priorities. Such priorities include improved job security, better registration mechanisms for informal enterprises and workers, extending state protection to the informal workforce, and increasing the productivity of informal enterprises and the incomes of informal workers (Chen, 2012). One organization following an approach that openly embraces informal work is the Durban-based NGO Asiye eTelufani (AeT), closely associated with the international network Women in Informal Employment: Globalizing and Organizing (WIEGO). We had the chance to speak to one of AeT's co-founders, Richard Dobson, and we share his testimony in Box 7.3 (see also Figure 7.3).

Box 7.3: Amplifying the voices of informal workers in Durban, South Africa: a conversation with Richard Dobson, AeT

Richard Dobson is an architect by training. He previously worked for eThekwini Municipality in Durban, supporting the Warwick Junction Urban Renewal Project in an area characterized by high levels of economic informality. In 2008 he co-founded AeT, an NGO focusing on promoting and developing good practice around inclusive design and facilitation services for those working in the informal economy in Durban.

Richard highlights how his approach towards informality is informed by a "hyperawareness of exclusion" linked to Durban's Apartheid past. It is guided by principles of inclusion and promotes the right to the city, livelihoods, and dignity for informal workers whose urban cultural preferences have been historically ignored. While such values align with South Africa's progressive post-Apartheid constitution, Richard recognizes that there remains "huge opposition to informality" among government officials who prioritize the interests of property owners and business lobbyists, focusing on "keeping the city clean and to showcase it for World Class events".

In contrast to dominant government responses, AeT's work centres around the principle of informal worker recognition: "If you're not going to recognize that this practice of an urban livelihood in a public space is a dignified and reasonable and legitimate activity, then you can't even start the debate." AeT positions itself "alongside informal workers" and seeks to "amplify the voice" of this under-represented stakeholder group. It does this through its role as "non-partisan urban communicator" that connects different stakeholders, including informal workers and municipal authorities but also academics and the wider citizenry. As part of urban education campaigns, the NGO serves as a "portal that academics and citizens can access" to learn about informal workers, for example through guided tours around Warwick's markets or through training urban planning students to better engage with economic informality from the perspective of workers.

AeT is "respectful of the street structures that are there" and recognizes that NGO workers "are definitely not the experts", but that expertise lies with informal workers. A lot of AeT's work focuses on gathering "urban intelligence" by observing worker activities and facilitating discussions with them. Emphasis is put on fostering worker-led bottom-up responses. AeT "trains informal workers to do their own research, and to identify their infrastructural needs". Richard emphasizes that "infrastructure is the pathway" towards inclusion of informal workers in the urban fabric:
'It's the appropriate infrastructure [for example, appropriate production and vending spaces, provision of toilets for workers, or existence of schools and daycare centres for the children of workers], which first of all gives some recognition that that activity that is there should be there from an urban presentation point of view. But not only that, from a user's point of view it actually dignifies the activity that they [workers] are engaged in, so they no longer are forced to work on salvaged packing crates and pieces of board to make their tables.'

Infrastructure is considered a starting point for interventions and design solutions that are co-produced with workers and address their needs and priorities in a culturally appropriate way. This requires a "huge level of inventiveness and multi-layered solutions. Sometimes it's an urban scale intervention. Other times, it's a tap. Other times, it's a cart. Other times, it's whatever". Responses always build on the "clues from the community" as to what infrastructural solutions work for them. Infrastructure also provides the key to establishing relations with the municipality. Having previously worked in the municipality, Richard and his AeT colleagues continue "to go to people [there] and have conversations with [them], and at times get support from them". In addition, AeT's work includes legal advocacy for informal workers, supporting them in their defence from illegal police actions or eviction threats. More recently, AeT's urban advocacy strategy attempts to "move away from permits and enforcement" as the primary regulatory instrument legitimizing public space trading, and to pay closer attention to advocating for integrated planning and placemaking solutions that not just address informal workers' needs but the quality of urban life more broadly.[2]

Richard's testimony provides a good overview of what responses that embrace informal work could look like. As he highlights, "It's not just about the location. It's about the people. It's about the local government. It's about the politics, it's about the finance, the law, education, and so many factors." Building on Richard's testimony, we structure the remainder of this chapter around the following interrelated themes, which all cohere with the notion of embracing informal work:

- governance and informal worker representation
- place-specific planning

Figure 7.3: Informal street vending activities in the Warwick Junction area in Durban, South Africa

Source: Philipp Horn

- financial solutions
- legal and social protections
- educational reform

Governance and informal worker representation

Embracing informal work means taking into consideration workers' interests, needs and priorities. Yet, as we have shown in previous sections, informal workers are often excluded from urban decision-making processes, which tend to remain top-down in nature or involve elite interest groups. This does not mean, however, that urban governance is only exercised by the state, private sector or elite groups. Urban informal workers often push for change through bottom-up interventions.

One way of intervening from the bottom-up is through aligning individual and collective survival activities with informal governance practices. An illustrative example is provided by Vargas Falla and Valencia (2019) who demonstrate how street vendors in Bogota engage in acts of 'quiet encroachment' (for a definition of this concept, see Chapter 5). In the specific context of their research, 'quiet encroachment' manifests through a practice referred to as '*acreditar*' (in English, accreditation), meaning that 'vendors need to come to the same place over and over again until they get accredited or recognised as the "rightful users" of that selling point' (Vargas Falla and Valencia, 2019: 94). The status of 'rightful user' does not *per se* refer to obtaining formal vending permission but rather represents a 'customary right' that vendors gain through, for example, obtaining help and advice from friends and relatives, respecting the spaces of already operating vendors, and obtaining informal recognition from government officials and police officers in the area (Vargas Falla and Valencia, 2019). This case study demonstrates that understanding governance and representation around informal work often requires looking at multiple tactics and at intersections with other articulations of urban informality, in this case governing informally.

Many informal workers are also affiliated with membership-based organizations (with some formally registered and others operating informally) including sector- or place-specific workers' associations, trade guilds or unions; national and international umbrella networks; and related support NGOs. Box 7.4 lists some prominent international organizations representing informal workers. Previous research highlights how, at the local level, such organizations often resist and oppose punitive responses (such as evictions) through public campaigns and protests, or through establishing clientelist alliances and *ad hoc* arrangements with municipal authorities to protect informal workers (for example, Bénit-Gbaffou [2016] shows how diverse street vendor organizations successfully undermined the 'Operation Clean Sweep' eviction campaign in Johannesburg). Many member-based organizations also advocate for better governance partnerships and seek to collaborate with state authorities. With support from national and international NGOs who provide capacity-building or serve as intermediaries, member-based organizations from across the globe have developed creative solutions to address challenges, and deployed innovative methods to improve their representation in formal governance channels at local, national and international levels – whether through organizing public stakeholder dialogues, engaging in political negotiations, or organizing awareness-raising campaigns. One example is the ratification of India's 2014 Street Vendor Law, a result of decades-long campaigning and political negotiations led by the National Association of Street Vendors in India and the Self-Employed Women's Association based in the same country. The 2014 Street Vendors Law 'requires cities to establish Town Vending Committees to regulate street vending, with at least 40 per cent representation of vendors on the committee' (UN-Habitat, 2016: 8), making this law exceptional in enabling the involvement of street vendors in governance processes that have a direct impact on their livelihood.

In short, then, these examples illustrate that informal workers increasingly do play a key role in urban governance and in improving livelihoods within their economic sectors – be that through self-help, 'quiet encroachment', collective acts of resistance, or efforts to establish more inclusive collaborative partnerships with key decision-makers. As we shall see, informal workers can also play an important role in urban planning.

Place-specific planning

Planning is concerned with shaping the future and achieving positive change in urban places through a mix of means, including the regulation of land uses and design of the built environment encompassing, among other elements, housing, transportation systems, water, electricity and energy infrastructure (Rydin, 2011). The specific land use and spatial needs of informal workers are rarely considered in top-down planning approaches guided by modernist city visions. But when conceived otherwise, for

Box 7.4: Key organizations supporting informal workers

- WIEGO: a global network dedicated to improving conditions of the working poor in the informal economy. The WIEGO website contains many reports, publications and workers' stories, as well as a catalogue of national and international worker-based organizations.
- HomeNet International: a global network of membership-based workers organizations representing thousands of home-based workers around the world.
- StreetNet International: a global organization of committed informal traders, with the goal to promote and leverage an autonomous and democratic alliance of street vendors, hawkers and cross-border traders in over 50 countries.
- International Alliance of Waste Pickers: a networking process supported by WIEGO, including thousands of waste picker organizations with groups in more than 28 countries, covering mainly Latin America, Asia and Africa.
- International Domestic Workers Federation: a membership-based global organization of domestic and household workers.

See alternative resource list (at the end of the chapter) for these organizations' websites.

---

example, through more collaborative and participatory approaches, planning can play a significant role in responding to the needs of informal workers.

An important starting point is to recognize that there is no single place-based planning response, as informal work occurs in a variety of places, including the home, informal neighbourhoods and public spaces. As each place has its distinct characteristics, appropriate planning solutions will vary for different settings. Regarding the home, Gautam Bhan (2020: 137) argues that planners should not just associate housing with being a 'dwelling unit' but 'an assemblage of location, services, work, and tenure'. The implications of embracing home-based work within planning are multiple. Planners, for example, could introduce zoning regulations that encourage mixed-use developments in residential areas and housing programmes that address the intersection of the home as space to live and work (UN-Habitat, 2016). The latter was evident in a large-scale housing improvement programme called the Local Development Programme (PRODEL) implemented in informal neighbourhoods in eight Nicaraguan cities between 1994 and 2008. In addition to improving basic services at neighbourhood scale, PRODEL engaged in collaborative micro-planning interventions with low-income households to incrementally improve their housing infrastructure and home-based microenterprises; this was financed through small microfinance loans for households (Stein, 2010). While this provided an opportunity for some households to improve their economic livelihoods, finance mechanisms were not viable nor accessible for every low-income household, excluding particularly the poorest of the urban poor. A careful engagement with financial solutions to informal work is therefore required – something explored further in the next section.

In cities of the global South, informal neighbourhoods are particularly vibrant hubs of informal economic activities. They are often comprised of home-based enterprises, shops and street traders, and many contain specialist economies that serve the city and feed into specific value chains (see, for example, Benjamin, 2000). Informal work is also key for the provision of core services in informal neighbourhoods, with landlords, healthcare facilities, schools, construction workers, carers, electricity, water and sanitation providers often operating informally and making a living from these activities. By calling for the demolition or relocation of such neighbourhoods, planners fail to acknowledge their strategic economic value as sites for job creation and contributors to wider city, national and global economies (UN-Habitat, 2016). But there increasingly exist examples of planning interventions that more effectively address the issue of informal work within informal neighbourhoods.

This is the case, for example, in Mukuru (already discussed in Chapters 5 and 6) – one of Nairobi's largest informal neighbourhoods – where a citizen-led enumeration was organized by local Shack/Slum Dwellers International affiliate Muungano wa Wanavijiji. This highlighted that 94 per cent of structures are informally owned and sublet by informally operating landlords, 150 schools in the area operate informally, and service provision is mainly undertaken by local cartels (informal service providers). While mainly inhabited by low-income residents, enumerations revealed that Mukuru represents a multi-million-dollar economy, as it is home to thousands of micro-enterprises and informal service providers. Since 2018, an innovative participatory and multi-sectoral informal neighbourhood upgrading process, based on the designation of the Mukuru Special Planning Area, has been unfolding. Instead of simply calling for formalization, this planning process recognizes the importance of informal businesses and service providers, both in terms of local expertise and economic potential for the area. As a result, novel service delivery models have been introduced that seek to sustain and better integrate informal service providers into public service provision, for example, by allocating these stakeholders responsibility and resources for managing and maintaining newly provided public water, electricity or sanitation infrastructure (see Horn et al, 2020). The Mukuru Special Planning Area hence illustrates how informal neighbourhood upgrading initiatives, which conventionally focus on living informally (see Chapter 6), can also address the intersection of multiple informalities and, specifically, working informally.

Public spaces such as streets, pavements and parks also represent important settings for informal economic activities by street vendors, waste pickers, rickshaw drivers and many more. Yet, the economic potential of public spaces, and the interests and needs of workers (for example, for toilets, storage spaces, security, ritual facilities, or day care and schools for workers' children), are often not considered in planning and design interventions. One factor explaining this is that public spaces are often administered by professionals from sectors not connected to socio-economic development. Parks tend to be operated by park authorities. Roads and sidewalks often fall under the realm of municipal traffic units composed by transport planners and road engineers who, as explicitly highlighted in the interview with Richard Dobson, "often lack the expertise to engage with workers, and come up with the wrong solutions". What is required, instead, are place-based interventions that combine expertise from different sectors and professions. AeT's work around collaborative planning and design in the Warwick Junction markets, involving informal traders and different municipal authorities from distinct sector units, shows how this can be achieved (see Dobson and Skinner, 2009). In short, then, urban planning should embrace the informal economy, and this requires creative place-specific solutions that address informal worker priorities through collaborative multi-sector responses.

Financial sector responses

Financial support is another key area required to better embrace working informally. This can include setting tax incentives that encourage informal enterprises to register their business, as evident in formalization efforts. Beyond formalization, informal workers often require access to financial services to sustain themselves in times of hardship, to pay bills associated with operating their business, or to make investments into goods, people, land, improved services and business infrastructure to better compete in the markets where they operate. To do this, informal workers often rely on a combination of different informal and formally provided financial services.

We conventionally associate informal financial services with the image of the 'loan shark', normally an individual who lends money at extremely high interest rates. Such lenders tend to offer credit out of their own pocket and, unlike banks or other formal financial institutions, lack significant reserves (Matin et al, 2002); although in Colombia, the colloquial term for this system, '*gota a gota*', or 'drop by drop', refers to a system in which criminal organizations are increasingly involved, raising the amount of credit available, but also the risks for borrowers. Despite high interest rates, 'loan sharks' remain a very popular route for informal workers to obtain a loan. This is particularly the case for extremely poor people who cannot access formal finance options such as micro-credits (Matin et al, 2002), discussed further below. Other informal financial mechanisms include savings groups where a group of people (for example, informal traders from a worker-based organization, friends or neighbours) come together to save money and pool their resources. Savings groups can be especially helpful for low-income informal workers who lack a steady income, as they can help build up savings gradually and, when a larger sum of money is needed, provide access to credit without the formalities associated with financial sector institutions (Mitlin et al, 2011). This practice has been a central component of the Shack/Slum Dwellers International movement's response to informality, as discussed in Chapter 6. Similarly, Tassi (2017: 1) notes how guilds of informal workers in El Alto rely on a 'system of rotating loans and credits' to make substantive investments, enabling them for example to establish 'their stalls on the side walks' or extend 'their commercial control over the neighbourhoods'.

Regarding formal financial services, research demonstrates that conventional banking options are often not accessible to low-income workers and small-scale enterprises operating informally (Chen, 2012). Throughout the last decades, however, a variety of finance solutions have emerged that seek to cater better for this group, with micro-credits perhaps being the best-known example. Microfinance institutions, whether operated by NGOs, private enterprises or state institutions, provide small- to medium-sized loans, often on relatively high interest rates, and permit small, frequent – often weekly – repayments that enable low-income borrowers to return money out of their existing income (Matin et al, 2002). Yet, as highlighted in the case of PRODEL, microcredits are often not an accessible option for the extremely poor, and can put extra financial pressures on low-income individuals and groups.

Other formal financial innovations include the emergence of mobile money transfer systems, with Kenya's M-Pesa – operated by the telecommunications provider Safaricom – being the most widely researched service that caters for those living and working informally. M-Pesa uses mobile phones to facilitate money transfers to workers who do not hold a bank account. In Kenya alone, there exist approximately 20 million M-Pesa accounts (Foster and Heeks, 2013). The case of M-Pesa also illustrates how formal and informal financial arrangements can connect. Informal savings groups (called *chamas* in Kenya), for example, make use of this platform for financial pooling and transfer activities (Meagher, 2018). Foster and Heeks (2013) also highlight how M-Pesa dealers have sometimes subcontracted their activities to informal sub-agents outside the Safari network to further their customer base and expand their product and service range – only to later centralize activities again to monopolize the gains.

In sum, then, there are a range of informal and formal financial services available to informal workers, with each of them characterized by different strengths and limitations. To meet their specific interests, informal workers tend to often make use of a combination of such services.

Legal and social protection

Whether through over-regulation, deregulation or a lack of regulation, the law often negatively affects informal workers. It may criminalize their activities, ignore their presence and everyday needs, and fail to protect them or include them in specific interventions, as those who operate informally are often considered outside the realm of government regulation. Embracing informal work through better legal and social protections, then, means deploying a rights-based framework that calls for the legal inclusion of informal workers (Brown, 2017). This is important because 'informal workers – like *all* workers – require a regulatory framework that protects their rights in the workplace, balances the needs of all stakeholders, and promotes a climate of stability and security' (UN-Habitat, 2016: 23, emphasis in original). Related to this are struggles for the recognition of informal workers' rights, including pressure for legal reform to increase their security and social protection. In line with what we discussed in Chapter 4, such activities are best undertaken in partnership between informal workers and local governments.

To identify reform pathways, there is a need to analyse existing legislation that directly or indirectly addresses informal work (UN-Habitat, 2016: 24–5). For example, the Universal Declaration of Human Rights grants every person the right to work and free choice of employment. The International Labour Organization provides guidelines for decent work. At the national level, constitutions also often incorporate the right to work as a universal right. Such international and national legal frameworks have in the past provided the basis for informal workers' organizations to engage in legal advocacy campaigns; for example, in Tanzania street vendors highlighted how legislation on street vending contradicts constitutional rights (UN-Habitat, 2016: 28). A reverse process was observed in Belo Horizonte in Brazil where legal advocacy began locally and shaped changes at higher levels. Here, waste pickers began to establish partnerships with municipal recycling programmes that were recognized in the 1990s as part of municipal norms; this was later integrated into state and federal law in the 2000s (UN-Habitat, 2016: 27).

Informal workers may also be affected by different sector-specific regulations, such as highway regulations controlling activities on roads and pavements, business licensing regulations, and sector-specific urban bylaws that are often used to justify evictions instead of protecting workers. Entry points to push for legal reform may also vary depending on the specific type of informal sector work, with domestic workers, home-based workers, street vendors and waste pickers all facing distinct legal challenges. Over the years, legal advocacy has led to important reforms in different sectors (for more detailed case studies on legal reforms for waste pickers and street traders, see UN-Habitat, 2016: 27–30). As part of its social protection programme, WIEGO is working with different informal workers' organizations across the globe to advocate for better social protection, social care and workplace services.[3]

The role of education

Finally, moving towards more inclusive responses towards working informally requires different ways of educating urban professionals. A review of curricula of planning schools in the global South by Watson (2011) demonstrated that 'all too often ... planners are educated ... to play a function in the city that is predominantly about control'. Training is often based on modernist, technical and Eurocentric understandings of cities that encourage practices such as evictions, which we discussed in previous sections. While informality is not covered at all in some planning schools, when it is included in curricula it is still not uncommon for informality to be presented as an obstacle to urban development (Watson, 2011).

There are multiple pathways to better capture informality in the training of urban professionals. Watson (2011: 19) emphasizes the need for conventional university lectures and theory courses to include the issue of informal work, drawing on the vast body of critical scholarship on this topic. Other solutions she proposes include the incorporation of case study material that shows why a particular approach towards working informally was or was not successful. She also advocates for experiential learning through engagements with informal workers, via field visits, studio work and inviting workers as topic experts to deliver lectures and seminars within universities and other educational institutions. The last point aligns closely with the priorities and interests of organizations composed of, or representing the needs of informal workers, such as AeT or WIEGO who are interested in working with academics to shape teaching programmes. Such engagements have the potential to influence future generations of urban professionals and prepare them to work with informal workers in a way that is more inclusive, horizontal and fair.

In our own work as university lecturers, we have tried to take on board these recommendations in our module called 'Urban Informality' and a connected class trip to Durban where we collaborated with AeT so that our students could learn directly from and with informal workers. This critical, engaged and experiential approach to informality also informs the way we wrote this book, and we hope it helps readers, among them current and future urban professionals, to critically reflect on their practice. We reflect further on issues of how to research and work with aspects of urban informality in Chapter 8.

Chapter summary

This chapter explored different responses to informal work. We began with a recap of core conceptual debates, outlining how different theoretical approaches could lead to distinct responses. The remainder of the chapter distinguished broadly between: (1) responses that consider informal work as a problem that should be eradicated via evictions, criminalization, and revanchism or resolved via formalization; and (2) responses that embrace informal work through governance, planning, financial solutions, legal and social protection, and education reform. What is clear from the review presented here is that there exists no single fit-for-purpose response, but rather, multiple responses towards informal work co-exist and coincide. Some of those are top-down, others are bottom-up, and some are more collaborative in nature. While providing effective solutions for some instances of informal work, many responses also generate divisions as they are often the result of conflicting priorities and uneven power relations. In order to address this, it is critical to centre the views of informal workers and their support organizations at the heart of responses to informal work.

Recommended reading

- Chen, M. and Carré, F. (2020) *The Informal Economy Revisited: Examining the Past, Envisioning the Future*, Abingdon: Routledge.
- UN-Habitat (2016) *Enhancing Productivity in the Urban Informal Economy*, Nairobi: UN Habitat.

EXERCISES

- As a recap, write down the key similarities and differences in definitions of and responses to the informal sector, informal employment and informal economy.

- Engage with solutions offered by different worker-based organizations (see alternative representations) and discuss to what extent and how they embrace informal work.

Alternative representations

Here we provide you with web links for key organizations supporting informal workers (see also Box 7.3). Organizations like WIEGO also provide first-hand testimonies from informal workers.

- WIEGO (https://www.wiego.org/)
- HomeNet International (https://www.homenetinternational.org/)
- StreetNet International (http://streetnet.org.za/)
- International Alliance of Waste Pickers (https://globalrec.org/)
- International Domestic Workers Federation (https://idwfed.org/about-us)

8

Emerging Alternatives

'I am stronger than I thought I was. ... The world is much much bigger than my neighbourhood. I feel content knowing that I am part of something so much bigger. I got clear ideas about what I want to do in our community and also ... seeing the Kenyan women and all the things that they'd achieved made me realize that I am capable of achieving much more than I have despite the circumstances.'

Community leader from Sheffield reflecting on the benefits of learning exchanges with organizations in the global South[1]

Throughout this book we have distinguished between processes relating to living, working and governing informally. Yet from the outset, in Chapter 1, we have acknowledged that while these categories may be helpful for ordering our knowledge, they do not always map neatly onto reality. Current and emerging approaches and alternatives to urban informality have sought to complicate and supersede the demarcations between what we have called living, working and governing informally, in this sense returning to our starting point in Chapter 1. Recent academic work in this field highlights the usefulness of heuristic categories – such as McFarlane and Waibel's (2012) identification of approaches to informality as spatial categorization, organizational form or governmentality – yet also emphasizes the need to transcend these categories, and even go beyond informality. At the same time, others emphasize 'the work that informality "does" for us', theoretically and in practice or policy terms, as Acuto et al (2019: 485) suggest. Again, this returns us to the need to pay attention to the conditions and underlying structures in which places, people and processes are labelled 'informal', as argued by Banks et al (2020) and highlighted in Chapter 1.

In this chapter we focus on emerging trends in theory and practice, exploring alternative understandings of and responses to informality. We examine recent debates which revive concerns to get beyond binaries and challenge dichotomous thinking. In particular, we engage with ideas that seek to go beyond the concept of informality, such as popular urbanization, collective life and solidarity economies, and look at alternative responses to urban informality, reflecting in particular on the New Urban

Agenda (NUA) as representative of contemporary top-down approaches that embrace informality, and emerging citizen-led approaches that emphasize South–North learning and the potential of urban reform coalitions. We reiterate the importance of including cultural responses towards informality, particularly through fiction, as different ways of representing it. We also review current and emerging approaches to researching informality and offer ideas for students on how to develop research in this area, briefly discussing ethical principles of conducting research on informality as well as innovative methodologies, from knowledge co-production and participatory approaches to digital research methods.

Beyond informality?

As outlined in Chapter 2, recent debates on urban informality have not only questioned the basis of the concept, but also the concept itself. In this section, we discuss emerging conceptual alternatives to informality that might take us beyond the concept and its constraints. We start by contextualizing such debates within wider urban theory, including Southern urban theory, before exploring some alternative conceptualizations, returning to our focus on living, working and governing practices, and finally considering calls to get beyond informality.

Developments in urban theory

A divergence in urban theory has been observed in recent decades, between approaches to urbanization that could be termed 'universalist', such as planetary urbanization, and those that are characterized as 'particularist', which can be associated with Southern (urban) theory (Derickson, 2015). Planetary urbanization suggests that urbanization and its associated processes are 'the defining, essential and necessary processes through which all planetary life can be understood' (Derickson, 2015: 649), drawing on Lefebvre and Marxist political economy to frame global capitalism as the 'context of context' of urbanization processes worldwide (Lefebvre, 2003 [1970]; Brenner, 2013).[2] Brenner and Schmid, key proponents of the theory, argue in their 2014 article that given the unreliability of world urban population estimates, and the conceptual vagueness of the term 'urban', we need a new vocabulary of urbanization. In particular, the penetration of 'urban' characteristics such as connectivity, dynamism and uncertainty into diverse contexts at a global scale suggests that 'the urbanization process has become a global condition rather than simply a "way of life"[3] that is confined to certain types of settlement spaces as opposed to others' (Brenner and Schmid, 2014: 747–8).

Planetary urbanization's lack of engagement with difference and inequality is often seen as counter to calls to 'provincialize' urban theory associated with theorists such as Robinson (2006), Watson (2003) and Simone (2004b). In line with postcolonial approaches mentioned in Chapter 2, these debates aim to rethink our understanding of the world (and in this case, cities) by centring the 'radical instability' of the South (Roy, 2014: 16) while moving away from the 'Eurocentric' underpinnings of social theory (Patel, 2014). Grounded in empirical examples derived from 'deep sustained conversation with those making the city in spaces of the Global South' (Derickson, 2015: 651–2), this perspective foregrounds everyday life and questions binaries such as modern/traditional, developed/developing and indeed formal/informal. It mistrusts planetary urbanization's totalizing tendencies, seeking instead to present 'counter-topographies' which aim to 'identify and nurture new solidarities and subjectivities, while troubling existing representations' (Derickson, 2015: 653).

Certainly, urban informality as a concept has remained marginalized within urban theory, perhaps due to the concept's imprecision (discussed in Chapter 2) and limited application outside the global South (Marx and Kelling, 2019). Writing in the same special issue as Marx and Kelling, Acuto et al (2019: 479–80) suggest that urban informality's continued 'othering' as a field of study reflects the enduring dominance of dualistic thinking which devalues informality, requiring researchers to work across categories, disciplines and sites for 'a better informality-informed urban theory'.

This aligns with the loosely defined body of 'Southern urban theory' that Bhan (2019) identifies as accumulating over the last decade. Southern urban theory critiques the 'rootless', universalizing theories 'built elsewhere', usually in city histories from the global North, which are applied to cities of the global South, obscuring everyday realities and limiting theorizing (Bhan, 2019: 641). Southern urban theory is '[w]ork that has sought to write *from* these [Southern] places rather than just *about* them' (Bhan, 2019: 642, emphasis in original). The South may be understood as diverse sites of knowledge production challenging dominant hegemonies, but also as a 'set of moving peripheries', highlighting shared experiences of colonialism, capitalism and precarity that extend to residents and places of global Northern cities (Bhan, 2019: 642), such as migrant workers in Manchester living and working in precarious legal, economic and material conditions (see, for example, Lombard, 2023).

Bhan (2019) concurs with Brenner and Schmid (2014) that new vocabularies are necessary to get beyond the constraints of urban theory. This suggests revisiting commonplace, taken-for-granted words and concepts, in a sociological tradition associated with Raymond Williams' (1976) influential book *Keywords* (see also Bennett et al, 2005), such as 'community', 'culture', 'participation' and – in our case – 'informality'. In urban studies, interrogating how key terms such as 'eviction', 'suburbs' and 'gentrification' can be reconstructed in Southern cities, beyond the Northern urban contexts where they originate, may help to transcend the conceptual divide between global North and South, while acknowledging the different historical and structural conditions that have determined diverse urban trajectories (Garrido et al, 2021). For example, Zeiderman (2018: 1120) asks how ideas such as 'global' and 'urban' are mobilized *by whom* and *for what purposes*, exploring these questions in the Colombian port city of Buenaventura where local officials pursue the 'world-class city' ideal through territorial development, while Afro-Colombian social movements embedded in 'global networks of racial justice activism' make counter-claims on the same urban territory. Bhan (2019: 640) suggests that vocabulary is 'a mode of theory-building', in which '[w]ords ... can [be] wielded and presented to amplify particular issues, places, and forms of knowledge at a particular time'.

This suggests the need to revisit and interrogate terms and concepts associated with 'urban informality', to reflect on their inferences and underlying power structures.

In this chapter we review recent conceptual alternatives relating to living, working and governing informally – namely popular urbanization, collective life, popular economies and infrastructural citizenship – to think about how (and whether) we might get beyond informality. A common feature of these approaches is to reverse the normative inference of dualisms, seeing informal processes from the perspective of those engaging in and with them, rather than outsiders, on the basis of sustained engagement with diverse empirical realities which may be brought into conversation with one another.

Emerging conceptual alternatives
Living informally: popular urbanization and collective life

Drawing on the Latin American idea of *'urbanización popular'*,[4] conceptualized in the 1980s to analyse marginalized urban areas and their underlying social processes, Streule et al (2020) redefine processes involved in the production of urban informality. Focusing on the role of (marginalized) urban residents in constructing and maintaining their homes and neighbourhoods, Streule et al (2020: 667) position them as 'the main protagonists of the urbanization process', foregrounding their collective action for the production, transformation and appropriation of urban space. The concept of popular urbanization thus emphasizes everyday processes and residents' agency, which play out in distinctive ways in diverse historical and geographical contexts – such as Mexico City, Lagos and Istanbul – while also acknowledging the role of the state.

The transposition of 'popular urbanization' into English-language debates takes up themes identified in Varley's (2013) important review of Latin American literature on urban informality, which highlights representations of informality as resistance, and shows how these challenge binary frameworks, while also arguing that such debates may nevertheless reproduce dualistic tropes of formal/informal (as discussed in Chapter 2). These include urban design studies celebrating informality's aesthetic dimensions (for example, Feireiss et al [2005] on Caracas), alongside work which places renewed emphasis on residents' agency (Hernández et al, 2010). Such critical debates include proposals to replace the concept of informality with 'marginality' (Hernández and Becerra, 2017), following debates such as a special issue of the *Latin American Research Review* (*LARR*, 2004) which in turn reprise discussions from the 1970s, such as Perlman's work in this area (also discussed in Chapter 2).

Alternative conceptions emerging from different regions take distinctive approaches. The idea of 'collective life', originating from work on Southern Africa, explains how people live and work in conditions characterized by inequality, precarity and instability. Collective life sees the 'continuous recombination of people's experiences and practices' as essential for understanding cities of the South (Simone, 2021: 1). 'Collective' does not refer to community or consensus, but plurality, diversity and density, conditions characterizing cities globally, which simultaneously hold many tensions and ambiguities (Bhan et al, 2020: 9). Instead of seeing informality as heroic or entrepreneurial, collective life emphasizes the highly fluid and unstable conditions that contextualize it, while identifying the possibility of 'remaking the social in ways that are more equal and just' (Simone, 2021: 7).

Figure 8.1: Responses to food insecurity in informal neighbourhoods in Cali, Colombia, during the COVID-19 pandemic

Source: Asomevid

Bhan et al (2020: 2), writing on Delhi, São Paulo, Jakarta and Johannesburg in the first six months of the COVID-19 pandemic, used the concept of 'collective life' to argue against totalizing narratives of pandemic responses and understand how 'the urban majority is trying to survive and cope within structures of inequality that now bear both the new imprint of COVID-19 while equally holding the continuities of older forms of distancing and exclusion' (as seen in Figure 8.1). Collective life offers a way to understand the everyday struggles of people living and working informally, linked in a meshwork of transactions which at times coalesce into solidarity:

> In these cities, getting by means being able to move, every day, both alone but also in concert with others, to stay open to the trade, the *skarrel*, the hustle to

arrange water, food, work, waste, childcare, data and identity for that day, that week, for just some more time. (Bhan et al, 2020: 3)

For example, finding food during the scarcity of the pandemic, when normal supply chains were disrupted, in a context where most people do not have access to a car, credit card or savings to buy in bulk, might mean:

> Borrowing cash from a friend down the road, who had to stand in a long line at the ATM to draw cash, handing over rickshaw or minibus fare, sometimes along a line of three or four other commuters until it gets to the driver, paying cash at the market at multiple stalls to get the best deals. (Bhan et al, 2020: 3)

Such ideas, while developed in the global South, may have global resonance; for example, communities in Manchester were also supporting each other during the pandemic in ways that responded to the precarity of their circumstances, including setting up informal support groups, to check on vulnerable or housebound residents, and addressing mental health needs outside of formal support services, for example, of elderly tenants living in high-rise flats (Community Savers 2020). Certainly, they echo other accounts highlighting the ingenuity and precarity that characterize life in many contemporary urban settings, whether emphasizing provisionality as a mode of living and working (Guma, 2021), the slow and uneven processes of 'autoconstrucción' involved in peripheral urbanization (Caldeira, 2016), or the persistently 'irregular' nature of such processes and places (Salazar, 2012).

Working informally: connections with social, solidarity and popular economies

The lens of collective life and provisionality is also deployed to move beyond a focus on working informally, in order to pay closer attention to formal–informal interactions, and investigate holistically how those alienated by the capitalist economy make ends meet and seek to transform not just economic but wider social, cultural and political relations in cities. Such trends are evident, for example, in scholarship on the social and solidarity economy, considered to at once incorporate informal economic practices and represent a possible pathway for addressing these. Originating in the global North, the concept of the social economy is defined as a way to 'respond to the alienation of needs by the traditional private sector or the public sector in times of socio-economic crisis' (Moulaert and Ailenei, 2005: 2041). Historical examples of the social economy in Europe, for example, include the formation of workers' mutual support collectives who resisted efforts to deregulate and enhance business competition in the 1840s and 1850s, as well as the emergence of food cooperatives for workers and unemployed people during the economic crisis of the 1920s and 1930s (Bouchard et al, 2000). The solidarity economy, often associated with the social economy (and for this reason referred to as the social and solidarity economy, or SSE), emphasizes efforts to enhance 'economic co-operation and reciprocity' (Moulaert and Ailenei, 2005: 2045). The SSE is made up of 'the voluntary, non-profit and co-operative sectors that are formally independent of the state' (Moulaert and Ailenei, 2005: 2042), and comprises of activities that transcend the market, for example by foregrounding social development efforts such as improving working conditions, incomes and overall livelihoods (ILO, 2022).

SSE perspectives transcend traditional dichotomies as they take into account the role and contribution of both market- and non-market actors, and informal and formal modes of organization. A common example of informal articulations within the SSE are self-help groups, defined as groups of individuals who join up to address mutual needs and goals. Savings groups represent a helpful illustration of self-help initiatives by informal workers or neighbourhood residents (see Chapters 6 and 7; see also Figure 8.2, and further discussion in this chapter). More formal SSE organizations include, among others, associations, defined as a 'legal entity principally engaged in producing non-market services for households or the community at large ... whose primary resources are voluntary contributions'; and social enterprises, defined as 'a unit that utilises market means but primarily to serve social purposes' (ILO, 2022: 13). Many people who live and work informally have formed or joined informal and formal SSE organizations such as workers' cooperatives or trade unions to improve their living conditions, for example, by accessing training, formal work, property, financial resources, information and other benefits. For this reason, international organizations such as Women in Informal Employment: Globalizing and Organizing (WIEGO; discussed also in Chapter 7) increasingly emphasize the potential of the SSE to support formalization in ways that benefit the workers involved, and enhance the rights of those living and working informally. For example, WIEGO now employs a dedicated specialist who explores the role of SSE in supporting informal workers.[5]

A collective life perspective, as discussed in the previous section, emphasizes that socio-economic practices of the urban majority are not reducible to informality

Figure 8.2: Women undertaking informal neighbourhood mapping in India

Source: Ana Holschuch/Shack/Slum Dwellers International

or even the SSE, but should be understood through the notion of urban popular economies, introduced in Chapter 4. Like popular urbanization, the term urban popular economy originally emerged from Latin America, in response to the economic crises following neoliberal reforms affecting cities in the late 20th and early 21st centuries (Gago, 2018). It refers to economic practices by the urban majority, defined as a highly diverse, mobile and heterogeneous group who bear 'the structural onus of having to make "their own way" in urban life' (Benjamin et al, 2022: 335). Practices associated with urban popular economies are considered to 'cross the boundaries between the formal and the informal, subsistence and accumulation, communal and profit calculations, and also those borders that are drawn between multiple scales and national boundaries' (Gago et al, 2018: 11). An example of such practices was introduced in Chapter 8, where we discussed how Indigenous Aymara traders, organizing around Indigenous communal and family ties, have developed trading relations with family-run businesses operating in the Chinese International Trade City of Yiwu to make bulk orders of goods which they subsequently sell on El Alto's Feria 16 de Julio – Latin America's largest informal street market (see also Tassi et al, 2012; Tassi, 2017).

A network of researchers affiliated with the Urban Popular Economies Collective[6] has further developed the notion of urban popular economies by applying it to distinct geopolitical contexts situated mainly, though not exclusively, within the global South. Benjamin et al (2022: 333) define 'urban popular economies to be platforms of alternative value creation where economic practices, forms of livelihoods, behavioural tactics, and strategies of connection, extension, and expansion coalesce to produce liveable territories for the urban majority', emphasizing practices that 'entail value creation beyond the strict economic sense of jobs or other income-generating activities, to include ways people care for each other, share resources, and capitalize on each other's connections to operate cities together'. From this perspective, urban popular economies tend to transcend formal–informal dualisms; additionally, while recognizing the importance of collective action, collective life may not always be formed around principles of solidarity (as emphasized by SSE research), but around hustling and other practices requiring 'mutual resourcefulness and shared opportunity' (Benjamin et al, 2022: 337). To illustrate this, the Urban Popular Economy Collective outlines the business tactics of clusters of electronics shops in Mumbai and Delhi, where hundreds of shops situated next to each other are connected by an internal telecoms system. Proximity and connectivity reduce the need for individual shops to maintain expensive inventories and, instead, shops often display empty boxes without having goods in stock. When a customer wants to purchase a product, shop-owners call nearby shops via the telecoms system to obtain the item for a marginal cut.

In short, then, an urban popular economy perspective highlights the practices of the urban majority as highly diverse, intersecting and situated in-between multiple domains such as formal/informal, individual/collective, market/non-market and socio-economic/politico-cultural, leading to variegated outcomes as some stakeholders promote social cohesion, solidarity and anti-capitalist alternatives, and others undermine such trends.

Governing informally: citizenship and infrastructure

In terms of governing informally, recent debates making more explicit links between the built environment and citizenship have explored 'the mutual relationship between the struggle for political inclusion and processes of informal urbanization' (Rocco and van Ballegooijen, 2018: 1), as cities increasingly become more significant than nation states for political struggles and processes (Purcell, 2003). Building on work by Holston (2008) on differentiated citizenship and Chatterjee (2004) on political and civil society (as discussed in Chapter 5), and debates around the Right to the City[7] (Lefebvre, 1996 [1967]; Harvey, 2008), which question the notion of citizenship in the context of widespread informality and inequality, Rocco and van Ballegooijen (2018) interrogate the political meaning of urban informality. They see the contextual conditions of people living and working informally as deriving from a lack of positive rights (for example, to land, housing and services), which can be taken as a measure of (lack of) democracy in a given context. In other words, '[i]nformal urbanization ... is the spatial expression of exclusion from citizenship' (Rocco and van Ballegooijen, 2018: 9), and people's efforts to provide themselves with housing and livelihoods through informal practices represent their political claims on the state for citizenship rights.

This resonates with other recent work which uses informality as a prism to understand state–society relations, in particular Lemanski's (2019) 'infrastructural citizenship' approach to understanding the connections between public infrastructure and citizenship, especially in contexts of spatial and economic marginalization. This approach highlights citizen-led practices to secure infrastructure provision (discussed in Chapter 6), while also understanding access to infrastructure as a citizenship issue (Lemanski, 2019: 2). Lemanski argues, however, for understanding the entanglement of infrastructure and citizenship claims through an everyday lens, rather than through episodic confrontations. This resonates with the notion of 'people as infrastructure', proposed in Simone's (2004a: 407–8) study of Johannesburg exploring 'economic collaboration among residents seemingly marginalized from and immiserated by urban life', who combine available resources, relationships, spaces and objects into specific yet contingent configurations offering 'a platform providing for and reproducing life in the city'. This idea is further developed in McFarlane and Silver's (2017) conceptualization of social infrastructure as the 'socio-material relations that sustain urban life', forged by ordinary urban residents in the absence or selective provision of infrastructure by the state. These accounts emphasize the agency of individuals in informal service provision processes, but also draw attention to the role of the state, if only through its deficiencies. The focus on citizenship highlights the governance dimension of informality, and its relevance for living and working informally, showing again how these categorizations do not always map neatly onto the messy complexity of everyday urban life.

The foregoing discussion gives some sense of emerging conceptual alternatives, which address critiques of urban informality as imprecise, over-generalized or theoretically marginalized. Nevertheless, while alternative conceptualizations are often inspiring and stimulating they entail, perhaps, the risk of over-abstraction, eclipsing the empirical phenomena which they purport to illuminate; in other words, of only seeing the 'slum as theory', as Rao (2006) puts it. Mabin (2014: 28) asks whether current theories are 'more opaque than helpful', suggesting that 'Southern theory' falls short of its claims both theoretically, as it does not deliver on the innovation it promises, but also empirically, as it fails to offer 'profound and substantial research on what is going on' in urban contexts.

Amid calls to theorize or learn from the South, we should therefore also retain a focus on practice, as well as a sense of space and time (and indeed of place). It is critical to acknowledge that the South is located in 'cities where the majority holds political, economic, spatial and ecological vulnerability' (Bhan, 2019: 643), suggesting the imperative to use theory to inform responses to these conditions. Indeed, Bhan (2019) suggests that the value of theorizing from the South cannot be separated from the need to formulate a 'Southern urban practice'. It may be, then, that the practical value of these theories is in their illumination of processes which, properly valued and supported, could inform rather than disrupt planning practice in these contexts and beyond (Guma, 2021). Building on these ideas, we discuss new developments in policy and practice in the next section.

New policy and practice approaches to informality

In this section, we engage with recent policy and practice approaches to informality that, rather than attempting to ignore, formalize, get beyond or deny it, recognize and engage with it frontally. We focus first on the NUA and its framing within wider development debates, as an example of 'top-down' or state-led initiatives, before examining two citizen-led initiatives with the potential for approaching informality differently at the city scale and beyond, as examples of urban reform coalitions.

State-led initiatives: the New Urban Agenda

The NUA 'sets out the goals for urban sustainable development within the UN's overall 2030 development framework' (Garschagen and Porter, 2018: 117), the 2030 Agenda for Sustainable Development, mentioned in Chapter 2. The NUA was the result of two years of meetings and discussions between United Nations (UN) member states and relevant organizations and agencies, including UN-Habitat (which led the process), intergovernmental organizations such as the World Bank, United Cities and Local Governments, and Cities Alliance, policy experts, local governments and civil society groups. As part of the process, 22 issue papers were written, including one on the 'informal [economic] sector' and one on 'informal settlements'.[8] The NUA was discussed and adopted at the Habitat III conference in Quito in October 2016 and endorsed by UN member states at a General Assembly in December 2016. It is a non-binding document which 'lays out standards and principles for the planning, construction, development, management, and improvement of urban areas' (United Nations, 2017: iv), expressed in a declaration of principles followed by an implementation plan. At its heart are three transformative commitments, relating to social inclusion and ending poverty; inclusive urban prosperity and opportunities; and environmental sustainability and resilience.

The NUA is part of the suite of agreements that make up the post-2015 development agenda, signalling the replacement of the Millennium Development Goals by the Sustainable Development Goals (SDGs). It aims to contribute to the implementation of the post-2015 agenda and the SDGs, particularly SDG 11, which seeks to make cities inclusive, safe and resilient (see Chapter 2). The 2030 Agenda for Sustainable Development is notable for its global approach, part of a wider 'universalisation' of development theory and practice beyond a limited concern with 'developing countries' in the global South (Horner and Hulme, 2017: 3). This is reflected in the SDGs' inclusive approach to global development, in recognition of 'the critical need for multi-directional learning' beyond dichotomies of developed/developing or global North/South, bolstered by the COVID-19 pandemic (Oldekop et al, 2020: 2) and growing recognition that inequality *within* countries may be as significant as inequality *between* them (Horner and Hulme, 2017).

The NUA represents an important urban element of these discussions, and its provisions apply to cities globally. It suggests that 'if well-planned and well-managed, urbanization can be a powerful tool for sustainable development for both developing and developed countries' (UN, 2017: iv). Nevertheless, its particular concern with 'different dimensions of sustainable development such as sanitation, housing, health, income generation or ecological quality' (Garschagen and Porter, 2018: 117) suggests its relevance in contexts where these aspects are deficient, particularly cities where urban informality is prevalent. During the development of the NUA, researchers argued for it to recognize the significance of urban informality in relation to diverse urban areas and actors around the world (Alfaro d'Alencon et al, 2018).

The NUA does incorporate a significant focus on urban informality, acknowledging the significance of 'slum and informal-settlement dwellers' (UN, 2017: 3), the need to support the 'social production of habitat' (UN, 2017: 12), and a commitment to recognize 'the contribution of the working poor in the informal economy' (UN, 2017: 12). Assessing this, Fraser (2018: 124) argues that the NUA's focus on informal neighbourhoods and work reflects 'shifts in intellectual thinking around urban informality ... away from conceptions of dysfunction and survivalism to a recognition of how informal systems work alongside and within formal systems' (as discussed in earlier chapters). This includes 'explicit reference to policies to prevent eviction and support for multiple forms of land and housing development', such as rental, alternative tenure and self-help housing, underpinned by co-produced data collected with urban residents (Fraser, 2018). This is in line with earlier Habitat conferences that sought to incorporate bottom-up perspectives while still emphasizing the role of planning in regulating urban space, as discussed in Chapter 6.

The NUA represents a milestone in terms of top-down recognition of the need for urban sustainability (Garschagen and Porter, 2018: 118). Innovative components include its focus on inclusive urbanization and recognition of city governments' role in enacting this through improved planning practice, accompanied by commitments from civil society and the private sector (Garschagen and Porter, 2018). However, the NUA has been critiqued for its lack of ambition in addressing the symptoms rather than causes of urban inequality, and its overburdening of local policy actors, suggesting it is unlikely to achieve its aims while the 'global political economy of development and the wider architecture for its financing remain unchanged' (Garschagen and Porter, 2018: 119). Moreover, it was launched against a backdrop of still unfulfilled 'old' urban agendas, including universal provision of adequate water and sanitation, and large-scale settlement upgrading (Satterthwaite, 2016: 4). In practice, 'dispossession, stigmatisation and denial too often characterise "formal" responses to "informal" systems', such as violent evictions of informal settlement residents in Lagos in 2016 and 2017 (Fraser, 2018: 124).

This suggests that the NUA must engage with the politics of informality (Fraser, 2018), or risk limiting its influence, as in the case of the previous Habitat agendas. As Satterthwaite (2018: 122) puts it, '[t]he power of non-binding commitments are in the scale and range of those who buy-in to them and act on them'. In this respect, the NUA's inattention to the role of urban government is problematic, given the importance of engagement at this level, particularly with regard to urban informality. In this respect, more consideration should be given to the support needed by urban governments to implement the NUA and the SDGs, alongside recognition that civil society and particularly grassroots organizations should be involved (Satterthwaite, 2018).

There has been limited systematic evaluation of the NUA's achievements so far. In 2022 a meeting of the UN General Assembly assessed progress on implementation, discussing a quadrennial (four-yearly) report which suggested some progress in meeting objectives, although also obstacles including the effects of the COVID-19 pandemic, and governance issues, particularly relating to the capacity and coordination of local governments, the strength of planning systems, and financing (UN General Assembly, 2022). A summary of national reports due to be submitted in March 2021 showed that only 40 out of 193 member states had submitted them.[9]

This suggests the ongoing significance of citizen-led initiatives, to which we now turn. We look at an example of South–North learning that draws on the experiences of Shack/Slum Dwellers International (SDI), discussed in the previous chapter, and in particular, the idea that communities must be central to responses to informal circumstances – which in the global North are often termed 'precarious' (Lombard, 2023).

Citizen-led responses: urban reform coalitions
Community Savers and Community-Led Action and Savings Support

Community Savers is a UK-based network of women-led neighbourhood and community groups that brings residents together 'to share ideas, experiences and strategies for addressing poverty and inequality in our neighbourhoods, towns and cities'.[10] Community Savers draws on the approaches outlined in Chapter 6, relating to citizen-led responses to informality. It is an example of South–North learning, as it has learned from the women-led approach of the international social movement SDI. Community Savers was founded in 2018 in Manchester, and currently has eight affiliates (CLASS/Community Savers, 2022). Affiliates are majority women-led independent organizations embedded in specific neighbourhoods whose members are neighbourhood residents. Their committee members, who are usually community leaders in some way (whether formally or informally recognized), form the Community Savers network leadership. The network works in alliance with and is supported by a separate professional organization called Community-Led Action and Savings Support (CLASS),[11] emulating the approach of SDI affiliates which comprise alliances between community federations and technical support non-government organizations (NGOs). The affiliates in the network are independent and work together on issues that they define as important in their neighbourhoods and cities.

There are several core components of the approach taken by Community Savers. It is based on organizing around savings as a regular practice, and it is women-led. It is grounded in processes of dialogue and learning exchange around experiences and strategies, with the aspiration over time to increase collective voice on city-wide and national policy (for example, through the establishment of a new coalition in Manchester campaigning for increased enforcement of developer obligations for social housing). It centres community-led consultation, data gathering and neighbourhood profiling to establish collective priorities of low-income urban residents within and across neighbourhood borders (for example, exploring neighbourhood losses and gains over time; evaluating gaps in provision, facilities and infrastructure against need and demographics; identifying public land where projects could be developed or green space could be saved/protected). Finally, it seeks the development of co-production projects and partnerships that can change internal cultures of practice; transform social power relations (such as citizen/state; tenant/landlord; and constituent/representative) and attract investment into community priorities for housing, services and infrastructure.

The practice of savings is central to many neighbourhood groups, as it can be a means of bringing people together, whether through an informal group of women who know each other, or an existing group that wants to try a new idea (CLASS/GM Savers, 2020). Weekly savings meetings allow women to pool resources and build trust alongside financial resilience. Coming together for this regular practice catalyses new perspectives on collective finance. Income generation and solidarity economy ideas develop, such as markets and food cooperatives which can create mutual benefit for members or generate income for community benefit, for example, using the turnover from market stall rental to take disadvantaged families on day trips and weekends away. This draws on practices of women-led savings in informal settlements across the global South, where the regular practice of savings builds trust through regular meetings (CLASS/GM Savers, 2020). The approach often appeals to women who frequently manage household finances and are often also involved in community activities, but may be less involved in formal decision-making processes locally due to gender-based barriers.

Together these processes enable place-based groups to come together and think about what is needed in their neighbourhood, as well as identifying what already exists. Groups are supported by regular learning exchanges with other groups, which enable them to share experiences and generate ideas. This has provided groups with a sense of 're-discovering community and re-igniting a belief that change is possible through collective action' (CLASS/Community Savers, 2022: 28). It has also generated neighbourhood- and city-wide networks with the capacity to form alliances with professionals and agencies in local authorities and other organizations, in support of achieving their aims, such as improving community involvement in neighbourhood planning, and securing better provision of social housing. As well as direct effects in the neighbourhoods where groups operate, the movement also seeks transformative change at the city and regional level, including partnerships with local and national public agencies, and through joint advocacy on urban challenges which affect cities around the world.

Drawing on the SDI model, exchanges may also be international, as well as taking place at the city or regional scale. The network originated with ideas that first began circulating in Greater Manchester after a series of exchanges between women's groups and South African and Kenyan activists associated with SDI (CLASS/GM Savers, 2020). The network has benefited throughout its existence from international exchanges with SDI affiliates, in person (in the UK) and online, but also through visiting groups in South Africa and Kenya. For example, in November 2022 eight leaders from Sheffield and Manchester visited Muungano Wa Wanavijiji[12] in Nairobi for an international learning visit, in order to share experiences and strategies (see Figure 8.3). As the testimony included at the start of the chapter highlights, seeing what can be achieved in Southern contexts can be inspiring for communities from places like the UK. The identification with established processes that have originated from and been proven to work in the global South results in 'renewed motivation for collective action' among UK-based groups (CLASS/Community Savers, 2022).

Figure 8.3: Members of Mum's Mart savings group from Wythenshawe, Manchester, UK, visiting the Ladies of Hope group in Mukuru, Nairobi, Kenya

Source: CLASS/Community Savers (2022)

Community Savers can therefore be seen as an example of South–North learning, through sharing different activist and public knowledges, beyond academic knowledge, in pursuit of more diverse urban imaginaries (McFarlane, 2010b).

The approaches pursued by the social movements discussed here also resonate with Mitlin's (2023) conceptualization of 'urban reform coalitions', which seeks to capture urban social movements' attempts to address urban issues at scale via resource redistribution. Urban reform coalitions are understood as 'groups of diverse stakeholders (potentially involving civil society, state agencies, private enterprises) who perceive benefits in coming together (for varying lengths of time) to achieve common goals' (Mitlin, 2023: 3), usually in pursuit of pro-poor reforms. As well as a concern for those living and working informally, such coalitions may include informal activities and relations, in an example of governing informally, and may also incorporate informal groups (such as informal vendors' networks). Mitlin (2023) acknowledges that while reform coalitions both emulate and seek to engage with the strategies of the private sector, this is often the hardest set of actors to engage with, and this is suggested by the examples here, of social movements which have predominantly sought alliances with the local state. Nevertheless, the concept is helpful for its potential to capture the work of such movements beyond their immediate constituencies, in an attempt to bring about longer-term change.

Box 8.1 offers another illustrative example of a citizen-led approach from the global South, which seeks transformative change at different scales, presenting the case of Catalytic Communities, a Rio-based NGO.

Box 8.1: Working with social leaders in Rio de Janeiro, Brazil: a conversation with Theresa Williamson, Catalytic Communities

Catalytic Communities is an NGO working with *favelas* in Rio de Janeiro. Its director, Theresa Williamson, shared insights into the organization's innovative approach to urban informality.

CatComm was established in 2000. After two years of doing local needs research, the NGO set up a community centre in 2002 in central Rio offering a space for *favela* leaders "to meet, to use the Internet before it was available, to develop projects, to do workshops, and it was all peer-to-peer organizing". Its work with Rio's *favelas* addresses the challenges of daily life such as access to adequate education, healthcare and sanitation, compounded by threats of eviction and displacement, particularly in the build-up to the Rio Olympics in 2016, and risks associated with armed actors' presence, particularly the police as well as militias and drug gangs.

Theresa explained that "the work of Catalytic Communities isn't directly with residents that are living their daily lives as individuals and families, it's with local organizers who are working on behalf of those residents, with those residents, in support of those residents". CatComm's four current programmes, "developed in response to community needs, co-created with community organizers", are *RioOnWatch*, a bilingual Portuguese/English community news reporting platform; the Sustainable Favela Network, "a network of hundreds of socio-environmental organizers across *favelas*, doing everything from solar panels to community museums, environmental education to biodigesters for sewage"; the Favela Community Land Trust Project, which applies this land tenure model to *favelas* (explored later in this box); and the Favelas Unified Dashboard, a citizen science research programme where communities collect their own data, from COVID-19 to water and energy.

The organization deploys an Asset-Based Community Development framework, founded on:

> '[A] basic understanding that *favelas* are in their essence solutions factories, beginning with addressing the need for shelter but expanding to all other areas, in the context of historic marginalization. The result is, despite their many challenges, an enormous variety of assets that they've built. ... So our focus is: how do we build on those? How do we address the deficiencies and challenges of informality without denying the qualities that it can bring to planning and to urban design?'

Informality is understood not in terms of a lack of formality, but through its own characteristics which can be valued (see Figure 8.4).

CatComm's approach acknowledges the complexity of informality alongside the authority of residents:

> 'Our work is founded on this understanding that informal settlements, *favelas*, are incredibly complex. And informal development brings both qualities and limitations. The only people who are really in a position to judge are the residents: the people who produce those qualities. They're the ones who know the value of those to them. And any sort of outside-in influence needs to be incredibly cognizant of that and careful not to dismantle those qualities under this guise of "We're solving the problem of informality" because, of course, there are problems associated with it as well.'

CatComm's work during the gentrification and displacement processes that accompanied the 2016 Rio Olympics led to the realization that:

> 'There's a hundred-year history, resulting from Brazil's unaddressed, dark history as the world's largest slave-holding country, of building a public sentiment that these communities shouldn't exist in the first place and therefore shouldn't exist now; that they're places of crime, that they're places of poverty, and that they'd be better off if everyone was moved to public housing. And so coming from this mindset, the public policies, whether it was the evictions, even in some cases with relocations to public housing, led to worse off outcomes as compared with their *favelas* of origin, in some cases by far. I mean, we saw people that I would say were pushed back 30 years in their family's development in that period.'

The processes of displacement, underpinned by disregard for communities and stigmatizing discourses led to the *RioOnWatch* project, which funds community journalists from *favelas* who present a more nuanced narrative about their neighbourhoods directly to a local and international audience. Communities have also been bolstered by social media which gives them a direct public voice. Such shifts are "critical for them to represent themselves. ... It has to come from the

Figure 8.4: 'Two different ways of life' from *How to Plan for Informality: The Experience of Catalytic Communities*

Two Different Ways of Life

'Informal' is not the absence of the 'formal'

When we choose one we must be aware of the qualities we are giving up.

Logic of the 'formal city'

- Regulation limits complexity
- Financial or bureaucratic barriers to entry
- Centralized or status-based master planning
- Pre-set architectural typologies
- Services and exchanges monetized
- 'Logic of privacy;' individual interests dominate
- Formal fixes, high tech approaches
- Market and state as coordinators (Abramo)
- Exchanges made through formal, regulated (and taxed) market logic

Logic of the 'informal city'

- Lack of regulation leads to increasing complexity
- Barriers can be removed through relationships
- Adaptive, iterative planning; urbanistic freedom
- Flexible architectural topologies adapted to territory
- Many necessary services demonetized and provided through mutual support/self-build (child care, water)
- 'Logic of proximity;' strong solidarity networks, sense of community; high degree of collective action
- Creative responses to challenges; 'hacks'
- Necessity and market as coordinators
- Pure market logic: 'Purest invisible hand' (at times more affordable; at others higher prices)

Source: Williamson (2021)

community first, it has to come from *favelas*, seeing their own value and recognizing their own role in the city and then standing up and pushing that message forward".

In order to address the challenges of informality while retaining its qualities, CatComm is piloting a community land trust model whereby land is owned and managed by a non-profit residents' association, which grants surface rights (rather than land titles) to residents, while the land remains in community ownership, giving them more control over neighbourhood development. As Theresa explained:

> 'The Community Land Trust is an opportunity to actually formalize *favelas* in a way that allows for their qualities to be maintained. So residents maintain and build on their collective history, neighbourhoods maintain their affordable nature, and they are developed according to resident priorities without displacement. A Community Land Trust can value and preserve what's on that land, the culture that's produced there. Residents create a non-profit that owns the land and fights for development that respects the community's history. So it allows them to formalize but not lose the qualities they built informally.'

This may also be supported by carefully planning the order of investments in *favelas* earmarked for formalization, starting with health, education and sanitation to reflect residents' priorities, and in order to 'allow people to grow economically so that they can pay and partake in the formalization', rather than being priced out as often happens.

The two examples provided here, in which organizations support leaders to make change at neighbourhood and city scale, including through negotiating with local authorities, illustrate the significance of urban reform coalitions in diverse contexts to support policy and practice addressing informality's challenges, while retaining the centrality of residents' voices, and focusing on addressing their priorities. In the next section, we explore this issue considering the ethics of engaging with informality as researchers and students in this field, focusing particularly on methodological and ethical considerations for researchers interested in urban informality, who may become the built environment professionals of tomorrow, charged with addressing these issues.

Engaging with informality

Throughout this book we have attempted to show that there are different ways of knowing urban informality (and urban phenomena more generally), that go beyond academic texts and accounts. For this reason, we have engaged with novels such as *A Fine Balance* (see Chapters 1 and 4), film representations such as *Roma* (see Chapter 4) and interview testimonies such as the one by Theresa Williamson in the above section, in order to suggest the significance of diverse representations of living, working and governing informally. There are many more fictional accounts that support this, such as those presented in Box 8.2, alongside accounts that 'cross over' between academic and journalistic or fictional approaches, such as Neuwirth's (2005) *Shadow Cities* and

Saunders' (2011) *Arrival City*. At the end of each chapter, we provide a list of alternative representations of informality, beyond the recommended academic readings, which will hopefully enrich and diversify your understanding of these phenomena. Yet while we strongly encourage you to engage with these secondary sources in order to know urban informality, we are aware that some of you may be planning or already engaging in primary research on urban informality, which involves gathering data for your own project (perhaps a dissertation or PhD). In this section, we therefore discuss some methodological and ethical considerations for engaging with informality, returning to the question of how we as researchers know urban informality.

Box 8.2: Representations of informality in fiction

Elizabeth Gaskell on Manchester, from *Mary Barton* (2011 [1848])

So they went along till they arrived in Berry Street. It was unpaved; and down the middle a gutter forced its way, every now and then forming pools in the holes with which the street abounded. ... As they passed, women from their doors tossed household slops of every description into the gutter; they ran into the next pool which overflowed and stagnated. Heaps of ashes were the stepping-stones, on which the passer-by, who cared in the least for cleanliness, took care not to put his foot. ... You went down one step ... into the cellar in which a family of human beings lived. It was very dark inside. The window-panes were, many of them, broken and stuffed with rags, which was reason enough for the dusky light that pervaded the place even at mid-day. After the account I have given of the state of the street, no one can be surprised that on going into the cellar ... the smell was so fœtid as almost to knock the two men down. Quickly recovering themselves, as those inured to such things do, they began to penetrate the thick darkness of the place, and to see three or four little children rolling on the damp, nay wet, brick floor, through which the stagnant, filthy moisture of the street oozed up; the fire-place was empty and black; the wife sat on her husband's lair, and cried in the dank loneliness. (Gaskell, 2011 [1848]: 71–2)

Upton Sinclair on Chicago, from *The Jungle* (2003 [1906])

Here was a population, low-class and mostly foreign, hanging always on the verge of starvation, and dependent for its opportunities of life upon the whim of men every bit as brutal and unscrupulous as the old-time slave-drivers; under such circumstances immorality was exactly as inevitable, and as prevalent, as it was under the system of chattel slavery. Things that were quite unspeakable went on there in the packing-houses all the time, and were taken for granted by everybody; only they did not show, as in the old slavery times, because there was no difference in colour between master and slave. (Sinclair, 2003 [1906]: 104)

Past endless blocks of two-story shanties he walked, along wooden sidewalks and unpaved pathways treacherous with deep slush-holes. Every few blocks there would be a railroad crossing on the level with the sidewalk, a death-trap for the unwary; long freight-trains would be passing, the cars clanking and crashing together. (Sinclair, 2003 [1906]: 167)

Patrick Chamoiseau describing Texaco, a fictional informal neighbourhood outside Fort-de-France, Martinique, from *Texaco* (1998)

The Western urban planner sees Texaco as a tumor on the urban order. Incoherent. Insalubrious. A dynamic contestation. A threat. It is denied any architectural or social value. Political discourse negates it. In other words, it is a problem. ... But to raze it is to send the problem elsewhere or worse: not to consider it. No, we must dismiss the West and re-learn to read: learn to re-invent the city. (Chamoiseau, 1998: 269)

While listening to the Lady, I suddenly got the feeling that in this entanglement, in this whole poetics of hutches devoted to the wish to live, nothing in Texaco was going against the grain of the city to such an extent as to make that site some sort of aberration. (Chamoiseau, 1998: 244)

Gregory David Roberts on Mumbai in *Shantaram* (2004)

Like brown and black dunes, the acres of slums rolled away from the roadside, and met the horizon with dirty heat-haze mirages. The miserable shelters were patched together from rags, scraps of plastic and paper, reed mats, and bamboo sticks. They slumped together, attached one to another, and with narrow lanes winding between them. Nothing in the enormous sprawl of it rose much above the height of a man.

It seemed impossible that a modern airport, full of prosperous and purposeful travellers, was only kilometres away from those crushed and cindered dreams. My first impression was that some catastrophe had taken place, and that the slums were refugee camps for the shambling survivors. I learned, months later, that they were survivors, of course, those slum-dwellers: the catastrophes that had driven them to the slums from their villages were poverty, famine, and bloodshed. And five thousand new survivors arrived in the city every week, week after week, year after year. (Roberts, 2004: 7)

Methodological considerations for researching informality

Given the ever-changing nature of informal urban growth and underlying processes, recent research suggests the importance of considering temporal dimensions of informality. Caldeira (2016) argues that a longitudinal perspective is important, and there is a growing body of longitudinal research by researchers who have engaged with this field over several decades. Notable examples include Janice Perlman's 2010 study of Rio de Janeiro, *Favela*, where she revisits the communities with whom she engaged for her groundbreaking study on the 'myth of marginality' (Perlman, 1976), discussed in Chapter 2. Similarly, Caroline Moser's (2009) book *Ordinary Families, Extraordinary Lives* traces the trajectories of households from a single settlement in Guayaquil, Ecuador over a generation, exploring the factors that facilitated or impeded social mobility. In some cases, other researchers have followed up earlier groundbreaking studies, such as the 2018 film *City Unfinished – Voices of El Ermitaño*, which traced some of the families involved in Turner's 1965 film *A Roof of One's Own* (see Chapter 2). Such approaches require a long-term engagement with communities, which may be less possible to students or researchers starting out their careers, and are usually confined to small studies (focusing on a handful of neighbourhoods at most) for practical reasons.

These approaches are particularly important given deficiencies in national data indices, which are often very broad, lacking detail at the neighbourhood scale (Samper et al, 2020). At the same time, large data sets can play a role in knowing urban informality; for example, monitoring progress towards the targets of the NUA and SDGs (Acuto and Parnell, 2016). Understanding the complexity of cities (and specifically informality) may necessitate approaches that are spatial rather than simply statistical, underlining the importance of geographic information system (GIS) methodologies (Acuto and Parnell, 2016). Emerging digital and GIS technologies hold the potential to know informality in new ways, including remote sensing (Brenner and Schmid, 2014) and urban land cover data (Angel, 2012).

For example, Connolly (2020) developed a methodology to measure the scale of informal neighbourhoods in Mexico City, using digital cartographic information cross-referenced with observation and field study. This relies on identifying a specific 'settlement type' associated with informality, using census and other data, such as date of urbanization, classification (as regular or not), density and socio-economic status of residents, to identify and map informal neighbourhoods (Connolly, 2020). Meanwhile, design-based approaches have used the spatial morphology of informal settlements to map informality at a global scale, seen in recent publications such as the *Atlas of Informal Settlement* (Dovey et al, 2023) and the *Atlas of Informality*, which aims to 'identify a standard global sample of informal neighbourhoods' (Samper et al, 2020: 1) by combining remote sensing data with urban morphology.

The increasing accessibility of digital mapping technologies, such as Google Maps, can be harnessed to understand informality; but it is important to be aware of how data is produced and used. For example, the project *Ta no Mapa*, a collaborative initiative between Google and a local NGO, claimed to map Rio de Janeiro's *favelas* for the purpose of inclusive citizenship; however, its focus mainly on businesses in 'pacified' *favelas* belied its objectives 'to re-define social exclusion as economic exclusion and incorporate spatial value' (Luque-Ayala and Neves Maia, 2019: 462). This contrasts sharply with participatory mapping, discussed in Chapter 6, a methodology that has been associated with SDI. In this approach, residents use available technology (such as handheld digital plotting devices) alongside traditional techniques (such as transect walks) to map their own settlements and generate data for their own purposes. This often occurs alongside enumeration through surveys, again owned by residents who define the questions, sampling strategy and how the information is used.

Finally, approaches to the everyday nature of urban informality are increasingly salient, often based on ethnographic methods (Elsheshtawy, 2011). For example, van Blerk et al (2023) applied a longitudinal ethnographic approach over three years to explore the micro-geographies of young people living and working informally in Accra, Bukavu and Harare, producing a richly detailed understanding of daily life in these circumstances. Ethnographic approaches are often increasingly used in combination with visual methods, as shown in Guma's (2021) account of 'shacks, shanties and micro-stalls', which offers a deep understanding of daily life in Kibera, enriched by photographic evidence. Auto-photography is also employed as a participatory method to understand people's living and working informally (Lombard, 2013; see also Figure 8.5). More recently, creative methods such as graphic novels and comics have been used to further understandings of how people live in informal contexts, including how they are affected by and respond to climate change (Sou et al, 2022).

Ethical considerations for researching informality

There exists lots of research ethics guidance for students embarking on social science research 'in the field', which for studies of urban informality often means research overseas, in a 'development' context, frequently in the global South. Such texts counsel students to maintain an awareness of cultural difference encompassing aspects of power, identity and language (Apentiik and Parpart, 2006). Basic research ethics require informed consent, transparency about objectives, and honesty about the benefits for respondents (Brydon, 2006). This may include consideration of whether

Figure 8.5: Photo of neighbourhood school taken by resident in Xalapa, Mexico

Source: Azucena Jiménez

to pay participants, an approach which is commonplace in medical research but less so in social research. Payment may raise issues such as incentivization, compromising consent, and issues of exploitation or increasing vulnerability (Head, 2009); however, it is increasingly recognized that communities should be compensated in some way for their expertise in research.

You are probably aware that it is important to reflect on our positionality as researchers. By positionality we mean aspects of our identity and context that we bring to the research experience, such as our ethnicity or race, gender, age and class, but also considerations such as our academic or professional background. These aspects may represent difference with regard to our research respondents, particularly in contexts of doing research overseas. At the same time, researchers should pay attention to issues of cross-cultural research which may arise in their home country as well as abroad (Smith, 2003). Whatever the context, issues of vulnerability, difference and positionality may arise, and researchers must remember that 'what enriches you may rob and violate others' (Nash, 2000 in Smith, 2003: 181). While sensitivity to positionality can help, it is also worth remembering that 'we can never not work with "others" who are separate and different from ourselves; difference is an essential aspect of all social interactions that requires that we are always everywhere in between or negotiating the worlds of me and not-me' (Nast, 1994: 57 in Smith, 2003: 188–9). This suggests that an awareness of our multiple positionalities as researchers may be necessary to deal with 'the politics of integration', in other words how to bridge the gap between the role of 'detached researcher' and active involvement with the research community; the solution for this may be a collaborative position where practical and flexible relations of solidarity are constructed through dialogue and struggle (Fuller, 1999).

The field of informality is particularly significant for built environment professionals, as planners (and other related professions) are often charged with responding to the 'problem' of informal living, working and governing. This relates to the question of ethics in planning, which has been addressed by scholars such as Campbell (2002) in the global North, and taken up by scholars such as Watson (2003) to explore how planning theory and ethics apply in contexts where 'modern' Western rationalities are confronted with conflicting versions of reality, or diverse contexts and subjectivities affect action and ethics (Winkler, 2018). Katherine Rankin suggests that planning as a discipline and practice must seek to recognize agency and resistance among the 'beneficiaries' of planning action, alongside the subjectivity of planners, and the conditions for collective action; this is particularly significant for planning students 'struggling to reconcile their commitment to do good in the world … [with] the complicity of planning action in imperialism, colonialism, neoliberalism, racism and other hegemonic projects' (Rankin, 2010: 182).

In order to avoid reproducing the practices of the past, future built environment researchers and practitioners must formulate their own ethics of practice and knowledge production, encompassing both postcolonial critique and a 'reflexive relationality' (Rankin, 2010). The poem by Arif Hasan (Box 8.3) is suggestive of some of the ethically difficult situations that professionals in the sphere of urban development may have to address.

Box 8.3: 'Development' by Arif Hasan

We play games
You and I and they
Play at reconciling what is irreconcilable
Agreeing on irrelevant details and grand concepts
But glossing over love and understanding
That the concepts embody
We play games
You and I and they
To preserve our little domains
And prevent them from blossoming
Into flowers that will free the world
Of you and I and they
We play games
You to survive and I to negotiate your survival
And they to plunder us both.
Karachi, February 1989

Source: Available from: http://arifhasan.com [Accessed 16 November 2023]

Planning research and practice has attempted to address these issues through adopting participatory methods. Deriving from the work of Freire on critical pedagogy and Fals Borda on participatory action research in the 1960s and 1970s, participatory research approaches emphasize methods that allow the researched to become active participants in the research. Participatory action research emerged from the ineffectiveness of top-down, externally designed and undertaken research and planning methods (Mansuri and Rao, 2013). Chambers (1983) was among the first to apply these methods in development research, proposing an approach known as participatory rural appraisal, which advocated increased participation by the rural poor, through reversals in learning and involving rural people as partners in research. This was later taken up in urban research, for example, through participatory urban appraisal approaches (Moser and McIlwaine, 1999). Bridging the gap between development research and practice, participatory techniques sought to recognize and include the most marginalized groups. Regardless of context, important elements for participatory research include knowledge of local community structures, existing organizations and hierarchies; awareness of the actors involved; sensitivity to cultures of decision-making; and a commitment to a flexible yet long-term approach (Hamdi, 2010).

Decades of participatory research have engendered critical debates around this, including questions about its effectiveness and potential harms. For example, debates on participatory research and practice in development suggested that participation was not radical but largely cosmetic, as it was 'used as a "hegemonic" device to secure compliance to, and control by, existing power structures' (Taylor, 2001: 137; see also Cooke and Kothari, 2001). Such factors are also emphasized by more recent debates on 'decolonial methodologies', whose advocates call for the decentred production of academic knowledge in order to dismantle historical relationships between knower and known (Smith, 2012).

In response, the potential of co-production has been emphasized. Co-production, discussed in Chapter 6, relates to the involvement of formal (state, other statutory or private) agencies and organizations, and communities and individual citizens, in specific initiatives or processes. It offers the potential for alliances in order to address urban issues, including informality and knowledge produced about this and other urban phenomena. Researchers are increasingly engaging in 'knowledge co-production' to improve urban development outcomes. A 'knowledge co-production' approach recognizes that it is not just academics or policy makers, but also 'citizens and communities [who obtain] knowledge about themselves, their preferences, their environment, and the dynamic interaction between society and the physical and ecological environment' (Castán Broto et al, 2022: 2). Co-production as a research method seeks to 'maintain long-term multi-actor negotiation processes and deliver positive societal outcomes', with emphasis put on 'place-based co-production processes whereby communities are involved in delivering outcomes that benefit them directly' (Castán Broto et al, 2022: 2).

Recent research applying a co-production perspective includes Knowledge in Action for Urban Inequality (KNOW), which between 2018 and 2022 sought to deliver knowledge that advances urban equality goals in six cities (Havana, Lima, Free Town, Kampala, Dar es Salaam, Yogyakarta) characterized by a significant population living and working informally.[13] A key strategy of the project was to generate city-based knowledge, with on-the-ground work led by local partners who involved community-based organizations as central collaborators (Castán Broto et al, 2022). Similarly, the African Cities Research Consortium, a major six-year investment by the United Kingdom's Foreign, Commonwealth and Development Office from 2020 until 2026, deploys a co-production perspective to co-create knowledge and turn research into meaningful action that tackles development challenges such as living and working informally.[14] It does this by supporting urban reform coalitions (introduced in previous sections) and multi-sectoral and multi-stakeholder alliances, with emphasis on the expertise of local residents.

While lauded for bringing ordinary people's concerns into knowledge exchange and decision-making processes, co-productive approaches can also have limitations. Mitlin et al (2020), for example, highlight how power dynamics within co-productive efforts often remain uneven, with resources distributed unfairly between academics and non-academic partners. Tensions also exist between different 'theories of change', with academics often seeking to promote more inclusive urban development through documenting findings from research in papers and policy reports, while organized communities tend to generate knowledge to foster mass mobilization around issues of concern. To overcome some of these tensions, future co-productive research on urban informality should, among other issues, critically interrogate status issues and resource allocation among different knowledge co-producers, reconcile theories of change, and improve accountability mechanisms between researchers and community representatives (Mitlin et al, 2020). Most importantly, they must foreground the voices of those engaged in living, working and governing informally.

Chapter summary

This chapter has explored emerging alternatives to some of the theoretical, policy and practice approaches that we have outlined in previous chapters. It explored questions of terminology within wider urban theory debates that centre informality as part of 'Southern' urban theory, and also examined attempts to transcend the category of informality, building on earlier critiques. What most of these emerging theoretical alternatives have in common – including popular urbanization, collective life and infrastructural citizenship – is an attempt to see from the South, drawing on concepts, contextual conditions and practices associated with Southern cities in their empirical diversity, and to centre people within this, attempting to understand informal processes from the perspective of those engaged in them. We explored recent shifts in responses to informality, examining state-led or top-down approaches through the NUA, and citizen-led processes through two examples of organizations which may be understood as urban reform coalitions. Both examples also make a strong case for recognizing the value of informal processes, for those engaged in them and for the wider city. Finally, we explored methodological and ethical considerations for researchers embarking on studying these phenomena, highlighting that the role of the reflective researcher should be framed within wider collaborative processes and alliances.

Recommended reading

- Bhan, G., Caldeira, T., Gillespie, K. and Simone, A. (2020) 'The pandemic, southern urbanisms and collective life', *Society and Space Magazine*, 3 August. Available from: https://www.societyandspace.org/articles/the-pandemic-southern-urbanisms-and-collective-life [Accessed 19 October 2023].
- Mitlin, D. (2023) 'The contribution of reform coalitions to inclusion and equity: lessons from urban social movements', *Area Development and Policy*, 8(1): 1–26.
- Benjamin, S., Castronovo, A., Cavallero, L., Cielo, C., Gago, V., Guma, P., Gupte, R., Habermehl, V., Salman, L. and Shetty, P. (2022) 'Urban popular economies: territories of operation for lives deemed worth living', *Public Culture*, 34(3): 333–57.

EXERCISES

- Based on the sources discussed in the first part of this chapter, consider whether 'urban informality' should be replaced as a concept, and if so, by what?

- Review the excerpts from novels presented in Box 8.2. What perspective is each author writing from, and how might this affect their interpretation of informality?

Alternative representations

- For fictionalized accounts of informality in different historic and geographic contexts, refer to any of the novels mentioned in Box 8.2.
- Have a look at Sou et al's (2022) *Everyday Stories of Climate Change* for a great example of using visual methods to represent living and working informally, through a comic book showing how communities adapt to climate change.
- For a different way of engaging with the NUA, explore UN-Habitat's *The New Urban Agenda Illustrated Handbook* (https://unhabitat.org/the-new-urban-agenda-illustrated).
- You might also like to engage with the related *New Urban Agenda Crash Course* (https://www.urbanagendaplatform.org/learning) which breaks down the contents of the NUA.

9

Conclusion: For Trans-Local, Multi-Voice Understandings of Urban Informality

Overarching arguments and conceptual framework

We hope that the preceding chapters have deepened your understanding of urban informality, enabling you to think critically about the underlying reasons for why much of the global urban population lives and works informally and engages in and/ or is affected by informal politics (referred to here as governing informally), as well as what can and should be done about this. While this book has covered a wide range of ideas and discussed diverse academic, policy and alternative representations, we have made four main arguments that contribute to and further advance existing scholarship on urban informality. We have introduced these arguments in Chapter 1 and we revisit them here in this concluding chapter.

The first argument is that informality, defined in basic terms as not being formal or official, or being beyond regulatory frameworks, affects us all in one way or the other. We unpacked this argument in Chapter 1 by reflecting on informal practices in our home countries, such as *Vitamin B* in Germany or *pulling strings* in the UK. While not everyone lives or works informally, most of us engage in the purchase and consumption of goods and services that can one way or another be associated with informality. Chapter 4 explored this argument in its discussion of formal–informal economic connections, whether through relationships between formal and informal enterprises (as illustrated through the case study of informal traders in El Alto, Bolivia, who engage with wholesale market enterprises in China, from Tassi et al [2012]), or through interactions in global value chains where different stages of production might be undertaken by formal and/or informal enterprises (as illustrated through the relationship between a home-based informal enterprise in Mumbai and the formal company Au Revoir Express, depicted in Mistry's [1995] novel *A Fine Balance*). Exploring such formal–informal relations is important as it reveals how informality is connected and integrated, though often on adverse terms, within the wider global political economic system and within everyday interactions that involve us all.

Our second argument, which we explored particularly in Chapter 2, is that an urban informality perspective helps to make sense of dynamics such as urban poverty, inequality and exclusion. Indeed, earlier conceptual accounts of urban informality between the 1950s and 1970s emerged out of work on poverty trends in rapidly urbanizing contexts in Africa, Asia and Latin America, with emphasis on the emergence of informal neighbourhoods in contexts where local and national governments were unable or unwilling to meet the demand for housing and services for low-income rural–urban migrants. Researching informal neighbourhoods in Ghana, Hart (1973) observed the emergence of informal sector work within highly unequal urban societies where formal employment opportunities remained limited. Prominent schools of thought developed in this period to make sense of informal neighbourhoods and informal employment offer distinct explanations of underlying reasons for urban informality. Dualists view the emergence of urban informality as a result of exclusion from industrialization and modernization due to rapid population growth in cities and mismatches between people's skills and requirements in new economic sectors (Hart, 1973). Structuralists consider urban informality as a subordinate feature of the global capitalist system that emerges particularly in situations in which states and enterprises favour profit over people, for example, reducing labour costs by cutting social and legal protections (Castells and Portes, 1989). Legalists consider urban informality to be the result of a hostile and exclusionary legal system, leaving low-income populations with no other choice than to live and work informally as bureaucratic procedures to participate in the formal economy are simply too complex (de Soto, 1989). Voluntarists, in contrast, assign responsibility to individuals who live or work informally, portraying them as free riders who avoid paying services, taxes or business registration fees and thereby generate unequal socio-economic relations (Levenson and Maloney, 1998). Despite differences, all these schools of thought share a view of urban informality as the result of wider political and socio-economic relations.

In this book we build on these perspectives while also critically interrogating them, arguing for a relational perspective towards urban informality that is grounded in political economy analysis in order to rethink its relationship with urban inequality and explore its relevance to all social sectors, including the urban poor but also other stakeholders such as elite groups. Building particularly on Banks et al (2020: 223), we suggest that viewing urban informality as a 'site of critical analysis' (in other words, paying attention to what and who is labelled informal under what circumstances) helps us to better understand 'how resources are distributed and power secured and consolidated' in urban settings, across multiple scales and involving diverse actors, including the state. In Chapter 2 and subsequent chapters we also demonstrated that no single conceptual perspective can make sense of urban informality holistically. We therefore propose that future urban informality scholarship draws on conceptual insights from multiple perspectives deriving from distinct social science disciplines, including more recent approaches that treat urban informality as the 'organising logic' of contemporary globalization and liberalization (AlSayyad, 2004: 26), as a form of 'collective opposition' by those excluded or adversely incorporated by globalization

(Boanada-Fuchs and Boanada, 2018), as state (in)action (Harris, 2018) or as a site for theory production mainly, though not exclusively, from the global South (Roy, 2011). Only by drawing together insights from a multiplicity of conceptual perspectives can we make sense of urban informality in all its complexity.

Our third argument, elaborated in Chapters 3 to 8 of the book, is that urban informality is a global issue characterized by a series of shared and interrelated features described here as living, working and governing informally, which must nevertheless be understood and addressed in a context-specific way. Shared features of living informally refer to particular characteristics of land (informally acquired, characterized by insecure tenure and/or residential status), housing (constructed incrementally and/or through self-help, often not complying with official building and planning standards, and characterized by poor structural quality), and services such as water, electricity, sanitation and public infrastructure (provided incrementally through self-help or informal providers and often inadequate in nature) – with each of these factors meriting particular attention and requiring specific responses (Chapters 3 and 6). Common characteristics of working informally – associated with the informal sector, informal employment and the informal economy – refer to economic activities, enterprises, jobs and workers that are neither regulated, nor receive legal or social protections from the state (Chapters 4 and 7). Moving beyond living and working informally, which is widely captured in the existing literature, we add politics to our critical analysis of urban informality. In doing so, we offer a novel and more holistic conceptual approach, which recognizes that informality does not emerge out of a vacuum but almost always derives from deliberate political choices. What we associate here with governing informally refers to informal institutions and practices that stand in contrast to and take place outside formal political channels, though often with the aim of influencing the formal structures and practices of urban politics, socio-economic relations and public life (Chapter 5).

While the distinct features of urban informality (living, working and governing) can be observed in diverse urban settings worldwide, their precise articulations and characteristics vary locally. To make sense of shared and context-specific characteristics we position discussions on urban informality in relation to wider debates around universalism and particularity in contemporary urban studies, highlighted in Chapter 8. A focus on universalism aligns with planetary urbanization approaches, which, departing from a Marxian perspective, emphasize general urbanization trends as a result of global capitalism. This perspective is also in line with structuralist accounts that consider urban informality to be the direct result of changes in the wider capitalist economic system, as outlined previously. Such perspectives help us, for example, to make sense of the rise of 'slums' in the global North as a consequence of capitalist industrialization (Chapter 2); of developments guided by 'world class city' imaginaries in places like Durban, Mumbai or Quito that seek to attract investors while displacing and criminalizing those living and working informally (Chapters 6 and 7); and of efforts to maximize capitalist profit through reducing labour costs via informalization (for example, the removal of social and legal worker protections), seen in the rise of the gig economy and platform urbanism, or in efforts to move production from formal to informal enterprises within global value chains (see Chapter 4).

While useful for identifying shared trends in geographically disparate settings, these accounts are criticized for limiting their analysis to global capitalism's structural and agential forces, overlooking contextual and local particularities and therefore offering only a partial understanding of urban phenomena such as informality (Buckley and Strauss, 2016). As discussed in Chapters 2 and 8, these limitations are acknowledged and addressed by urban theory projects emerging out of specific geopolitical contexts and drawing on postcolonial approaches. These approaches share an aspiration to move beyond purely Marxian political economy analysis, offering a critique of 'Northern' or 'Western' schools of thought, and deconstructing global urban theory by emphasizing the particularities of specific urban settings and processes, with attention to the global South, and processes of South–South and South–North learning (Simone, 2010; McFarlane, 2011; Robinson and Roy, 2016; Watson, 2016). Building on this diverse body of scholarship, in this book we have traced the particularities of urban informality in different geopolitical settings. Among other issues, we have paid particular attention to the role of (post)colonial history and regional and place-specific geopolitical variations.

In relation to (post)colonial history, we highlighted for example how specific features of living informally in Latin America must be understood in relation to legacies of Spanish and Portuguese colonialism that distinguished between 'planned' inner cities for predominantly 'White' settlers and 'disorderly' urban peripheries, home to Indigenous populations and African slaves (Connolly, 2017: 41). Such ethno-spatial divisions have to some degree been maintained and continue to characterize the 'planned' and formal parts of the central Latin American city and its 'disorderly' and 'informal' peripheral neighbourhoods (Chapters 1 to 4). Colonial legacies in Latin America also help explain why, up to the present day, it is often Indigenous and Black women who work informally as domestic workers in 'White' and '*mestizo*' urban households (Chapter 4; see also Wade, 2013). Cities elsewhere in the global South experience distinct colonial histories, with different effects on urban informality, as highlighted, for example, in our discussion on links between informal work and caste in urban India (Chapter 4; see also McFarlane, 2008), apartheid and articulations of working and living informally in South Africa (Chapter 7), and deliberate efforts by local authorities in Israel to declare the land-use patterns of Bedouin groups as illegal while legalizing the land occupation practices of Jewish settlers (Chapter 5; see also Yiftachel, 2009). Despite a shared history of colonialism across many countries in the global South, then, distinctive (post)colonial trajectories lead to diverse urban informality outcomes that require context-specific responses (Chapters 6 and 7).

Urban informality is also perceived, represented and addressed differently in diverse geopolitical contexts. Taking again the example of Latin America, in different countries and cities, informal neighbourhoods are named differently, and the specificities of such denominations are not easily translatable into English, for example: '*barriadas, pueblos jóvenes, favelas, loteamientos, barrios, barrios de rancho, barrios populares, comunas, lotificaciones irregulares, asentamientos humanos autoproducidos, asentamientos urbanos (o humanos) irregulares, populares, no-controlados o precarios, colonias populares o proletarias, villas miseria, callampas, urbanización informal, fraccionamientos clandestinas, fraccionamientos piratas, urbanización popular*' (Connolly, 2017: 24). Latin America is also a region where more than half of the urban population lives and works in situations which could be characterized as 'informal'. However, in a context where informality is the norm, the term 'informality' itself is rarely heard, as ordinary people but also government authorities often refer to such phenomena as 'popular' economies, habitat and urbanization, as discussed in Chapter 8 (see also Gago et al, 2018).

Similar to context-specific understandings emanating from Latin America, we have reflected on the rich repertoire of Africanist, South Asian and Middle Eastern perspectives that theorize from 'slums' and informal marketplaces in these geopolitical settings, with each body of work highlighting unique cultural, political, geographic and socio-economic features. We also paid attention to the growing emergence of informality in the 'global North', whether through the rise of the gig economy and platform urbanism (Chapter 4) or through the emergence of informal housing in 'beds and sheds' in the UK or refugee camps in France (Chapter 3). Unlike in the global South, where informality is a reality for the urban majority and where, in response, governments often tolerate or even support it, urban informality in the global North is still treated as an exception and often remains subject to strict regulatory enforcement. What is clear, then, is that geopolitical context matters in terms of how urban informality is understood and addressed. Regional and place-specific variations mitigate against standardized frameworks and solutions; instead, we argue for embracing local context and taking seriously geographic, historical, cultural, socio-economic and political particularities.

Our fourth and final argument is that a more holistic understanding of urban informality requires engaging with and promoting a greater diversity of representations. Throughout the different chapters of this book, we introduced diverse perspectives from distinct sources. Our intention was to move beyond specific siloes of knowledge production, promote alternative voices (for example, by including interview testimonies with practitioners and residents involved in living and working informally in Chapters 2, 3, 6, 7 and 8), and engage in a critical dialogue with popular, academic, policy and community-focused knowledges on urban informality. Reflecting on methodological and ethical concerns relating to informality scholarship, we also discussed approaches to researching informality, highlighting recent shifts towards more longitudinal, multi-voice, mixed-method and co-productive approaches.

Within the limited scope of this book, which is further narrowed by the always limited knowledge of its authors – in this case two European academics who predominantly work in Latin America – we can of course only provide a partial overview of the significant knowledge produced on urban informality. Therefore, we suggest treating this book simply as a starting point on your journey of learning about and engaging with urban informality. You may want to follow our reading and viewing suggestions, but also to identify additional sources yourself, perhaps on or from the place where you are from or where you currently live, thereby deepening your understanding of the issues introduced here.

Evaluating responses to urban informality

Informality is not only a lived reality for many urban residents worldwide; it also represents a key issue within global development agendas that guide national and local government policy and planning practice. For example, both Sustainable Development Goal 11 on Sustainable Cities and Communities and the New Urban Agenda acknowledge and engage with informality, proposing the need to improve the conditions of those living and working informally while recognizing their right to exist in the city. A key objective of this book has been to provide a critical overview of how informality has been and is being addressed through different responses, be that through top–down or state-led interventions initiated by governments or international agencies, bottom-up or citizen-led initiatives by those who work and live informally, or efforts that promote co-produced solutions (Chapters 6, 7 and 8).

We highlighted how state-led or top-down responses towards urban informality have shifted over time, from initial efforts seeking to stamp out informal markets and neighbourhoods through evictions and criminalization. Later responses sought to encourage formalization, for example, through granting tenure rights and business permits, or embrace informality, for example, through aided self-help, upgrading and regularization efforts, or through enhancing representation of informal workers and residents in participatory and co-productive planning processes, and within university curricula to train the next generation of urban professionals. International organizations like UN-Habitat, the World Bank, the International Monetary Fund and the International Labour Organization, as well as international summits such as the Habitat conferences I, II and III, have played diverse yet significant roles in pushing for shifts in policy interventions by national governments. Yet, at the local level, such shifts are by no means linear, as distinct types of interventions often co-exist. For example, in Nairobi in Kenya, innovative interventions that seek to embrace urban informality such as the Mukuru Special Planning Area co-exist with punitive responses such as the 2018 eviction of approximately 20,000 residents in the informal neighbourhood Kibera[1] – an intervention to make space for the construction of a road to reduce traffic congestion in the adjacent upper-middle-class neighbourhood of Kilimani (which as shown in Figure 3.6 has also been subject to informal middle-class development).

Punitive interventions like the one in Kibera continue to exist because top-down responses occur in contexts of uneven power relations, in which government authorities deal with conflicting priorities, often opposing informality in lower-income areas, while prioritizing the interests of property owners, business elites, and middle- and upper-class residents. Practices that favour elite interests were discussed in Chapter 5, where we reflected on how governments may generate situations of calculated informality that often serve to 'whiten' and 'legalize' illegal land occupations, construction and business practices by elites while contributing to the 'darkening' and 'illegalization' of the everyday practices of low-income groups. Such examples demonstrate again that informality is not a natural state but a result of political action. We therefore need to pay attention to how top-down policy and planning responses not only respond to, but also create, urban informality.

Independent from their underlying intentions and practical effects, we highlighted that top-down interventions are unlikely to resolve urban informality entirely. This is suggested by the scale and size of the phenomenon: urban informality represents a lived reality for most people living in cities, especially in the global South, but also increasingly in the global North. After decades of research, policy and practice around how to address informality, it is important to recognize that it is an enduring phenomenon that is here to stay, especially in contexts where living and working informally is often the only option for people to make a living in the city. We therefore support calls to recognize, rather than to question and undermine, people's right to live and work informally. Indeed, most contemporary top-down responses tend to move in this direction, even if this occurs through a 'double-faced policy' where government authorities pronounce living and working informally as 'illegal and undesirable while at the same time providing the institutional framework, land and other resources for their creation and consolidation' (Connolly, 2017: 41) – whether through aided self-help, upgrading, titling, regularization, the social production of habitat, corrupt practices or fostering patron–client relations (Chapters 5, 6 and 7).

We also highlighted the importance of recognizing the enormous efforts expended by those living and working informally. Our discussions of citizen-led or bottom-up responses showed how it is often residents of informal neighbourhoods, street vendors and other informal workers who take things into their own hands to resolve the necessities of urban life. Such actions may align with self-help practices, but they may also (or alternatively) include subtle individual acts of appropriation and/ or resistance – such as the 'quiet encroachment' observed by Bayat (2000: 545) – particularly in contexts where repressive political regimes dominate. Other bottom-up responses are more collective in nature, ranging from 'insurgent' protests and actions to the formation of grassroots and civil society networks that promote community-led developments in informal neighbourhoods, or informal workers' rights. Such grassroots organizations, sometimes supported by international networks and professionals working in non-government organizations (such as Shack/Slum Dwellers International and Women in Informal Employment: Globalizing and Organizing), have managed to address some of the priorities and needs of those living and working informally. Initially focusing mainly on the global South, we also noted a growing emphasis on South–North learning, with organizations such as Community Savers in Manchester emerging from exchanges with Shack/Slum Dwellers International affiliates in South Africa and Kenya. By necessity, grassroots interventions tend to be small in scale, while larger initiatives such as the improvement of infrastructure and services in informal neighbourhoods and markets usually require state involvement and cooperation, something that is increasingly achieved through more co-productive interventions and the promotion of urban reform coalitions. These issues were introduced and discussed in Chapters 6, 7 and 8.

Many citizen-led responses to informality implicitly or explicitly mobilize an asset-based approach, which starts from the position of evaluating existing benefits and strengths in contexts of living and working informally, rather than seeing them simply as 'not formal', or defined in negative terms. This offers individuals and communities a basis from which to organize and advocate for their right to exist in the urban environment, or to resist attempts to remove them. Organizations such as Catalytic Communities in Rio and Asiye eTelufani in Durban argue that informality is not just a lack of formality, but has its own specific qualities which should be valued and supported in their own right. These qualities are often hard to understand without engaging with the people who live and work informally, but they are important to recognize and protect, not only for the good of those living and working there, but also because they have potential benefits and learnings for the whole city (and beyond it, in other contexts).

In sum, then, a multiplicity of top-down, bottom-up and co-productive responses to urban informality co-exist, with varying results. We finish this section by sharing some fundamental principles that we, based on our critical analysis throughout this book, consider essential for the development of more progressive responses that better address the priorities and needs of those working and living informally:

- Responses should follow a 'do no harm' strategy. Evictions should be avoided, but local and national governments also need to recognize that formalization alone is insufficient to address urban informality, as this phenomenon is likely to continue to exist in many urban contexts characterized by inequality around the world.
- Context and place matters. Responses should therefore engage with relevant historical, political, economic, social, cultural and place-specific particularities in order to provide actions that are sensitive to these issues, rather than attempting a 'one-size-fits-all' approach.
- Single-sector responses are likely to fail in addressing urban informality, particularly given its intersections with other policy challenges. It is therefore crucial to join up expertise from different policy sectors and to involve stakeholders operating at different scales – from local to international – and from public, private and civil society spheres.
- The involvement of people who live and work informally, and organizations representing them, through more participatory engagements, collaborative governance and partnership building is essential in addressing urban informality, as it can enable more targeted and inclusive responses that foreground their interests and needs, and build on their existing innovations.

Future directions

By structuring this book around three core themes (living, working and governing informally), there are, inevitably, other important and emerging aspects of urban informality that have not been addressed sufficiently. In Chapter 8 we discussed some contemporary trends such as new approaches to urban informality informed by Southern (urban) theory, guided by global approaches to development as well as South–North and South–South learning. Chapter 8 also discussed current work that questions urban informality and promotes alternative conceptualizations such as popular and peripheral urbanization and economies, social and solidarity economies, collective life, and infrastructural citizenship. We want to conclude this book by reflecting on three contemporary trends that we consider important for future scholarship, activism and policy advocacy around urban informality. These are the climate emergency, the permacrisis, and the role of artificial intelligence (AI) and technological innovation in shaping the future of informal working, living and governing.

When writing the final pages of this book in summer 2023, nearly every country and many cities on this planet were affected by severe environmental disasters or climate-related events such as heat waves, extreme cold spells, torrential rain, storms, volcanic eruptions, landslides, wildfires, floods and earthquakes. This indicates that we are indeed living in a climate emergency of apparently increasingly apocalyptic character (Cohen, 2020). Recent research demonstrates that those who live and work informally are particularly vulnerable to the effects of the climate emergency, as they often occupy land that is prone to flooding or landslides, lack access to adequate housing and infrastructure, and do not have adequate social and healthcare support to help them protect themselves or recover from environmental disasters (Dodman et al, 2023). At the same time, those living and working informally are not passively accepting this crisis. For example, by engaging in economic activities such as waste picking, urban agriculture or recycling, informal workers are at the forefront of providing solutions for improved environmental sustainability (Dodman et al, 2023). More attention must be paid to the effects of the climate emergency on urban informality and the potential contribution towards urban climate action by those living and working informally.

The second trend we wish to foreground is the permacrisis. Declared as word of the year 2022 by the *Collins Dictionary*, the term permacrisis refers to 'an extended period of instability and insecurity, especially one resulting from a series of catastrophic events'.[2] At the current juncture, such catastrophic events include, among others, the climate emergency discussed previously, the after-effects of the COVID-19 pandemic, the global economic crisis, and wars in countries like Ethiopia, Israel/Palestine, Syria and Ukraine. As elaborated in Chapters 3, 4 and 8, COVID-19 had a particularly negative effect on those living and working informally, for whom social distancing and isolating at home is hardly a possibility. The economic, social and political after-effects of this crisis are still being determined (see, for example, Simon et al, 2021). We also know from previous research that economic crises are normally accompanied by significant increases in informal sector work, as those laid off from their jobs search for other means to get by (Chapter 3; see also Chen, 2012). It remains to be seen whether similar trends occur at the current juncture. What is evident already, though, is that the current global economic crisis and ongoing wars are uprooting people across the world, with millions migrating from the countryside to cities or from one city to another urban setting, domestically or abroad. All this occurs in a geopolitical context characterized by a re-emergence of right-wing and populist governments that advocate for a hostile approach towards migrants and refugees. Often denied rights to asylum, many migrants are unable to access public housing, social and legal protections, and the right to work, whether at transit points or in destination cities. In such contexts, living and working informally often remains the only available option. In response to the permacrisis, however, we can also denote a rise in campaigns and activities relating to migrants' rights, housing and climate change action, anti-war movements, and informal worker organization. Future research would do well to investigate the distinct yet interconnected urban popular struggles that share a desire to find ways out of the permacrisis, focusing particularly on what this means for the future of urban informality.

The third trend we focus on here refers to AI-related technological innovations and their variegated implications for the future of informal working and living. In a seminal paper on AI-induced automation, Frey and Osborne (2013) estimate that 47 per cent of existing jobs in the United States are susceptible to automation, with similar trends reported for other countries in the global North and South (Raval, 2019). On the one hand, AI-induced automation tends to be associated with a rise in job insecurity, informalization (as observed in the rise of the gig economy and platform urbanism discussed in Chapter 3), and an increase in surveillance dynamics to track at a granular level worker movement, communication between workers and customers, and rest times. Such surveillance practices often have harmful impacts on workers' stress levels and privacy rights (Raval, 2019). On the other hand, more positive accounts highlight how app-based informal work can lead to greater flexibility, enabling workers to choose or refuse work or to engage in forms of flexi-work by 'freelancing' for multiple platforms (Kenney and Zysman, 2016). Relating to living informally, organizations such as the Inter-American Development Bank consider AI a helpful tool for incorporating informal neighbourhoods in official city maps, for example through using algorithms that analyse satellite images and identify 'characteristic visual patterns' of informal neighbourhoods from space,[3] building on geographic information systems techniques outlined in Chapter 8. Such innovations may help local authorities to identify and integrate informal settlements into planning and service provision schemes. At the same time, such innovations can also be problematic as they may, by visibilizing informality, enable punitive actions like evictions by more hostile governments, or infringe upon the rights of residents who may want to remain informal and even invisible (Chapter 4). What becomes clear, then, is that AI urban techno-futures have the potential to generate empowering outcomes, but they can also re-entrench precarity and reinforce the exclusion of those who live and work informally.

The brief review of contemporary trends discussed here (to which we are sure you can add others) demonstrates that urban informality is likely to prevail in a rapidly urbanizing world characterized by multiple environmental, political, socio-economic and technological transformations. We hope that this book has inspired you to further engage with urban informality, and that it encourages you to embrace deeper understanding of the priorities and needs of those living, working and governing informally – be that through research, art-based interventions, activism, policy and planning practice, or other means.

Notes

Chapter 1
1. Interview conducted by Philipp Horn in 2021.
2. Available from: https://ageofzinc.wordpress.com/2018/08/08/a-poem-written-by-the-late-patrick-magebhula/ [Accessed 16 November 2023].
3. Available from: www.sdgs.un.org [Accessed 29 January 2024].
4. Available from: https://www.un.org/millenniumgoals [Accessed 24 January 2024].

Chapter 2
1. Interview conducted by Jaime Hernández and Daniela Mosquera Camacho in 2019, for *Improbable Dialogues* project, in which Melanie Lombard was co-investigator.
2. This chapter draws on the following previously published works: Lombard (2014; 2015).
3. Distinguishable from the period of 'early urbanization' from 1800 to around 1949 characterized by the 'sustained growth of urban populations' which led to 'permanent transitions towards predominantly urban living' in North America, Europe, Japan and Australasia, late urbanization is characterized by 'sustained increases in urban populations in virtually all countries' from the 1950s onwards (Fox and Goodfellow, 2021: 5).

Chapter 3
1. Interview conducted by Carlos Tobar Tovar in 2020, part of *Paz en Aguablanca* project, in which Melanie Lombard was co-investigator.
2. Here, we distinguish between pavement dwelling and street homelessness, as we are mainly concerned with the phenomenon of semi-permanent residence on pavements, accompanied by some form of spatial construction. For an in-depth discussion on the meaning of homelessness in the global South, see Tipple and Speak (2005).
3. Here, we use both terms depending on their use in the debates we discuss; however, we are mindful of McFarlane and Silver's (2017: 459) observation that '[t]he term "neighbourhood" rather than "settlement" serves to remind us that informal settlements are more than just sites and shelter; they are actual urban places with lives and going ons, much like other neighbourhoods'.
4. Care must be taken with this terminology, as not all informal residents are squatters, despite the prevalence of the term in some debates (see, for example, Satterthwaite's [2008] review of Neuwirth [2005]).
5. There are some parallels with the recent phenomenon of short-term renting via online platforms, most notably Airbnb, that have enabled occupants in cities around the world, particularly in the global North, to capitalize on their housing as an asset.

Chapter 4
1. Interview conducted by Philipp Horn in 2021.

Chapter 5

1. Interview conducted by Lilian Odongo in 2019 as part of a research project led by Philipp Horn that documented participation in the Mukuru Special Planning Area in Nairobi, Kenya.
2. We follow French cultural critic de Certeau (1984: 37) who defines tactics as follows: 'The space of tactic is the space of the other. Thus it must play on and with a terrain imposed on it and organised by the law of a foreign power. … It is a manoeuvre "within the enemy's field of vision". … It operates in isolated actions, blow by blow. It takes advantage of "opportunities" and depends on them.' In our context, we deploy the concept of tactics to refer to the everyday engagements of ordinary people who live and work informally to deploy, modify and transform formal governance institutions and practices to meet their basic needs.
3. See also https://www.transparency.org/en/what-is-corruption [Accessed 1 March 2024].
4. Agency refers to the 'ability or capacity of an actor to act consciously and, in doing so, to attempt to realise his or her intentions' (Hay, 2002: 94).
5. The term social structure refers to the historical context and to established rules and procedures which characterize a society (Hudson and Leftwich, 2014).
6. Invited spaces refer to platforms for citizen participation designed and controlled by states, NGOs or donors.
7. This section draws on Horn (2022).
8. Thanks to Tom Goodfellow for this reference.

Chapter 6

1. Interview conducted by Lilian Odongo in 2019 as part of a research project led by Philipp Horn that documented participation in the Mukuru Special Planning Area in Nairobi, Kenya.
2. Good governance is a set of governance ideals pursued by the World Bank and other agencies, promoting active citizenship, more participatory forms of democracy and greater decentralization; critical debates have highlighted its entanglement with neoliberalization agendas (Guarneros-Meza and Geddes, 2010; see also Chapter 1).
3. New Public Management refers to an approach, often applied under the good governance framework and specifically under decentralization, which attempted to make local government more efficient; in urban settings, this often translated into a focus on 'management, operational efficiency and property rights' (Jones and Ward, 1994: 16).
4. https://www.hic-net.org [Accessed 1 March 2024].
5. https://sdinet.org/ [Accessed 1 March 2024].
6. This paragraph draws on Horn et al (2020) and Horn (2021).

Chapter 7

1. Interview conducted by Carlos Tobar Tovar in 2021, part of the *Paz en Aguablanca* project, in which Melanie Lombard was co-investigator.
2. You can find more information about different interventions by AeT on its website: https://aet.org.za/ [Accessed 1 March 2024].
3. For detailed case studies and further references on this topic see: https://www.wiego.org/our-work-impact/core-programmes/social-protection [Accessed 1 March 2024].

Chapter 8

1. Interview conducted by Sophie King in 2022 as part of impact evaluation for Community Savers network.
2. Such a perspective is put forward by Brenner (2013: 95) who defines planetary urbanization dynamics as follows: 'The urban [is considered] as "concrete abstraction" in which the contradictory socio-spatial relations of capitalism (commodification, capital circulation, capital accumulation and associated forms of political regulation/contestation) are at once territorialized (embedded within

concrete contexts and thus fragmented) and generalized (extended across place, territory and scale) and thus universalized.'
3. Here Brenner and Schmid (2014) refer to Wirth's (1938) seminal article, 'Urbanism as a way of life', on the social characteristics of cities, which they draw on to frame their argument.
4. As Connolly (2020: 122) points out, the Spanish term '*popular*' denotes 'of the people', distinguishing them from 'the ruling classes', and is therefore 'preferred as a non-deprecatory adjective'.
5. See https://www.wiego.org/blog/qa-wiego-social-and-solidarity-economy-specialist-federico-parra [Accessed 29 January 2024].
6. The collective is comprised of Solomon Benjamin, Alioscia Castronovo, Luci Cavallero, Cristina Cielo, Véronica Gago, Prince Guma, Rupali Gupte, Victoria Habermehl, Lana Salman, Prasad Shetty, AbdouMaliq Simone, Constance Smith and João Tonucci.
7. The Right to the City is a contested term. Conceptually, it does not refer to a legal approach to urban development, but rather represents 'a cry and a demand' (Lefebvre, 1996 [1967]: 158) by historically marginalised groups to appropriate urban space according to their interests and needs; to participate in decisions concerning urban planning, design, and management; and to be at the core of urban life. For further explanation see Marcuse (2009).
8. https://habitat3.org/documents-and-archive/preparatory-documents/issue-papers/ [Accessed 29 January 2024].
9. https://www.urbanagendaplatform.org/member-states [Accessed 29 January 2024].
10. https://communitysavers.net/ [Accessed 29 January 2024].
11. One of the authors of this book, Melanie Lombard, is a board member for this organization.
12. We discussed the work of this organization in relation to efforts in the informal Mukuru area in Chapters 5–7.
13. https://www.urban-know.com/ [Accessed 29 January 2024].
14. https://www.african-cities.org/about-us/ [Accessed 29 January 2024].

Chapter 9

1. https://www.aljazeera.com/news/2018/7/24/kenya-kibera-demolitions-leave-thousands-homeless [Accessed 1 March 2024].
2. https://www.collinsdictionary.com/dictionary/english/permacrisis [Accessed 1 March 2024].
3. https://blogs.iadb.org/ciudades-sostenibles/en/can-artificial-intelligence-help-reducing-urban-informality/ [Accessed 1 March 2024].

References

Abahlali baseMjondolo (2009) 'Abahlali baseMjondolo will challenge the KZN Slums Act in the Constitutional Court on 14 May 2009', *Abahlali baseMjondolo*, 14 May. Available from: https://abahlali.org/node/5120/ [Accessed 14 November 2023].

Abramo, P. (2010) 'Mercado Informal de Alquiler: nueva puerta de acceso a los asentamientos populares', *Revista Praiavermelha*, 20: 67–84.

Abrams, C. (1964) *Man's Struggle for Shelter in an Urbanizing World*, Cambridge, MA: MIT Press.

Abrams, C. (1965) *The City Is the Frontier*. New York: Harper and Row.

Acemoglu, D. and Robinson, J. (2012) *Why Nations Fail: The Origins of Power, Prosperity, and Poverty*, London: Profile Books.

Acuto, M. and Parnell, S. (2016) 'Leave no city behind', *Science*, 352(6288): 873.

Acuto, M., Dinardi, C. and Marx, C. (2019) 'Transcending (in)formal urbanism', *Urban Studies*, 56(3): 475–87.

Agbiboa, D.E. (2018) 'Informal urban governance and predatory politics in Africa: the role of motor-park touts in Lagos', *African Affairs*, 117(466): 62–82.

Agnew, J. and Oslender, U. (2010) 'Overlapping territorialities, sovereignty in dispute: empirical lessons from Latin America', *Tabula Rasa*, 13: 191–213.

Alfaro d'Alencon, P., Smith, H., Alvarez, E., Cabrera, C., Fokdal, J., Lombard, M., Mazzolini, A., Michelutti, E., Moretto, L. and Spire, A. (2018) 'Interrogating informality: conceptualisations, practices and policies in the light of the New Urban Agenda', *Habitat International*, 75: 59–66.

Alfasi, N. (2014) 'Doomed to informality: familial versus modern planning in Arab towns in Israel', *Planning Theory & Practice*, 15(2): 170–86.

Alfers, L., Galvani, F., Grapsa, E., Juergens, F. and Sevilla, A. (2021) 'Older informal workers in the COVID-19 crisis', *WIEGO COVID-19 Crisis and the Informal Economy Policy Insights 5*. Available from: https://www.wiego.org/sites/default/files/resources/file/PolicyInsights5.pdf [Accessed 19 October 2023].

AlSayyad, N. (2004) 'Urban informality as a "new" way of life', in A. Roy and N. AlSayyad (eds) *Urban Informality: Transnational Perspectives from the Middle East, Latin America and South Asia*, New York: Lexington Books, pp 7–30.

Alvarez, J.A. and Pizzinelli, C. (2021) 'COVID-19 and the informality-driven recovery: the case of Colombia's labor market', IMF Working Paper No. 2021/235. Available from: https://www.imf.org/en/Publications/WP/Issues/2021/09/17/COVID-19-and-the-Informality-driven-Recovery-The-Case-of-Colombia-s-Labor-Market-465831 [Accessed 22 November 2023].

Anderson, B. (2000) *Doing the Dirty Work? The Global Politics of Domestic Labour*, London: Palgrave Macmillan.

Angel, S. (2012) *Planet of Cities*, Cambridge, MA: Lincoln Institute of Land Policy.

Apentiik, C. and Parpart, J. (2006) 'Working in different cultures: issues of race, ethnicity and identity', in V. Desai and R. Potter (eds) *Doing Development Research*, London: SAGE, pp 34–43.

Appadurai, A. (2001) 'Deep democracy: urban governmentality and the horizon of politics', *Environment and Urbanization*, 13(2): 23–43.

Appendini, K. (2001) *Land Regularization and Conflict Resolution: The Case of Mexico*, Mexico City: FAO Rural Development Division.

Arbona, J.M. and Kohl, B. (2004) 'City profile: La Paz – El Alto', *Cities*, 21(3): 255–65.

Arimah, B. (2010) 'The face of urban poverty: explaining the prevalence of slums in developing countries', in J. Beall, B. Guha-Khasnobis and R. Kanbur (eds) *Urbanization and Development: Multidisciplinary Perspectives*, Oxford: Oxford University Press, pp 144–65.

Austin (1994) 'The Austin Memorandum on the reform of Article 27, and its impact upon the urbanization of the *ejido* in Mexico', *Bulletin of Latin American Research*, 13(3): 327–35.

Austin, R. (1993) 'Honest living: street vendors, municipal regulation, and the black public sphere', *The Yale Law Journal*, 103(8): 2119–31.

Auyero, J. (1999a) '"From the client's point(s) of view": how poor people perceive and evaluate political clientelism', *Theory and Society*, 28(2): 297–334.

Auyero, J. (1999b) '"This is a lot like the Bronx, isn't it?" Lived experiences of marginality in an Argentine slum', *International Journal of Urban and Regional Research*, 23(1): 45–69.

Auyero, J. (2000) 'The logic of clientelism in Argentina: an ethnographic account', *Latin American Research Review*, 35(3): 55–81.

Azuela, A. and Tomas, F. (eds) (1996) *El acceso de los pobres al suelo urbano*, Mexico City: Centro de Estudios Mexicanos y Centramericanos.

Azuela, A. and Duhau, E. (1998) 'Tenure regularisation, private property and public order in Mexico', in E. Fernandes and A. Varley (eds) *Illegal Cities: Law and Urban Change in Developing Countries*, London: Zed, pp 157–71.

Balchin, P. and Stewart, J. (2001) 'Social housing in Latin America: opportunities for affordability in a region of housing need', *Journal of Housing and the Built Environment*, 16(3/4): 333–41.

Bangasser, P. (2000) *The ILO and the Informal Sector: An Institutional History*, Geneva: International Labour Organization.

Banks, N. (2016a) 'Livelihoods limitations: the political economy of urban poverty in Dhaka, Bangladesh', *Development and Change*, 47(2): 266–92.

Banks, N. (2016b) 'Youth poverty, employment and livelihoods: social and economic implications of living with insecurity in Arusha, Tanzania', *Environment and Urbanization*, 28(2): 437–54.

Banks, N., Lombard, M. and Mitlin, D. (2020) 'Urban informality as a site of critical analysis', *The Journal of Development Studies*, 56(2): 223–38.

Baumgart, S. and Kreibich, W. (2011) 'Informal urbanization: historical and geographical perspectives', *disP – The Planning Review*, 47(4): 12–23.

Bayat, A. (2000) 'From "dangerous classes" to "quiet rebels": politics of the urban subaltern in the global south', *International Sociology*, 15(3): 533–57.

Bayat, A. (2004) 'Globalization and the politics of the informals in the global south', in A. Roy and N. Alsayyad (eds) *Urban Informality: Transnational Perspectives from the Middle East, Latin America and South Asia*, New York: Lexington Books, pp 79–102.

Beard, V.A., Miraftab, F. and Silver, C. (2008) *Planning and Decentralization: Contested Spaces for Public Action in the Global South*, Abingdon: Routledge.

Bendiksen, J. (2008) *The Places We Live*, London: Aperture Foundation.

Bénit-Gbaffou, C. (2016) 'Do street traders have the "right to the city"? The politics of street trader organisations in inner city Johannesburg, post-Operation Clean Sweep', *Third World Quarterly*, 37(6): 1102–29.

Benjamin, S. (2000) 'Governance, economic settings and poverty in Bangalore', *Environment and Urbanization*, 12(1): 35–56.

Benjamin, S. (2004) 'Urban land transformation for pro-poor economies', *Geoforum*, 35(2): 177–87.

Benjamin, S. (2008) 'Occupancy urbanism: radicalizing politics and economy beyond policy and programs', *International Journal of Urban and Regional Research*, 32(3): 719–29.

Bennett, T., Grossberg, L. and Morris, M. (2005) *New Keywords: A Revised Vocabulary of Culture and Society*, Oxford: Blackwell.

Berg, J., Furrer, M., Harmon, E., Rani, U. and Silberman, M.S. (2018) *Digital Labour Platforms and the Future of Work: Towards Decent Work in the Online World*, Geneva: ILO.

Bhan, G. (2019) 'Notes on a southern urban practice', *Environment and Urbanization*, 31(2): 639–54.

Bhan, G. (2020) 'Informality, housing and work: the view from Indian cities', in M. Chen and F. Carré (eds) *The Informal Economy Revisited*, Abingdon: Routledge, pp 136–40.

Bhan, G., Caldeira, T., Gillespie, K. and Simone, A. (2020) 'The pandemic, southern urbanisms and collective life', *Society and Space*, 3 August. Available from: https://www.societyandspace.org/articles/the-pandemic-southern-urbanisms-and-collective-life [Accessed 19 October 2023].

Blanchard Jerrold, W. and Doré, G. (1872) *London: A Pilgrimage*, London: Grant and Co/British Library.

Boanada-Fuchs, A. and Boanada, V. (2018) 'Towards a taxonomic understanding of informality', *International Development Planning Review*, 40(4): 397–420.

Bogaards, M. (2019) 'Formal and informal consociational institutions: a comparison of the national pact and the Taif agreement in Lebanon', *Nationalism and Ethnic Politics*, 25(1): 27–42.

Bonnet, F., Vanek, J. and Chen, M. (2019) *Women and Men in the Informal Economy: A Statistical Brief*, Geneva: ILO.

Boonjubun, C. (2017) 'Conflicts over streets: the eviction of Bangkok street vendors', *Cities*, 70: 22–31.

Booth, C. (1889) *Life and Labour of the People in London*, London: Macmillan.

Bouchard, M., Bourque, G. and Lévesque, B. (2000) *L'évaluation de l'économie sociale dans la perspective des nouvelles formes de régulation socio-économique de l'intérêt général*, Working Paper No. 0013, Cahiers du CRISES. Available from: https://www.erudit.org/en/journals/crs/2001-n35-crs1517017/1002235ar.pdf [Accessed 19 October 2023].

Breeze, M. (2023) 'Temporary sheltering, empowering design, and the jungle: a case for architects', in G. Karunaratne (ed), *Informal Settlements of the Global South*, Abingdon: Routledge, pp 29–46.

Brenner, N. (2013) 'Theses on urbanisation', *Public Culture*, 25(1): 85–114.

Brenner, N. and Schmid, C. (2014) 'The "urban age" in question', *International Journal of Urban and Regional Research*, 38(3): 731–55.

Brett, E.A. (2009) *Reconstructing Development Theory: International Inequality, Institutional Reform and Social Emancipation*, London: Palgrave Macmillan.

Bromley, R. (1978) 'The urban informal sector: why is it worth discussing?', *World Development*, 6(9/10): 1033–9.

Brown, A. (2017) *Rebel Streets and the Informal Economy: Street Trade and the Law*, Abingdon: Taylor & Francis.

Brydon, L. (2006) 'Ethical practices in doing development research', in V. Desai and R. Potter (eds) *Doing Development Research*, London: SAGE, pp 25–33.

Buckley, M. and Strauss, K. (2016) 'With, against and beyond Lefebvre: planetary urbanization and epistemic plurality', *Environment and Planning D*, 34(4): 617–36.

Burgess, R. (1978) 'Petty commodity housing or dweller control? A critique of John Turner's view on housing policy', *World Development*, 6(9/10): 1105–33.

Caldeira, T. (2016) 'Peripheral urbanization: autoconstruction, transversal logics, and politics in cities of the global south', *Environment and Planning D*, 35(1): 3–20.

Campbell, H. (2002) 'Planning: an idea of value', *Town Planning Review*, 73(3): 271–88.

Carr, M., Chen, M. and Tate, J. (2000) 'Globalization and home-based workers', *Feminist Economics*, 6(3): 123–42.

Carré, F. (2020) 'Informal employment in developed countries: relevance and statistical measurement', in M. Chen and F. Carré (eds) *The Informal Economy Revisited*, Abingdon: Routledge, pp 52–9.

Carrieri, A. and Murta, I. (2011) 'Cleaning up the city: a study on the removal of street vendors from downtown Belo Horizonte, Brazil', *Canadian Journal of Administrative Sciences*, 28(2): 217–25.

Castán Broto, V., Ortiz, C., Lipietz, B., Osuteye, E., Johnson, C., Kombe, W. and Levy, C. (2022) 'Co-production outcomes for urban equality: learning from different trajectories of citizens' involvement in urban change', *Current Research in Environmental Sustainability*, 4(4): 100179.

Castells, M. (1983) *The City and the Grassroots: A Cross-Cultural Theory of Urban Social Movements*, Berkeley: University of California Press.

Castells, M. and Portes, A. (1989) 'World underneath: the origins, dynamics, and effects of the informal economy', in A. Portes, M. Castells and L. Benton (eds) *The Informal Economy: Studies in Advanced and Less Developed Countries*, Baltimore: Johns Hopkins University Press.

Cerf, M. (2021) 'Everything dey scatta', *Otherwise Magazine*, November 2020–February 2021. Available from: https://www.otherwisemag.com/everything [Accessed 19 October 2023].

Chambers, R. (1983) *Rural Development: Putting the Last First*, Harlow: Longman.

Chambers, R. (1995) 'Poverty and livelihoods: whose reality counts?', *Environment and Urbanization*, 7(1): 173–204.

Chamoiseau, P. (1998) *Texaco*, New York: Random House.

Chan, K.W. and Zhang, L. (1999) 'The *hukou* system and rural-urban migration in China: processes and changes', *The China Quarterly*, 160: 818–55.

Chatteraj, S. (2024) 'Jugaad (India)'. Global Informality Project. Available from: https://www.in-formality.com/ [Accessed 29 January 2024].

Chatterjee, P. (2004) *The Politics of the Governed: Reflections on Popular Politics in Most of the World*, New York: Columbia University Press.

Chatterjee, P. (2008) 'Democracy and economic transformation in India', *Economic and Political Weekly*, 43(16): 53–62.

Chen, M. (2012) 'The informal economy: definitions, theories and policies', WIEGO Working Paper 1. Available from: https://www.wiego.org/sites/default/files/publications/files/Chen_WIEGO_WP1.pdf [Accessed 19 October 2023].

Chen, M. and Vanek, J. (2013) 'Informal employment revisited: theories, data & policies', *Indian Journal of Industrial Relations*, 48(3): 390–401.

Chen, M., Sebstad, J. and O'Connell, L. (1999) 'Counting the invisible workforce: the case of homebased workers', *World Development*, 27(3): 603–10.

Cherry, M.A. (2016) 'Beyond misclassification: the digital transformation of work', *Comparative Labor Law & Policy Journal*, 2016–2: 577–602.

Cheung, S. (2000) 'Speaking out: days in the lives of three Hong Kong cage dwellers', *positions: east asia cultures critique*, 8(1): 235–62.

Chiodelli, F. (2016) 'International housing policy for the urban poor and the informal city in the global south: a non-diachronic review', *Journal of International Development*, 28(5): 788–807.

Chiodelli, F., Coppola, A., Belotti, E., Berruti, G., Clough Marinaro, I., Curci, F. and Zanfi, F. (2021) 'The production of informal space: a critical atlas of housing informalities in Italy between public institutions and political strategies', *Progress in Planning*, 149: 100495.

Chitekwe-Biti, B., Patel, S. and Mitlin, D. (2014) 'The transnational experience of community-led development', in J. Bredenoord, P. van Lindert and P. Smets (eds) *Affordable Housing in the Urban Global South*, Abingdon: Earthscan, pp 117–32.

CLASS/Community Savers (2022) *Outcomes, Learning, and Next Steps*. Available from: https://communitysavers.net/2023/05/community-savers-2022-outcomes-learning-next-steps/ [Accessed 15 November 2023].

CLASS/GM Savers (2020) *Greater Manchester Savers, Our Story So Far*. Available from: https://communitysavers.net/2020/05/greater-manchester-savers-our-story-so-far/ [Accessed 15 November 2023].

Cohen, D.A. (2020) 'Confronting the urban climate emergency: critical urban studies in the age of a green new deal', *City*, 24(1–2): 52–64.

Collord, M., Goodfellow, T. and Asante, L. (2021) 'Uneven development, politics and governance in urban Africa: an analytical literature review', African Cities Research Consortium Working Paper 2. Available from: https://www.african-cities.org/wp-content/uploads/2021/12/ACRC_Working-Paper-2_November-2021.pdf [Accessed 20 November 2023].

Community Savers (2020) 'Looking out for each other during lockdown'. Available from: https://communitysavers.net/2020/05/looking-out-for-each-other-during-lockdown/ [Accessed 29 January 2024].

Connolly, P. (2017) 'Latin American informal urbanism: contexts, concepts and contributions with specific reference to Mexico', in F. Hernández and A. Becerra (eds) *Marginal Urbanisms: Informal and Formal Development in Cities of Latin America*, Newcastle: Cambridge Scholars Publishing, pp 22–47.

Connolly, P. (2020) 'Informal settlements in the age of digital cartography', *Bulletin of Latin American Research*, 38(2): 116–38.

Cooke, B. and Kothari, U. (eds) (2001) *Participation: The New Tyranny?*, New York: Zed.

Copisarow, R. and Barbour, A. (2004) *Self-Employed People in the Informal Economy – Cheats or Contributors: Evidence, Implications and Policy Recommendations*, Birmingham: Community Links.

Cordera, R., Ramírez Kuri, P. and Ziccardi, A. (eds) (2008) *Pobreza, Desigualdad y Exclusión Social en la Ciudad del Siglo XXI*, Mexico City: Siglo XXI.

Datta, A. (2011) '"Mongrel city": cosmopolitan neighbourliness in a Delhi squatter settlement', *Antipode*, 44(3): 745–63.

Davis, M. (2006) *Planet of Slums*, London: Verso.

D'Cruz, C. and Mitlin, D. (2005) *Shack/Slum Dwellers International: One Experience of the Contribution of Membership Organizations to Pro-Poor Urban Development*, London: IIED.

De Carli, B. and Frediani, A. (2016) 'Insurgent regeneration: spatial practices of citizenship in the rehabilitation of inner-city São Paulo', *GeoHumanities*, 2(2): 331–53.

de Certeau, M. (1984) *The Practice of Everyday Life*, Berkeley: University of California Press.

Demissie, F. (2007) 'Imperial legacies and postcolonial predicaments: an introduction', *African Identities*, 5(2): 155–65.

Derickson, K. (2015) 'Urban geography I: locating urban theory in the "urban age"', *Progress in Human Geography*, 39(5): 647–57.

de Soto, H. (1989) *The Other Path: The Economic Answer to Terrorism*, New York: HarperCollins.

de Soto, H. (2000) *The Mystery of Capital: Why Capitalism Triumphs in the West and Fails Everywhere Else*, New York: Basic Books.

de Souza, F. (2001) 'The future of informal settlements: lessons in the legalization of disputed urban land in Recife, Brazil', *Geoforum*, 32(4): 483–92.

Devkar, G., Rajan, A., Narayanan, S. and Elayaraja, M. (2019) 'Provision of basic services in slums: a review of the evidence on top-down and bottom-up approaches', *Development Policy Review*, 37(3): 331–47.

Dobson, R. and Skinner, C. (2009) *Working in Warwick: Including Street Traders in Urban Plans*, Durban: University of KwaZulu-Natal.

REFERENCES

Dodge, T. (2020) 'Iraq's informal consociationalism and its problems', *Studies in Ethnicity and Nationalism*, 20(2): 145–52.

Dodman, D., Sverdlik, A., Agarwal, S., Kadungure, A., Kothiwal, K., Machemedze, R. and Verma, S. (2023) 'Climate change and informal workers: towards an agenda for research and practice', *Urban Climate*, 48: 101401.

Dorries, H., Hugill, D. and Tomiak, J. (2022) 'Racial capitalism and the production of settler colonial cities', *Geoforum*, 132: 263–70.

Dovey, K. and King, R. (2011) 'Forms of informality: morphology and visibility of informal settlements', *Built Environment*, 37(1): 11–29.

Dovey, K., van Oostrum, M., Shafique, T., Chatterjee, I. and Pafka, E. (2023) *Atlas of Informal Settlement: Understanding Self-Organized Urban Design*, London: Bloomsbury.

du Toit, D. (2013) *Exploited, Undervalued – and Essential: Domestic Workers and the Realisation of Their Rights*, Pretoria: PULP.

Durand, J. (1983) *La ciudad invade al ejido. Proletarización, urbanización y lucha política en el Cerro del Judío, D.F.*, Mexico City: Ediciones de la Casa Chata.

Durand-Lasserve, A. and Royston, L. (eds) (2002) *Holding their Ground: Secure Land Tenure for the Urban Poor in Developing Countries*, London: Earthscan.

Durst, N. and Wegmann, J. (2017) 'Informal housing in the United States', *International Journal of Urban and Regional Research*, 41(2): 282–97.

Elsheshtawy, Y. (2011) 'The informal turn', *Built Environment*, 37(1): 5–10.

Engels, F. (1969 [1887]) *The Condition of the Working Class in England*, London: Panther Books.

Environment and Urbanization (1990) 'NGO profile: Habitat International Coalition', *Environment and Urbanization*, 2(1): 105–12.

Escobar de Pabón, S.E., Aponte, G.H. and Rojas, B. (2015) *Un futuro en riesgo: jóvenes y trabajo en el municipio de El Alto*, La Paz: Centro de Estudios para el Desarrollo Laboral y Agrario.

Everett, M. (2001) 'Evictions and human rights: land disputes in Bogota, Colombia', *Habitat International*, 25(4): 453–71.

Fairbanks II, R. (2011) 'The politics of urban informality in Philadelphia's Recovery Housing Movement', *Urban Studies*, 48(12): 2555–70.

Fawaz, M. (2017) 'Exceptions and the actually existing practice of planning: Beirut (Lebanon) as case study', *Urban Studies*, 54(8): 1938–55.

Feireiss, K., Brillembourg, A. and Klumpner, H. (eds) (2005) *Informal City: Caracas Case*, Munich: Prestel.

Fernandes, E. (2002) 'The influence of de Soto's "The mystery of capital"', *Land Lines*, 14: 5–8.

Fernandes, E. (2007) 'Urban land regularization programs: state of knowledge', in A. Garland, M. Massoumi and B. Ruble (eds) *Global Urban Poverty: Setting the Agenda*, Washington, DC: Woodrow Wilson International Center, pp 181–8.

Fernandes, E. (2011) *Regularization of Informal Settlements in Latin America*, Policy Focus Report, Cambridge, MA: Lincoln Institute of Land Policy.

Few, R., Gouvaia, N., Mathee, A., Harpham, T., Cohn, A., Swart, A. and Coulson, N. (2004) 'Informal sub-division of residential and commercial buildings in São Paulo and Johannesburg: living conditions and policy implications', *Habitat International*, 28(3): 427–42.

Foster, C. and Heeks, R. (2013) 'Analyzing policy for inclusive innovation: the mobile sector and base-of-the-pyramid markets in Kenya', *Innovation and Development*, 3(1): 103–19.

Fox, S. (2014) 'The political economy of slums: theory and evidence from sub-Saharan Africa', *World Development*, 54: 191–203.

Fox, S. and Goodfellow, T. (2016) *Cities and Development* (2nd edition), London: Routledge.

Fox, S. and Goodfellow, T. (2021) 'On the conditions of "late urbanisation"', *Urban Studies*, 59(10): 1959–80.

Fraser, A. (2018) 'Informality in the new urban agenda: from the aspirational policies of integration to a politics of constructive engagement', *Planning Theory and Practice*, 19(1): 124–6.

Frediani, A. and Cociña, C. (2019) '"Participation as planning": strategies from the south to challenge the limits of planning', *Built Environment*, 45(2): 143–61.

Frediani, A., de Carli, B., Barbosa, B.R., de Assis Comaru, F. and de Sousa Moretti, R. (2018) 'São Paulo: occupations – a pedagogy of confrontation – informal building occupations in São Paulo's central neighbourhoods', in R. Rocco and J. van Ballegooijen (eds) *The Routledge Handbook on Informal Urbanization*, Abingdon: Routledge, pp 259–69.

Freire, M. and Stren, M. (2001) *The Challenge of Urban Government: Policies and Practices*, Washington, DC: World Bank.

Frey, C.B. and Osborne, M. (2013) *The Future of Employment: How Susceptible are Jobs to Computerisation?*, Oxford: Oxford Martin School, University of Oxford.

Friedmann, J. (1998) 'The new political economy of planning: the rise of civil society', in M. Douglass and J. Friedmann (eds) *Cities for Citizens: Planning and the Rise of Civil Society in a Global Age*, Chichester: John Wiley and Sons, pp 19–35.

Fuller, D. (1999) 'Part of the action or "going native"? Learning to cope with the politics of integration', *Area*, 31(3): 221–7.

Gago, V. (2018) 'What are popular economies? Some reflections from Argentina', *Radical Philosophy*, 202: 32–8.

Gago, V., Cielo, C. and Gachet, F. (2018) 'Economía popular: entre la informalidad y la reproducción ampliada Presentación del dossier', *Íconos. Revista de Ciencias Sociales*, 62: 11–20.

Garrido, M., Ren, X. and Weinstein, L. (2021) 'Towards a global urban sociology: keywords', *City & Community*, 20(1): 4–12.

Garschagen, M. and Porter, L. (2018) 'The new urban agenda: from vision to policy and action', *Planning Theory and Practice*, 19(1): 117–21.

Gaskell, E. (2011 [1848]) *Mary Barton*, London: Harper Press.

Gereffi, G., Humphrey, J., Kaplinsky, R. and Sturgeon, T.J. (2001) 'Introduction: globalisation, value chains and development', *IDS Bulletin*, 32(3): 1–8.

REFERENCES

Ghertner, D.A. (2011) 'Gentrifying the state, gentrifying participation: elite governance programs in Delhi', *International Journal of Urban and Regional Research*, 35(3): 504–32.

Ghertner, D.A. (2012) 'Nuisance talk and the propriety of property: middle-class discourses of a slum-free Delhi', *Antipode*, 44(4): 1161–87.

Gibson-Graham, J.K., Cameron, J. and Healy, S. (2013) *Take Back the Economy: An Ethical Guide for Transforming Our Communities*, Minneapolis: University of Minnesota Press.

Gilbert, A. (2007) 'The return of the slum: does language matter?', *International Journal of Urban and Regional Research*, 31(4): 697–713.

Gilbert, A. (2014) 'Housing the urban poor', in V. Desai and R. Potter (eds), *The Companion to Development Studies*, London: Arnold, pp 306–10.

Gilbert, A. (2016) 'Rental housing: the international experience', *Habitat International*, 54(3): 173–81.

Giovannini, F. (2008) 'Towards an intellectual leadership: rediscovering the role of the United Nations in the 21st century', *Planning Theory and Practice*, 9(2): 254–60.

GLTN (2023) *Access to Land and Tenure Security*. Available from: https://gltn.net/access-to-land-and-tenure-security/# [Accessed 15 November 2023].

Goldstein, D.M. (2005) 'Flexible justice: neoliberal violence and "self-help" security in Bolivia', *Critique of Anthropology*, 25(4): 389–411.

Goldstein, D.M. (2012) *Outlawed: Between Security and Rights in a Bolivian City*, Durham, NC: Duke University Press.

Goldstein, D.M. (2016) *Owners of the Sidewalk: Security and Survival in the Informal City*, Durham, NC: Duke University Press.

Goodfellow, T. (2020) 'Political informality: deals, trust networks, and the negotiation of value in the urban realm', *The Journal of Development Studies*, 56(2): 278–94.

Goodfellow, T. (2022) *Politics and the Urban Frontier: Transformation and Divergence in Late Urbanizing East Africa*, Oxford: Oxford University Press.

Gough, K. and Kellett, P. (2001) 'Housing consolidation and home-based income generation: evidence from self-help settlements in two Colombian cities', *Cities*, 18(4): 235–47.

Griffiths, J. (1986) 'What is legal pluralism?', *The Journal of Legal Pluralism and Unofficial Law*, 18(24): 1–55.

Guarneros-Meza, V. and Geddes, M. (2010) 'Local governance and participation under neoliberalism: comparative perspectives', *International Journal of Urban and Regional Research*, 34(1): 115–29.

Gulyani, S. and Talukdar, D. (2008) 'Slum real estate: the low-quality high-price puzzle in Nairobi's slum rental market and its implications for theory and practice', *World Development*, 36(10): 1916–37.

Guma, P. (2021) 'Recasting provisional urban worlds in the global south: shacks, shanties and micro-stalls', *Planning Theory & Practice*, 22(2): 211–26.

Gupte, J., te Lintelo, D., Patel, S., Rao, V., McGregor, A. and Laksham, R. (2019) *Global Report on Internal Displacement*, Internal Displacement Monitoring Centre, Institute of Development Studies. Available from: https://www.internal-displacement.org/global-report/grid2019/downloads/background_papers/Jaideep_FinalPaper.pdf [Accessed 20 October 2023].

Hackenbroch, K. and Hossain, S. (2012) 'The organised encroachment of the powerful: everyday practices of public space and water supply in Dhaka, Bangladesh', *Planning Theory and Practice*, 13(3): 397–420.

Hall, P. (2002) *Cities of Tomorrow*, Oxford: Blackwell.

Hamdi, N. (2010) *The Placemaker's Guide to Building Community*, London: Earthscan.

Hardoy, J.E. (1973) *Pre-Colombian Cities*, Toronto: Fitzhenry & Whiteside.

Hardoy, J. and Satterthwaite, D. (1989) *Squatter Citizen: Life in the Urban Third World*, London: Earthscan.

Hardy, D. and Ward, C. (1984) *Arcadia for All: The Legacy of a Makeshift Landscape*, London: Continuum International Publishing.

Harris, R. (2018) 'Modes of informal urban development: a global phenomenon', *Journal of Planning Literature*, 33(3): 267–86.

Hart, K. (1973) 'Informal income opportunities and urban employment in Ghana', *The Journal of Modern African Studies*, 11(1): 61–89.

Harvey, D. (2008) 'The right to the city', *New Left Review*, 53: 23–40.

Harvey, D. and Reed, M. (1996) 'The culture of poverty: an ideological analysis', *Sociological Perspectives*, 39(4): 465–495.

Hay, C. (2002) *Political Analysis*, Basingstoke: Palgrave.

Head, E. (2009) 'The ethics and implications of paying participants in qualitative research', *International Journal of Social Research Methodology*, 12(4): 335–44.

Heeks, R. (2017) 'Decent work and the digital gig economy: a developing country perspective on employment impacts and standards in online outsourcing, crowdwork, etc.', Development Informatics Working Paper, 71. Available from: https://papers.ssrn.com/sol3/papers.cfm?abstract_id=3431033 [Accessed 20 October 2023].

Helmke, G. and Levitsky, S. (2004) 'Informal institutions and comparative politics: a research agenda', *Perspectives on Politics*, 2(4): 725–40.

Hernández, F. (2017) 'Locating marginality in Latin American cities', in F. Hernández and A. Becerra, *Marginal Urbanisms: Informal and Formal Development in Cities of Latin America*, Newcastle-upon-Tyne: Cambridge Scholars Publishing, pp ix–xl.

Hernández, F. and Becerra, A. (2017) *Marginal Urbanisms: Informal and Formal Development in Cities of Latin America*, Newcastle-upon-Tyne: Cambridge Scholars Publishing.

Hernández, F., Kellett, P. and Allen, L. (2010) *Rethinking the Informal City: Critical Perspectives from Latin America*, Oxford: Berghahn.

Herrle, P. and Fokdal, J. (2011) 'Beyond the urban informality discourse: negotiating power, legitimacy and resources', *Geographische Zeitschrift*, 99(1): 3–15.

HIC (1987) 'Limuru declaration', Habitat International Coalition. Available from: https://www.hic-net.org/limuru-declaration/ [Accessed 20 October 2023].

HIC (2003) 'Social production of habitat: conceptual framework', Habitat International Coalition. Available from: https://www.hic-net.org/social-production-of-habitat-conceptual-framework/ [Accessed 14 November 2023].

Hilbrandt, H., Alves, S.N. and Tuvikene, T. (2017) 'Writing across contexts: urban informality and the state in Tallinn, Bafata and Berlin', *International Journal of Urban and Regional Research*, 41(6): 946–61.

REFERENCES

Holston, J. (2008) *Insurgent Citizenship: Disjunctions of Democracy and Modernity in Brazil*, Princeton: Princeton University Press.

Holston, J. (2009) 'Insurgent citizenship in an era of global urban peripheries', *City & Society*, 21(2): 245–67.

Holzinger, K., Kern, F.G. and Kromrey, D. (2016) 'The dualism of contemporary traditional governance and the state: institutional setups and political consequences', *Political Research Quarterly*, 69(3): 469–81.

Home, R. (2014) 'Shaping cities of the global south: legal histories of planning and colonialism', in S. Parnell and S. Oldfield (eds) *The Routledge Handbook on Cities of the Global South*, London: Routledge, pp 75–85.

Horn, P. (2019) *Indigenous Rights to the City: Ethnicity and Urban Planning in Bolivia and Ecuador*, London: Routledge.

Horn, P. (2021) 'Enabling participatory planning to be scaled in exclusionary urban political environments: lessons from the Mukuru Special Planning Area in Nairobi', *Environment and Urbanization*, 33(2): 519–38.

Horn, P. (2022) 'The politics of hyperregulation in La Paz, Bolivia: speculative peri-urban development in a context of unresolved municipal boundary conflicts', *Urban Studies*, 59(12): 2489–505.

Horn, P., Kimani, J., Makau, J. and Njoroge, P. (2020) 'Scaling participation in informal settlement upgrading: a documentation of community mobilisation and consultation processes in the Mukuru Special Planning Area, Nairobi, Kenya', Working Paper, University of Manchester. Available from: http://hummedia.manchester.ac.uk/institutes/gdi/publications/workingpapers/scaling-participation-horn-et-al.pdf [Accessed 20 October 2023].

Horner, R. and Hulme, D. (2017) 'Converging divergence? Unpacking the new geography of 21st century global development', GDI Working Paper Series, Global Development Institute, University of Manchester.

Huang, G., Zhang, H. and Xue, D. (2018) 'Beyond unemployment: informal employment and heterogenous motivations for participating in street vending in present-day China', *Urban Studies*, 55(12): 2743–61.

Huchzermeyer, M. (2004) *Unlawful Occupation: Informal Settlements and Urban Policy in South Africa and Brazil*, Trenton: Africa World Press.

Huchzermeyer, M. (2007) 'Elimination of the poor in KwaZulu-Natal', *Pambazuka News: Weekly Forum for Social Justice in South Africa*, 4 July. Available from: https://www.pambazuka.org/governance/elimination-poor-kwazulu-natal [Accessed 20 October 2023].

Huchzermeyer, M. (2011) *Cities with 'Slums': From Informal Settlement Eradication to a Right to the City in South Africa*, Claremont: UCT Press.

Hudson, D. and Leftwich, A. (2014) 'From political economy to political analysis', Development Leadership Program Research Paper 25, University of Birmingham.

International Labour Organization (ILO) (1972) *Employment, Incomes and Equality: A Strategy for Increasing Productive Employment in Kenya*, Geneva: International Labour Organization.

International Labour Organization (ILO) (2019) *Women and Men in the Informal Economy*, Geneva: International Labour Organization.

International Labour Organization (ILO) (2020) *Impact of Lockdown Measures on the Informal Economy*. ILO Briefing Note. Available from: https://www.ilo.org/global/topics/employment-promotion/informal-economy/publications/WCMS_743523/lang--en/index.htm [Accessed 25 January 2024).

International Labour Organization (ILO) (2022) *Decent Work and the Social and Solidarity Economy*, Geneva: International Labour Organization.

Jaffe, R. and Koster, M. (2019) 'The myth of formality in the global north: informality-as-innovation in Dutch governance', *International Journal of Urban and Regional Research*, 43(3): 563–8.

Jaglin, S. (2017) 'Regulating service delivery in southern cities: rethinking urban heterogeneity', in S. Parnell and S. Oldfield (eds) *Handbook of Cities of the Global South*, Abingdon: Routledge, pp 434–47.

Jones, G. and Ward, P. (1994) *Methodology for Land & Housing Market Analysis*, London: UCL Press.

Kamete, A.Y. and Lindell, I. (2010) 'The politics of "non-planning" interventions in African cities: unravelling the international and local dimensions in Harare and Maputo', *Journal of Southern African Studies*, 36(4): 889–912.

Kasarda, J. and Crenshaw, E. (1991) 'Third world urbanization: dimensions, theories, and determinants', *Annual Review of Sociology*, 17: 467–501.

Keivani, R. and Werna, E. (2001) 'Refocusing the housing debate in developing countries from a pluralist perspective', *Habitat International*, 25(2): 191–208.

Kenney, M. and Zysman, J. (2016) 'The rise of the platform economy', *Issues in Science and Technology*, 32(3): 61–9.

Kiddle, G. (2010) 'Key theory and evolving debates in international housing policy: from legalisation to perceived security of tenure approaches', *Geography Compass*, 4(7): 881–92.

Kingman, E. (2012) 'Ciudad, seguridad y racismo', in E. Kingman (ed) *San Roque: indígenas urbanos, seguridad y patrimonio*, Quito: FLACSO, pp 175–209.

Koechlin, L. (2018) 'Vetterliwirtschaft', in A. Ledeneva (ed) *The Global Encyclopaedia of Informality, Volume 1: Towards Understanding of Social and Cultural Complexity*, London: UCL Press, pp 267–70.

Kohl, B. (2003) 'Democratizing decentralization in Bolivia: the law of popular participation', *Journal of Planning Education and Research*, 23(2): 153–64.

Kuyucu, T. (2014) 'Law, property and ambiguity: the uses and abuses of legal ambiguity in remaking Istanbul's informal settlements', *International Journal of Urban and Regional Research*, 38(2): 609–27.

Langston, J. (2003) 'The formal bases of informal power: Mexico', paper presented at Informal Institutions and Politics in Latin America conference, Kellogg Institute for International Studies, University of Notre Dame, 24–25 April.

LARR (2004) 'From the marginality of the 1960s to the "new poverty" of today: a LARR research forum', *Latin American Research Review*, 39(1): 183–97.

Lazar, S. (2008) *El Alto, Rebel City: Self and Citizenship in Andean Bolivia*, Durham, NC: Duke University Press.

Ledeneva, A. (2018a) *The Global Encyclopaedia of Informality, Volume 1: Towards Understanding of Social and Cultural Complexity*, London: UCL Press.

REFERENCES

Ledeneva, A. (2018b) 'Blad', in A. Ledeneva (ed) *The Global Encyclopaedia of Informality, Volume 1: Towards Understanding of Social and Cultural Complexity*, London: UCL Press, pp 40–3.

Lefebvre, H. (1996 [1967]) 'The right to the city', in E. Kofman and E. Lebas (eds) *Writings on Cities*, Oxford: Blackwell, pp 63–181.

Lefebvre, H. (2003 [1970]) *The Urban Revolution*, Minneapolis: University of Minnesota Press.

Legg, S. and McFarlane, C. (2008) 'Ordinary urban spaces: between postcolonialism and development', *Environment and Planning A*, 40(1): 6–14.

Lemanski, C. (2009) 'Augmented informality: South Africa's backyard dwellings as a by-product of formal housing policies', *Habitat international*, 33(4): 472–84.

Lemanski, C. (2019) 'Introduction: the infrastructure of citizenship', in C. Lemanski (ed) *Citizenship and Infrastructure: Practices and Identities of Citizens and the State*, Abingdon: Routledge, pp 1–7.

Lemanski, C. and Lama-Rewal, T. (2012) 'The "missing middle": class and urban governance in Delhi's unauthorised colonies', *Transactions of the IBG*, 38(1): 91–105.

Levenson, A.R. and Maloney, W.F. (1998) *The Informal Sector, Firm Dynamics, and Industrial Participation (No. 1988)*, Washington, DC: World Bank Publications.

Lewis, O. (1952) 'Urbanization without breakdown: a case study', *The Scientific Monthly*, 75(1): 31–41.

Lewis, O. (1961) *The Children of Sánchez*, Harmondsworth: Penguin.

Lewis, O. (1967a) *La Vida: A Puerto Rican Family in the Culture of Poverty – San Juan and New York*, New York: Random House.

Lewis, O. (1967b) 'The culture of poverty', *Scientific American*, 215(4): 19–25.

Lewis, W.A. (1954) 'Economic Development with Unlimited Supplies of Labour', *The Manchester School*, 2(2): 139–191.

Lijphart, A. (1975) *The Politics of Accommodation: Pluralism and Democracy in the Netherlands*, Berkeley: University of California Press.

Lindell, I. (2010) *Africa's Informal Workers: Collective Agency, Alliances and Transnational Organizing in Urban Africa*, London: Zed Books.

Linz, J. (2021) 'Where crises converge: the affective register of displacement in Mexico City's post-earthquake gentrification', *Cultural Geographies*, 28(2): 285–300.

Lloyd, P. (1979) *Slums of Hope? Shanty Towns of the Third World*, London: Penguin.

Lombard, M. (2009) *Making a Place in the City: Place-Making in Urban Informal Settlements in Mexico*, PhD thesis, University of Sheffield.

Lombard, M. (2013) 'Using auto-photography to understand place: reflections from research in urban informal settlements in Mexico', *Area*, 45(1): 23–32.

Lombard, M. (2014) 'Constructing ordinary place: place-making in urban informal settlements in Mexico', *Progress in Planning*, 94: 1–53.

Lombard, M. (2015) 'Discursive constructions of low-income neighbourhoods', *Geography Compass*, 9(12): 648–59.

Lombard, M. (2016) 'Land conflict in peri-urban areas: exploring the effects of land reform on informal settlement in Mexico', *Urban Studies*, 53(13): 2700–20.

Lombard, M. (2019) 'Informality as structure or agency? Exploring shed housing in the UK as informal practice', *International Journal of Urban and Regional Research*, 43(3): 569–75.

Lombard, M. (2023) 'The experience of precarity: low-paid economic migrants' housing in Manchester', *Housing Studies*, 38(2): 307–26.

Lombard, M. and Meth, P. (2016) 'Informalities and the city', in M. Jayne and K. Ward (eds) *Urban Theory: New Critical Perspectives*, Routledge: Abingdon, pp 158–171.

Lombard, M. and Rakodi, C. (2016) 'Urban land conflict in the global south: towards an analytical framework', *Urban Studies*, 53(13): 2683–99.

Lombard, M., Hernández, J. and Lopez, A. (2021) 'Informal rental housing in Colombia: an essential option for low-income households', *International Development Planning Review*, 43(2): 257–77.

Lomnitz, L. (1977) *Networks and Marginality: Life in a Mexican Shanty Town*, New York: Academic Press.

Luque-Ayala, A. and Neves Maia, F. (2019) 'Digital territories: Google Maps as a political technique in the re-making of urban informality', *Environment and Planning D, Society and Space*, 37(3): 449–67.

Mabin, A. (2014) 'Grounding southern city theory in time and place', in S. Parnell and S. Oldfield (eds) *The Routledge Handbook on Cities of the Global South*, Abingdon: Routledge, pp 21–36.

Maloney, W.F. (2004) 'Informality revisited', *World Development*, 32(7): 1159–78.

Mangin, W. (1967) 'Latin American squatter settlements: a problem and a solution', *Latin American Research Review*, 2(3): 65–98.

Mansuri, G. and Rao, V. (2013) *Localizing Development: Does Participation Work?* Policy Research Report, Washington, DC: World Bank.

Marcuse, P. (2009) 'From critical urban theory to the right to the city', *City*, 13(2–3): 185–97.

Marx, C. and Kelling, E. (2019) 'Knowing urban informalities', *Urban Studies*, 56(3): 494–509.

Matin, I., Hulme, D. and Rutherford, S. (2002) 'Finance for the poor: from microcredit to microfinancial services', *Journal of International Development*, 14(2): 273–94.

Matos Mar, J. (1966) *Estudio de las Barriadas Limeñas*, Lima: United Nations.

Mayne, A. (2017) *Slums: The History of a Global Injustice*, London: Reaktion Books.

McFarlane, C. (2004) 'Geographical imaginations and spaces of political engagement: examples from the India alliance', *Antipode*, 36(5): 890–916.

McFarlane, C. (2008) 'Governing the contaminated city: infrastructure and sanitation in colonial and post-colonial Bombay', *International Journal of Urban and Regional Research*, 32(2): 415–35.

McFarlane, C. (2009) 'Translocal assemblages: space, power and social movements', *Geoforum*, 40(4): 561–7.

McFarlane, C. (2010a) 'Infrastructure, interruption, and inequality: urban life in the global south', in S. Graham (ed) *Disrupted Cities: When Infrastructure Fails*, Abingdon: Routledge, pp 131–44.

McFarlane, C. (2010b) 'The comparative city: knowledge, learning, urbanism', *International Journal of Urban and Regional Research*, 34(4): 725–42.

McFarlane, C. (2011) 'Assemblage and critical urbanism', *City*, 15(1–2): 204–24.

McFarlane, C. (2012) 'Rethinking informality: politics, crisis, and the city', *Planning Theory and Practice*, 13(1): 89–108.

McFarlane, C. and Silver, J. (2017) 'Navigating the city: dialectics of everyday urbanism', *Transactions of the Institute of British Geographers*, 42(3): 458–71.

McFarlane, M. and Waibel, M. (2012) *Urban Informalities: Reflections on the Formal and Informal*, Farnham: Ashgate.

McGranahan, G., Mitlin, D. and Satterthwaite, D. (2008) 'Land and services for the urban poor in rapidly urbanizing countries', in G. Martine, G. McGranahan, M. Montgomery and R. Fernández-Castilla (eds) *The New Global Frontier: Urbanization, Poverty and Environment in the 21st Century*, London: Earthscan, pp 77–98.

Meagher, K. (2007) 'Introduction: special issue on "informal institutions and development in Africa"', *Africa Spectrum*, 42(3): 405–18.

Meagher, K. (2018) 'Cannibalizing the informal economy: frugal innovation and economic inclusion in Africa', *The European Journal of Development Research*, 30: 17–33.

Mearns, A. (1969 [1883]) *The Bitter Cry of Outcast London: An Inquiry into the Condition of the Abject Poor*, Bath: Chivers.

Menon, G. (2018) 'People out of place: pavement dwelling in Mumbai', *Review of Urban Affairs*, 53(12): 85–92.

Mercer, M. (2006) 'Working with partners: NGOs and CBOs', in V. Desai and R. Potter (eds) *Doing Development Research*, London: SAGE, pp 94–103.

Meth, P. (2013) 'Millennium Development Goals and urban informal settlements: unintended consequences', *International Development Planning Review*, 35(1): v–xiii.

Mills, C.W. (1956) *The Power Elite*, Oxford: Oxford University Press.

Miraftab, F. (2009) 'Insurgent planning: situating radical planning in the global south', *Planning Theory*, 8(1): 32–50.

Miranda, L. (2002) 'A new mystery from de Soto? A review of "The mystery of capital", Hernando de Soto, 2001', *Environment and Urbanization*, 14(1): 263–4.

Mistry, R. (1995) *A Fine Balance*, London: Faber & Faber.

Mitlin, D. (2008) 'With and beyond the state: co-production as a route to political influence, power and transformation for grassroots organizations', *Environment and Urbanization*, 20(2): 339–60.

Mitlin, D. (2014) 'Politics, informality and clientelism: exploring a pro-poor urban politics', ESID Working Paper 34, Manchester University.

Mitlin, D. (2023) 'The contribution of reform coalitions to inclusion and equity: lessons from urban social movements', *Area Development and Policy*, 8(1): 1–26.

Mitlin, D. and Satterthwaite, D. (eds) (2004) *Empowering Squatter Citizen: Local Government, Civil Society and Urban Poverty Reduction*, London: Earthscan.

Mitlin, D. and Satterthwaite, D. (2013) *Urban Poverty in the Global South: Scale and Nature*, London: Earthscan.

Mitlin, D. and Walnycki, A. (2020) 'Informality as experimentation: water utilities' strategies for cost recovery and their consequences for universal access', *Journal of Development Studies*, 56(2): 259–77.

Mitlin, D., Satterthwaite, D. and Bartlett, S. (2011) *Capital, Capacities and Collaboration: The Multiple Roles of Community Savings in Addressing Urban Poverty*, London: Human Settlements Group, International Institute for Environment and Development.

Mitlin, D., Bennett, J., Horn, P., King, S., Makau, J. and Nyama, G.M. (2020) 'Knowledge matters: the potential contribution of the coproduction of research', *The European Journal of Development Research*, 32(3): 544–59.

Moatasim, F. (2019) 'Entitled urbanism: elite informality and the reimagining of a planned modern city', *Urban Studies*, 56(5): 1009–25.

Monkkonen, P. (2011) 'The housing transition in Mexico: expanding access to housing finance', *Urban Affairs Review*, 8 March.

Montaño, J. (1976) *Los Pobres de la Ciudad en los Asentamientos Espontáneos*, Mexico City: Siglo Veintiuno.

Morse, R.M. (1978) 'Latin American intellectuals and the city, 1860–1940', *Journal of Latin American Studies*, 10(2): 219–38.

Moser, C. (1978) 'Informal sector or petty commodity production: dualism or dependence on urban development', *World Development*, 6(9/10): 1041–64.

Moser, C. (1994) 'The informal sector debate, part 1: 1970–1983', in C. Rakowski (ed) *Contrapunto: The Informal Sector Debate in Latin America*, Albany: State University of New York Press, pp 11–29.

Moser, C. (2009) *Ordinary Families, Extraordinary Lives*, Washington, DC: Brookings Institution Press.

Moser, C. and Peake, L. (eds) (1987) *Women, Human Settlements and Housing*, London: Tavistock Publications.

Moser, C. and McIlwaine, C. (1999) 'Participatory urban appraisal and its application for research on violence', *Environment and Urbanisation*, 11(2): 203–26.

Moulaert, F. and Ailenei, O. (2005) 'Social economy, third sector and solidarity relations: a conceptual synthesis from history to present', *Urban Studies*, 42(11): 2037–53.

Müller, F.I. (2017) 'Urban informality as a signifier: performing urban reordering in suburban Rio de Janeiro', *International Sociology*, 32(4): 493–511.

Murray, C. and Clapham, D. (2015) 'Housing policies in Latin America: overview of the four largest economies', *International Journal of Housing Policy*, 15(3): 347–64.

Musembi, C.N. (2007) 'De Soto and land relations in rural Africa: breathing life into dead theories about property rights', *Third World Quarterly*, 28(8): 1457–78.

Mwau, B. (2019) 'The rise of Nairobi's concrete tenement jungle', *Age of Zinc*, 10 October. Available from: https://ageofzinc.wordpress.com/2019/10/10/the-rise-of-vertical-slums-in-nairobi/ [Accessed 20 October 2023].

Mwau, B. and Sverdlik, A. (2020) 'High rises and low-quality shelter: rental housing dynamics in Mathare Valley, Nairobi', *Environment and Urbanization*, 32(2): 481–502.

Myers, G.A. (2003) *Verandahs of Power: Colonialism and Space in Urban Africa*, Syracuse: Syracuse University Press.

Nazha, N. (2018) 'Beirut: Dahiye – an active space for social justice and resistance – re-imagining informality in light of growing urban marginality', in R. Rocco and J. van Ballegooijen (eds) *The Routledge Handbook on Informal Urbanization*, Abingdon: Routledge, pp 44–53.

Neuwirth, R. (2005) *Shadow Cities: A Billion Squatters, a New Urban World*, Abingdon: Routledge.

REFERENCES

Nthambi Jimmy, E. (2023) *Reconsidering Informality: Informal Housing Practices, Illegal Actors, and Planning Response Strategies within Middle-Income Neighbourhoods in Nairobi City Kenya*, PhD thesis, Gran Sasso Science Institute.

Oguttu, J.W., McCrindle, C.M., Makita, K. and Grace, D. (2014) 'Investigation of the food value chain of ready-to-eat chicken and the associated risk for staphylococcal food poisoning in Tshwane Metropole, South Africa', *Food Control*, 45: 87–94.

Ohnsorge, F. and Yu, S. (2022) *The Long Shadow of Informality: Challenges and Policies*, Washington, DC: World Bank Publications.

Oldekop, J., Horner, R., Hulme, D., Adhikari, R., Agarwal, B., Alford, M. et al (2020) 'COVID-19 and the case for global development', *World Development*, 134: 105044.

Omoegun, A.O., Mackie, P. and Brown, A. (2019) 'The aftermath of eviction in the Nigerian informal economy', *International Development Planning Review*, 41(1): 107–28.

Ostrom, E. (1996) 'Crossing the great divide: co-production, synergy and development', *World Development*, 26(6): 1073–87.

Our World in Data (2023) 'Ensure access to water and sanitation for all', SDG Tracker. Available from: https://ourworldindata.org/sdgs/clean-water-sanitation [Accessed 15 November 2023].

Özdemirli, Y.K. (2018) 'Ankara: struggles for housing – legitimate, self-contradictory or both? Impacts of clientelism and rights-seeking on informal housing in Ankara', in R. Rocco and J. van Ballegooijen (eds) *The Routledge Handbook on Informal Urbanization*, Abingdon: Routledge, pp 22–33.

Painter, J. and Jeffrey, A. (2009) *Political Geography*, New York: SAGE.

Park, J.F. (2019) 'Abolish rent', *Radical Housing Journal*, 1(2): 179–84.

Parnell, S. (2016) 'Defining a global urban development agenda', *World Development*, 78: 529–40.

Patel, K. (2016) 'Sowing the seeds of conflict? Low income housing delivery, community participation and inclusive citizenship in South Africa', *Urban Studies*, 53(13): 2738–57.

Patel, S. (2014) 'Is there a "south" perspective to urban studies?', in S. Parnell and S. Oldfield (eds) *The Routledge Handbook on Cities of the Global South*, Abingdon: Routledge, pp 37–47.

Payne, G. (2001) 'Urban land tenure policy options: titles or rights?', *Habitat International*, 25(3): 415–29.

Payne, G. (2004) 'Land tenure and property rights: an introduction', *Habitat International*, 28(2): 167–79.

Payne, G., Durand-Lasserve, A. and Rakodi, C. (2009) 'The limits of land titling and home ownership', *Environment and Urbanization*, 21(2): 443–62.

Peattie, L.R. (1970) *The View from the Barrio*, Ann Arbor: University of Michigan Press.

Perlman, J. (1976) *Myth of Marginality: Urban Poverty and Politics in Rio de Janeiro*, Berkeley: University of California Press.

Pierre, J. (1999) 'Models of urban governance: the institutional dimension of urban politics', *Urban Affairs Review*, 34(3): 372–96.

Platt, T. (1982) *Estado boliviano y ayllu andino: tierra y tributo en el Norte de Potosí*, Lima: Instituto de Estudios Peruanos.

Porter, L. (2010) *Unlearning the Colonial Cultures of Planning*, Farnham: Ashgate.

Portes, A. (1972) 'Rationality in the slum: an essay on interpretive sociology', *Comparative Studies in Society and History*, 14(3): 268–86.

Portes, A. (1983) 'The informal sector: definition, controversy, and relation to national development', *Review (Fernand Braudel Center)*, 7(1): 151–74.

Potter, R., Binns, T., Elliott, J., Nel, E. and Smith, D. (2008) *Geographies of Development: An Introduction to Development Studies*, Abingdon: Routledge.

Pritchett, L., Werker, E. and Sen, K. (2018) *Deals and Development: The Political Dynamics of Growth Episodes*, Oxford: Oxford University Press.

Purcell, M. (2003) 'Citizenship and the right to the global city: reimagining the capitalist world order', *International Journal of Urban and Regional Research*, 27(3): 564–90.

Quiros-Romero, G., Alexander, T. and Ribarsky, J. (2021) 'Measuring the informal economy', IMF Policy Paper, 2021(002).

Raju, S. (2013) 'The material and the symbolic: intersectionalities of home-based work in India', *Economic and Political Weekly*, 48(1): 60–8.

Rakowski, C.A. (1994) 'Convergence and divergence in the informal sector debate: a focus on Latin America, 1984–92', *World Development*, 22(4): 501–16.

Ranganathan, M. (2014) '"Mafias" in the waterscape: urban informality and everyday public authority in Bangalore', *Water Alternatives*, 7(1): 89–105.

Rankin, K. (2010) 'Reflexivity and post-colonial critique: toward an ethics of accountability in planning praxis', *Planning Theory*, 9(3): 181–99.

Rao, V. (2006) 'Slum as theory: the South/Asian city and globalisation', *International Journal of Urban and Regional Research*, 30(1): 225–32.

Raval, N. (2019) 'Automating informality: on AI and labour in the global south', in Global Information Society Watch (ed) *Artificial Intelligence: Human Rights, Social Justice and Development*. Available from: https://giswatch.org/sites/default/files/gisw2019_artificial_intelligence.pdf [Accessed 20 October 2023].

Ren, X. (2018) 'Governing the informal: housing policies over informal settlements in China, India, and Brazil', *Housing Policy Debate*, 28(1): 79–93.

Riis, J. (1997 [1890]) *How the Other Half Lives*, New York: Penguin.

Risør, H. (2010) 'Twenty hanging dolls and a lynching: defacing dangerousness and enacting citizenship in El Alto, Bolivia', *Public Culture*, 22(3): 465–85.

Roberts, G. (2004) *Shantaram*, London: Abacus.

Robinson, J. (2002) 'Global and world cities: a view from off the map', *International Journal of Urban and Regional Research*, 26(3): 531–54.

Robinson, J. (2006) *Ordinary Cities: Between Modernity and Development*, Abingdon: Routledge.

Robinson, J. and Roy, A. (2016) 'Debate on global urbanisms and the nature of urban theory', *International Journal of Urban and Regional Research*, 40(1): 181–6.

Rocco, R. and van Ballegooijen, J. (2018) *The Routledge Handbook of Informal Urbanization*, Abingdon: Routledge.

Rojas-García, G. and Toledo González, M.P. (2018) 'Paid domestic work: gender and the informal economy in Mexico', *Latin American Perspectives*, 45(1): 146–62.

Romero, J.L. (1976) *Latinoamérica, Las ciudades y las ideas*, Buenos Aires: Siglo XXI.

Romero, G. (2003) 'Social production of habitat: reflections on its history, conceptions and proposals', *Trialog*, 3(78): 8–15.

Roy, A. (2003) *City Requiem, Calcutta: Gender and the Politics of Poverty*, Minneapolis: University of Minnesota Press.

Roy, A. (2005) 'Urban informality: toward an epistemology of planning', *Journal of the American Planning Association*, 71(2): 147–58.

Roy, A. (2009) 'Why India cannot plan its cities: informality, insurgence and the idiom of urbanization', *Planning Theory*, 8(1): 76–87.

Roy, A. (2011) 'Slumdog cities: rethinking subaltern urbanism', *International Journal of Urban and Regional Research*, 35(2): 223–38.

Roy, A. (2014) 'Worlding the south: towards a post-colonial urban theory', in S. Parnell and S. Oldfield (eds) *The Routledge Handbook on Cities of the Global South*, Abingdon: Routledge, pp 9–20.

Roy, A. and AlSayyad, N. (2004) *Urban Informality: Transnational Perspectives from the Middle East, Latin America and South Asia*, Lanham: Lexington Books.

Rydin, Y. (2011) *The Purpose of Planning: Creating Sustainable Towns and Cities*, Bristol: Policy Press.

Salazar, C. (ed) (2012) *Irregular. Suelo y mercado en América Latina*, Mexico City: Colegio de Mexico.

Samper, J., Shelby, J. and Behary, D. (2020) 'The paradox of informal settlements revealed in an ATLAS of informality: findings from mapping growth in the most common yet unmapped forms of urbanization', *Sustainability*, 12(22): 9510.

Sassen, S. (2018) *Cities in a World Economy*, New York: SAGE.

Satterthwaite, D. (2008) 'Review of Robert Neuwirth 2005: *Shadow cities: a billion squatters, a new urban world*. New York and London: Routledge', *International Journal of Urban and Regional Research*, 32(1): 233–5.

Satterthwaite, D. (2012) 'Upgrading informal settlements', in S. Smith (ed) *International Encyclopaedia of Housing and Home*, Oxford: Elsevier, pp 206–11.

Satterthwaite, D. (2016) 'Editorial: a new urban agenda?', *Environment and Urbanization*, 28(1): 3–12.

Satterthwaite, D. (2018) 'Will the new urban agenda have any positive influence on governments and international agencies?', *Planning Theory and Practice*, 19(1): 121–3.

Satterthwaite, D. and Mitlin, D. (2013) *Reducing Urban Poverty in the Global South*, Abingdon: Routledge.

Saunders, D. (2011) *Arrival City: How the Largest Migration in History Is Reshaping Our World*, London: Windmill Books.

Scheba, A. and Turok, I. (2020) 'Informal rental housing in the south: dynamic but neglected', *Environment and Urbanization*, 32(1): 109–32.

Schiller, M. and Raco, M. (2021) 'Postcolonial narratives and the governance of informal housing in London', *International Journal of Housing Policy*, 21(2): 268–90.

Schneider, F. (2012) 'Size and measurement of the informal economy in 110 countries', paper presented at the Workshop of Australian National Tax Centre, Canberra: ANU.

Schütz, E. (2003) 'Stones in the way: on self-determination in housing in times of globalisation', *Trialog*, 3(78): 5–7.

Scott, J.C. (1998) *Seeing Like a State, How Certain Schemes to Improve the Human Condition Have Failed*, London: Yale University Press.

Sen, A. (2005) 'Human rights and capabilities', *Journal of Human Development*, 6(2): 151–66.

Sheppard, E., Sparks, T. and Leitner, H. (2020) 'World class aspirations, urban informality, and poverty politics: a north–south comparison', *Antipode*, 50(2): 393–407.

Simon, D., Arano, A., Cammisa, M., Perry, B., Pettersson, S., Riise, J., et al (2021) 'Cities coping with COVID-19', *City*, 25(1): 129–70

Simone, A. (2000) *On Informality and Considerations for Policy*, Dark Roast Occasional Paper Series 3, Cape Town: Isandla Institute.

Simone, A. (2004a) 'People as infrastructure: intersecting fragments in Johannesburg', *Public Culture*, 16(3): 407–29.

Simone, A. (2004b) *For the City Yet to Come, Changing African Life in Four Cities*, London: Duke University Press.

Simone, A. (2010) *City Life from Jakarta to Dakar: Movements at the Crossroads*, Abingdon: Routledge.

Simone, A. (2019) 'Contests over value: from the informal to the popular', *Urban Studies*, 56(3): 616–19.

Simone, A. (2021) 'Ritornello: people as infrastructure', *Urban Geography*, 42(9): 1341–8.

Sinclair, U. (2003 [1906]) *The Jungle*, London: Penguin.

Singer, H.W. (1970) 'Dualism revisited: a new approach to the problems of the dual society in developing countries', *The Journal of Development Studies*, 7(1): 60–75.

Skinner, C. and Watson, V. (2020) 'The informal economy in urban Africa: challenging planning theory and praxis', in M. Chen and F. Carré (eds) *The Informal Economy Revisited*, Abingdon: Routledge, pp 123–31.

Slocum, S.L., Backman, K.F. and Robinson, K.L. (2011) 'Tourism pathways to prosperity: perspectives on the informal economy in Tanzania', *Tourism Analysis*, 16(1): 43–55.

Smith, F. (2003) 'Working in different cultures', in N. Clifford and G. Valentine (eds) *Key Methods in Geography*, London: SAGE, pp 179–93.

Smith, N. (1996) *The New Urban Frontier: Gentrification and the Revanchist City*, Abingdon: Routledge.

Smith, P. (1994) 'Assessing the size of the underground economy: the Statistics Canada perspectives', *Canadian Economic Observer*, 7(5): 11–37.

Smith, P.R. (2011) 'The pitfalls of home: protecting the health and safety of paid domestic workers', *Canadian Journal of Women and the Law*, 23(1): 309–39.

Smith, T.L. (2012) *Decolonizing Methodologies: Research and Indigenous People*, London: Zed Books.

Sou, G., Risha, A.N., Sims, C. and Ziervogel, G. (2022) *Everyday Stories of Climate Change*, Manchester and Melbourne: RMIT University and the University of Manchester.

SPARC (1988) *We, the Invisible: A Census of Pavement Dwellers*, Mumbai: Society for the Protection of Area Resource Centres.

Staab, S. (2020) 'Social protection for women informal workers: perspectives from Latin America', in M. Chen and F. Carré (eds) *The Informal Economy Revisited*, Abingdon: Routledge, pp 215–20.

Stein, A. (2010) *Urban Poverty, Social Exclusion and Social Housing Finance: The Case of PRODEL in Nicaragua*, PhD thesis, Lund University.

Stokes, C. (1962) 'A theory of slums', *Land Economics*, 38(3): 187–97.

REFERENCES

Streule, M., Karaman, O., Sawyer, L. and Schmid, C. (2020) 'Popular urbanization: conceptualizing urbanization processes beyond informality', *International Journal of Urban and Regional Research*, 44(4): 652–72.

Sud, N. and Sánchez-Ancochea, D. (2022) 'Southern discomfort: interrogating the category of the global south', *Development and Change*, 53(6): 1123–50.

Swanson, K. (2007) 'Revanchist urbanism heads south: the regulation of indigenous beggars and street vendors in Ecuador', *Antipode*, 39(4): 708–28.

Talukdar, D. (2018) 'Cost of being a slum dweller in Nairobi: living under dismal conditions but still paying a housing rent premium', *World Development*, 109: 42–56.

Tassi, N. (2017) *The Native World-System: An Ethnography of Bolivian Aymara Traders in the Global Economy*, Oxford: Oxford University Press.

Tassi, N., Arbona, J.M., Ferrufino, G. and Rodríguez-Carmona, A. (2012) 'El desborde económico popular en Bolivia: comerciantes aymaras en el mundo global', *Nueva sociedad*, 241: 93–105.

Taylor, H. (2001) 'Insights into participation from critical management and labour process perspectives', in B. Cooke and U. Kothari (eds) *Participation: The New Tyranny?*, New York: Zed, pp 122–138.

Tibaijuka, A. (2005) *Report of the Fact-Finding Mission to Zimbabwe to Assess the Scope and Impact of Operation Murambatsvina by the UN Special Envoy on Human Settlement Issues in Zambia*, Nairobi: UN-Habitat.

Tipple, G. and Speak, S. (2005) 'Definitions of homelessness in developing countries', *Habitat International*, 29(2): 337–52.

To, W.M. and Lai, L.S. (2015) 'Crowdsourcing in China: opportunities and concerns', *IT Professional*, 17(3): 53–9.

Tokman, V.E. (1984) 'The employment crisis in Latin America', *International Labour Review*, 123: 585–98.

Triandafyllidou, A. (2013) *Irregular Migrant Domestic Workers in Europe*, Farnham: Ashgate.

Turner, J. (1967) 'Barriers and channels for housing development in modernizing countries', *Journal of the American Institute of Planners*, 33(3): 167–81.

Turner, J. (1968) 'Uncontrolled urban settlement: problems and policies', in G. Breese (ed) *The City in Newly Developing Countries: Readings on Urbanism and Urbanisation*, Englewood Cliffs: Prentice Hall, pp 507–534.

Turner, J. (1972) 'Housing as a verb', in J. Turner and R. Fichter (eds) *Freedom to Build: Dweller Control of the Housing Process*, New York: Collier-Macmillan, pp 148–75.

Turner, J. and Fichter, R. (eds) (1972) *Freedom to Build: Dweller Control of the Housing Process*, New York: Collier-Macmillan.

UN General Assembly (2022) *Progress in the Implementation of the New Urban Agenda*, report of the Secretary-General for General Assembly Seventy-sixth session, 23 July. Available from: https://documents-dds-ny.un.org/doc/UNDOC/GEN/N22/278/72/PDF/N2227872.pdf?OpenElement [Accessed 20 October 2023].

UN-Habitat (1992) *Multilingual Glossary of Human Settlement Terms*, Nairobi: UN-Habitat.

UN-Habitat (2003) *The Challenge of the Slums: Global Report on Human Settlements 2003*, London: Earthscan.

UN-Habitat (2016) *Enhancing Productivity in the Urban Informal Economy*, Nairobi: UN-Habitat.

UN-Habitat (2020) *The New Urban Agenda Illustrated*, Nairobi: UN-Habitat.

United Nations (UN) (2015) *Transforming Our World: The 2023 Agenda for Sustainable Development*, New York: United Nations.

United Nations (UN) (2017) *New Urban Agenda*, New York: United Nations. Available from: https://habitat3.org/the-new-urban-agenda/ [Accessed 15 November 2023].

United Nations (UN) (2021) *The Sustainable Development Goals Report 2021*, New York: United Nations.

Urban Popular Economy Collective, Benjamin, S., Castronovo, A., Cavallero, L., Cielo, C., Gago, V., Guma, P., Gupte, R., Habermehl, V., Salman, L. and Shetty, P. (2022) 'Urban popular economies: territories of operation for lives deemed worth living', *Public Culture*, 34(3): 333–57.

van Blerk, L., Hunter, J., Shand, W. and Prazeres, L. (2023) 'Creating stories for impact: co-producing knowledge with young people through story mapping', *Area*, 55(1): 99–107.

Vanek, J. (2020) 'Advances in statistics on informal employment: an overview highlighting WIEGO's contributions', in M. Chen and F. Carré (eds) *The Informal Economy Revisited*, Abingdon: Routledge, pp 47–51.

Vanek, J., Chen, M., Carré, F., Heintz, J. and Hussmanns, R. (2014) 'Statistics on the informal economy: definitions, regional estimates & challenges', WIEGO Working Paper 2. Available from: https://www.wiego.org/sites/default/files/publications/files/Vanek-Statistics-WIEGO-WP2.pdf [Accessed 20 October 2023].

van Gelder, J. (2010) 'What tenure security? The case for a tripartite view', *Land Use Policy*, 27(2): 449–56.

Vargas Falla, A.M. and Valencia, S.C. (2019) 'Beyond state regulation of informality: understanding access to public space by street vendors in Bogotá', *International Development Planning Review*, 41(1): 85–105.

Varley, A. (1998) 'The political uses of illegality: evidence from urban Mexico', in E. Fernandes and A. Varley (eds) *Illegal Cities: Law and Urban Change in Developing Countries*, London: Zed, pp 172–90.

Varley, A. (2007) 'Gender and property formalization: conventional and alternative approaches', *World Development*, 35(10): 1739–53.

Varley, A. (2013) 'Postcolonialising informality?', *Environment and Planning D*, 31(1): 4–22.

Varley, A. (2016) 'Property titles and the urban poor: from informality to displacement?', *Planning Theory and Practice*, 18(3): 385–404.

von Benda-Beckmann, F. (2002) 'Who's afraid of legal pluralism?', *The Journal of Legal Pluralism and Unofficial Law*, 34(47): 37–82.

Ward, P. (ed) (1982) *Self-Help Housing: A Critique*, London: Mansell.

Ward, P. (1989) 'Political mediation and illegal settlement in Mexico City', in A. Gilbert (ed) *Housing and Land in Urban Mexico*, San Diego: Centre for US-Mexican Studies, University of California.

Ward, P. (1990) *Mexico City: The Production and Reproduction of an Urban Environment*, New York: Macmillan.

Wade, P. (2009) *Race and Sex in Latin America*, London: Pluto Press.

Wade, P. (2013) 'Articulations of eroticism and race: domestic service in Latin America', *Feminist Theory*, 14(2): 187–202.

REFERENCES

Watson, V. (2003) 'Conflicting rationalities: implications for planning theory and ethics', *Planning Theory and Practice*, 4(4): 395–407.

Watson, V. (2009) 'Seeing from the south: refocusing urban planning on the globe's central urban issues', *Urban Studies*, 46(11): 2259–75.

Watson, V. (2011) 'Inclusive urban planning for the working poor: planning education trends and potential shifts', WIEGO Urban Policies Research Report 11. Available from: https://www.wiego.org/publications/inclusive-urban-planning-working-poor-planning-education-trends-and-potential-shift [Accessed 20 October 2023].

Watson, V. (2012) 'Planning and the "stubborn realities" of global south-east cities: some emerging ideas', *Planning Theory*, 12(1): 81–100.

Watson, V. (2016) 'Shifting approaches to planning theory: global north and south', *Urban Planning*, 1(4): 32–41.

Webb, J. (2018) 'Cash for access', in A. Ledeneva (ed) *The Global Encyclopaedia of Informality, Volume 1: Towards Understanding of Social and Cultural Complexity*, London: UCL Press, pp 184–7.

Weinstein, L. (2008) 'Mumbai's development mafias: globalization, organized crime and land development', *International Journal of Urban and Regional Research*, 32(1): 22–39.

Wigle, J. (2009) 'Shelter, location and livelihoods: exploring the linkages in Mexico City', *International Planning Studies*, 13(3): 197–222.

Williams, R. (1976) 'Community', in R. Williams (ed) *Keywords*, London: Fontana, pp 75–6.

Williamson, T. (2021) *Lessons on How to Plan for Informality: The Experience of Catalytic Communities*. Presentation.

Winkler, T. (2018) 'Rethinking scholarship on planning ethics', in M. Gundar, A. Madanipour and V. Watson (eds) *The Routledge Handbook of Planning Theory*, London: Routledge, pp 81–92.

Wirth, L. (1938) 'Urbanism as a way of life', *The American Journal of Sociology*, 44(1): 1–24.

Wright, E.O. (2019) *How to be an Anticapitalist in the Twenty-First Century*, London: Verso Books.

Yelling, J.A. (1986) *Slums and Slum Clearance in Victorian London*, London: Allen & Unwin.

Yeoh, B. and Kong, L. (1994) 'Reading landscape meanings: state constructions and lived experiences in Singapore's Chinatown', *Habitat International*, 18(4): 17–35.

Yiftachel, O. (2006) 'Re-engaging planning theory? Towards "south-eastern" perspectives', *Planning Theory*, 5(3): 211–22.

Yiftachel, O. (2009) 'Theoretical notes on "gray cities": the coming of urban apartheid?', *Planning Theory*, 8(1): 88–100.

Yiftachel, O. (2020) 'From displacement to displaceability: a southeastern perspective on the new metropolis', *City*, 24(1–2): 151–65.

Zeiderman, A. (2016) *Endangered City: The Politics of Security and Risk in Bogota*, Durham, NC: Duke University Press.

Zeiderman, A. (2018) 'Beyond the enclave of urban theory', *International Journal of Urban and Regional Research*, 42(6): 1114–26.

Zibechi, R. (2010) *Dispersing Power: Social Movements as Anti-State Forces*, Edinburgh: AK Press.

Index

A

Abrams, C. 16, 28, 29
abuse 75
academic representations 16–17
Accra 31, 69
Acuto, M. 41, 155, 157
Addams, J. 17
AeT (Asiye eTelufani) 144–5, 150, 153, 189
'affordability,' defining 59
affordable housing 10, 53, 111, 120, 130
Africa
  'collective life' 158
  contribution of informal economy to GDP 82–3
  'differentiated citizenship' 93
  economic crises 80
  informal employment 78–9
  inner-city informal housing 48
  middle classes 63
  urban informal neighbourhoods 50
  vertical slums 63–4
African Cities Research Consortium 179
Agbiboa, D.E. 97, 104
agency 38, 96, 158
agency working 74–5
aid agencies 116
'aided self-help' 113, 116–19
Ailenei, O. 160
Alfaro d'Alencon, P. 62, 64, 165
alliances 92, 168
AlSayyad, N. 12, 20, 33, 34, 36, 40–1, 184
Amsterdam 102
Ankara 104
anti-capitalist struggles 137, 163
anti-urban bias 30
Appadurai, A. 47
artificial intelligence (AI) 190, 191–2
artistic accounts 15–16, 172–4
asentamiento informales 49
asset accumulation 58, 119, 126
Athens 64
austerity 42, 64
autonomous political organization 96–7
auto-photography 176
Auyero, J. 38, 106
Aymara 80, 84, 162
Azuela, A. 34, 121

B

Bangalore 104
Bangasser, P. 30, 31, 32
Bangkok 139
Bangladesh 107
Bani Gala, Islamabad 63
banking 97, 102, 150–1
Banks, N. 9, 10, 12, 13, 41, 79, 96, 104, 107, 155, 184
barriadas 28–9
basic services 59, 118, 126, 131
Bayat, A. 33, 38, 98, 99, 189
'beds in sheds' 42, 43, 46, 65, 187
Behind the Beautiful Forevers (Boo) 106
Beirut 99–100, 102
Belo Horizonte 140, 152
Bendiksen, J. 35
Benjamin, S. 106, 149, 162
Berg, J. 76
beyond informality 40–3, 156–72
Bhan, G. 144, 148, 157, 158, 159–60, 164
Boanada, V. 37, 40, 185
Boanada-Fuchs, A. 37, 40, 185
Bogota 48, 94, 95, 115, 146
Bolivia 25, 67, 68, 79, 84, 94, 97, 99, 100, 102, 103
Bonnet, F. 73, 76, 77
Boo, K. 106
Booth, C. 16, 26
bottom-up perspectives 96–101, 137, 146, 165, 189
boundary conflicts 103
Brazil 93, 100, 122, 131, 142, 152, 169–72, 189
Breeze, M. 97
Brenner, N. 156, 157, 175
bribes 106
  see also corruption
Bromley, R. 32, 35
Buenos Aires 38, 48, 106
'bundle of rights' 55
bureaucracy 71, 119

C

'cage'/'coffin' housing 49
calculated informality 101–4
Calcutta 101
Caldeira, T. 175

Cali 51, 57, 135, 159
Campbell, H. 177
Cape Town 64, 116
capitalism 35, 69, 70, 71, 85, 119–20, 137, 156, 186
  see also neoliberalization
Caracas 56
cartels 149
'cash for access' 91
Castán Broto, V. 179
caste relations 75
Castells, M. 70, 96, 97, 137, 184
Catalytic Communities 169–72, 189
categorization 9–13
CBOs (community-based organizations) 123, 125, 126, 129, 144
Chambers, R. 178
Chamoiseau, P. 174
Charco Azul 51–2
Chatteraj, S. 17
Chatterjee, P. 93–4, 106, 163
Chen, M. 5, 6, 11, 35, 69, 70, 71, 73, 81, 84, 135, 142, 143, 150–1, 191
Cheung, S. 49
Chicago 173–4
China 50, 71–2, 78, 84, 116, 162
Chiodelli, F. 43, 115, 116, 117, 118, 119
Chitekwe-Biti, B. 127, 129, 131
Cities Alliance 116
'Cities without Slums' 37, 116
citizen organizations 100
citizen-led responses 123–31, 163, 166–72, 189
citizenship 90, 92, 93, 163
Ciudad Bolivar 95
Ciudadela San Antonio, Buenaventura 23
civil society organizations
  citizen-led responses 123, 129
  cooperative, multi-actor responses 14
  governing informally 93–4
  living informally 114
  neighbourhood associations 99
  New Urban Agenda 164, 166
CLASS (Community-Led Action and Savings Support) 167–8
class relations 75, 78
clientelism 12, 34, 53, 91–2, 101, 104–7
climate emergency 190–1
Cochabamba 94, 97, 102
Cociña, C. 125, 126, 129
'collective life' 158–60, 162
collective opposition 37–40, 184, 190
collective organization 98–100
collective ownership 55
Collord, M. 12
Colombia 23, 45, 50–2, 58, 95, 135, 150, 159
colonial urbanism 24–5, 41, 53
colonialism
  eviction 139
  and the 'global South' 5
  governing informally 92–5, 96
  hyperregulation 103

  legacy 186
  living informally 58, 115
  working informally 75, 137
commercial buildings, settlements in 48
community knowledge 18
community mobilizers 89, 128
community organization 118
Community Savers 160, 166–7, 169, 189
community-focused accounts of informality 17–18
conditional cash transfers 17
Connolly, P. 53, 54, 175, 186, 189
consociationalism 91
consolidation processes 60–2
cooperative, multi-actor responses 14, 183–92
co-production 129–31, 179, 187, 188
Cordera, R. 34
'cordon sanitaire' 25
CORETT (Comisión para la Regularización de la Tenencia de la Tierra) 121
corruption 12, 63, 67, 91–2
cosmopolitanism 42
COVID-19 80, 81, 144, 159–60, 165, 166, 191
credit, access to 34, 53, 118, 119, 120, 151
criminalization 11, 15, 53, 138, 139, 150, 151, 185, 188
cultural norms 53
'culture of poverty' 30, 96
customary rights 146–7

D

Dahiye, Beirut 99–100
daily savings 127–8
data gathering complexities
  evictions 115
  informal economy's contribution to the overall economy 82–3
  informality generally 18, 175
  living informally 11, 49, 55
  working informally 76–7
Datta, A. 37
Davis, M. 34, 35, 36
de Certeau, M. 194n2
de Soto, H. 34, 35, 71, 119, 120, 184
'dead capital' 34, 71, 119
decolonization 42, 137
definitions 2, 158, 183
Delhi 37, 106, 159, 162
Delhi Group 76
democratization 14, 137, 163
demolition 31, 37, 47, 101, 112, 114–15, 118
deregulation 52, 101, 104, 138
Derickson, K. 156, 157
'Development' (Hasan) 178
development planning 30, 41, 119, 139
Devkar, G. 14, 118, 129
Dhaka 107
'differentiated citizenship' 92–3, 163
digital cartography 175
dimensions of informality 9–13
Dirty Pretty Things 75
'dirty work' 75

INDEX

displacement 28, 29, 115, 124–5
disregulation 102
'do no harm' 190
Dobson, R. 144–5, 149–50
Dodman, D. 191
domestic workers 73, 74–5, 77
Dovey, K. 57, 175
drinking water 59–60, 128
drug trafficking 82
du Toit, D. 75
dualist approaches
   21st century debates 35
   developments in urban theory 157, 158
   formal/informal 9, 17, 184
   governing informally 90, 93
   working informally 70, 136
Durand-Lasserve, A. 55, 56
Durban 139, 140, 144, 146, 189
Durst, N. 42–3, 65

E

economic crises 80, 191
economic growth 69
Ecuador 48, 139, 141–2
education 152–3
El Alto 67, 68, 79, 84, 97–8, 99, 100, 162
electricity supplies 29, 46, 59, 97, 98, 118, 128
elites
   citizenship 92
   governing informally 91, 103–4, 188
   living informally 62–4
   revanchist responses to informal work 139
   top-down informal governance 146
   urban informality as collective opposition to 38, 40
   urban revitalization 141–2
   see also middle- and high-income communities
enabling approaches 119–23
Engels, F. 3, 25–6, 27
entrepreneurial informality 34–5, 71
   see also micro-entrepreneurialism
enumeration tools 128
environmental regulations 40
eradication policies 29, 37, 112, 114–16
   see also eviction
'escapist' responses to informal work 137
essentialization 38
ethical considerations in research 176–80
ethnography 38, 40, 176
Everett, M. 115
eviction
   governing informally 100
   living informally 55, 62, 112, 114–15, 122
   market evictions 55, 116
   responses to informality 15, 17, 18, 188, 190
   working informally 138–42
exploitation 34, 71, 72, 75, 118

F

Fairbanks II, R. 64
Favela Bairro programme 122

favelas 32, 37–8, 45, 49, 169–72
Fawaz, M. 102
Fernandes, E. 53, 122, 123
Few, R. 48
financial institutions 97, 102, 127–8, 148–9, 150–1, 168
Fine Balance, A (Mistry, 1995) 74, 84, 106, 172, 183
flexibilization 71
floods 40, 62
food security 159–60
FORLAC (Program for the Promotion of Formalization in Latin America and the Caribbean) 142
formalization 62, 100, 112, 135, 136, 138, 142–3, 150, 188, 190
Foster, C. 151
Fox, S. 28, 30, 53
Fraser, A. 165, 166
Frear, S. 75
Frediani, A. 100, 125, 126, 129
Freire, P. 178
Frey, C.B. 192
Friedmann, J. 123
funding agencies 116, 117, 118

G

Gago, V. 84, 162
Garschagen, M. 165, 166
Gaskell, E. 173
GDP, contribution of informal economy to 82–3
gender
   domestic workers 75, 77
   informal employment 78
   legal titles 120
   working informally 12
   see also women
gentrification 116, 122, 124–5
geographic information systems (GIS) 18, 175
geopolitics 91, 186, 187
Germany 2
Ghana 31–2, 184
Ghertner, D.A. 106
Gibson-Graham, J.K. 137
gig economy 6, 67, 75–8, 84, 185, 192
Gilbert, A. 36, 37, 51, 57, 112
Giovannini, F. 112
Glasgow 4
global economic crisis 2008 80, 191
global North
   contribution of informal economy to GDP 82–3
   informal employment 78
   informal settlements 3
   informal work 6
   living informally 64–5, 97
Global Report on Human Settlements (UN-Habitat, 2003) 36
global scale informality 42–3
global South
   governing informally 90, 92, 94
   informal neighbourhoods 11

radical instability 156
Southern urban theory 5, 16–17, 42, 65, 156–7, 164, 190
South-North comparisons/learning 42, 65, 166, 169, 186, 189
South-South comparisons 42, 186
  as term 5
  urbanization 28
  working informally 69
global urban agenda 112–14
global value chains 84, 149, 185
globalization 36, 38, 52, 184
Goldstein, D.M. 94, 98, 102
Goodfellow, T. 28, 90, 91, 92, 94
governing informally 12, 89–109, 146–7, 163–4, 185
  autonomous political organization 96–7
  calculated informality 101–4
  clientelism 12, 34, 53, 91–2, 101, 104–7
  collective organization 98–100
  corruption 12, 63, 67, 91–2
  insurgent politics 98, 100–1
  hyperregulation 102–3
  quiet encroachment 38, 98–9, 146, 147, 189
'gray spaces' 101–2
Guangzhou 72
Guayaquil 57, 97, 139, 141–2, 175
guilds 147, 150
Guma, P. 160, 164, 176
Gupte, J. 115

H

Habitat International Coalition (HIC) 125, 126–7
Hackenbroch, K. 60
Hall, P. 26, 28, 30
Hardoy, J. 24, 34, 46, 47, 48, 49, 52, 53, 56, 58
Hardy, D. 64
Harris, R. 40, 43, 53, 94, 95, 96, 185
Hart, K. 31, 69, 70, 184
Hasan, A. 123, 124–5, 177–8
health and safety regulations 75
Heeks, R. 151
Helmke, G. 89, 90, 91
Hernández, F. 25, 158
heroism 35
heuristic categorization 155
Hill, O. 17
Holston, J. 92, 93, 100, 163
Holzinger, K. 93
home-based work 58, 73–4, 81, 148, 149
homelessness 47, 117, 126
Hong Kong 49
Horn, P. 58, 79, 103, 104, 149
Hossain, S. 60
'House of Wonders,' Zanzibar 93
housing 57–8
  see also affordable housing; living informally
Housing for All Movement 100
housing quality 57, 62, 64
Huang, G. 72
Huchzermeyer, M. 40, 112, 114, 115–16

hukou 72
human rights 112, 126, 151
human trafficking 82, 102
Hunsley, P.M. 8–9

I

Illegal (Patrick Magebhula Hunsley) 8–9
illegal/semi-legal economic practices/work 11, 81–2
ILO (International Labour Organization) 5, 30, 31, 69, 70, 72, 76, 77, 78, 80, 142, 151, 160, 188
immigration status 75, 97
improvement of housing (existing) 57, 60–1
India
  affordable housing 130
  co-production 131
  domestic workers 75
  governing informally 93–4, 101
  living informally 37, 39, 47, 127, 130
  pavement dwelling 47
  'slums' 37, 39
  street vending 147
  working informally 5–6, 74
Indian Alliance 127
Indigenous populations
  colonial urbanism 24–5
  'differentiated citizenship' 93
  domestic workers 75
  'gray spaces' 102
  informal employment 79–80, 84
  'traditional' governance 93
  urbanization 28
  working informally 137, 162
industrialization 25, 28, 69, 70
informal economic practices
  characteristics of 5–6, 31
  under-estimations of 30
  informal assets as 'dead capital' 34
  legal and illegal 81–2
  see also working informally
informal employment 73–80
  see also working informally
informal neighbourhoods 3–4, 10, 11, 25–30, 35–41, 45–66, 104
  see also living informally; services to informal neighbourhoods
'infrastructural citizenship' 163, 190
infrastructure 59–60, 163
  see also services to informal neighbourhoods
inner-city informal housing 47–8
Institute for Liberty and Democracy 120
insurgent politics 98, 100–1
Inter-American Development Bank 192
intergenerational assets 58
International Conference of Labour Statisticians (ICLS) 76
International Expert Group on Informal Sector Statistics 72, 76
International Monetary Fund 36, 52, 112, 188
invisibility 18
Islamabad 63
Israel 80, 93, 101, 186

Istanbul 102, 158
Italy 43

J

Jaffe, R. 102
Jaglin, S. 60
Jakarta 43, 159
Jeffrey, A. 12
job creation 69, 149
Johannesburg 48, 68, 139, 147, 159, 163
'jugaad' 17
Jungle, The (Sinclair, 1906) 173–4

K

Kamete, A.Y. 139
Karachi 123, 124–5
Keivani, R. 117, 118, 119
Kelling, E. 2, 157
Kenya
 alternative approaches 168, 188
 governing informally 89, 93, 100–1, 104, 105
 informal neighbourhoods 3, 63, 111, 128
 working informally 149, 151
Kenya Mission 30, 69, 70
Kibera 188
Kiddle, G. 111, 112, 113, 114, 119
King, R. 57
kinship cultures 84, 93, 107
KNOW (Knowledge in Action for Urban Inequality) 179
Koechlin, L. 91
Koster, M. 102
Kuyucu, T. 102

L

La Paz 25, 97, 103
labour protections 67, 70, 74, 76, 143, 144, 151–2
Lagos 97, 104, 139, 158, 166
land acquisition 46, 49, 55–7, 94–5, 103, 105, 112, 117–18, 185
land invasion/squatting 56, 97, 98, 102, 104, 117
land tenure 55
 see also legal titles; tenure security
land values 55
Langston, J. 91
Latin America
 collective life 162
 colonial legacies 186
 colonial urbanism 24–5
 contribution of informal economy to GDP 82–3
 domestic workers 75
 economic crises 80
 eradication policies 114
 informal economic practices 31–2
 informal work 142
 inner-city informal housing 48
 Latin American research 17, 33–4
 living informally 186–7
 rapid urbanization 28–30
 regularization 122–3
 urbanización popular 158

Lebanon 99–100, 102
Ledeneva, A. 91
Lefebvre, H. 156, 163
legal advocacy 152
legal pluralism 90, 102–3
legal titles 34, 55, 62, 105, 113, 119–20
legalist approaches 9, 17, 35, 70, 71, 138, 184
legalization of assets 34
Legg, S. 42
Lemanski, C. 163
Levenson, A.R. 71, 184
Levitsky, S. 89, 90, 91
Lewis, O. 30, 96
Lewis, W.A. 69
liberalization 36, 38, 184
Lima 28, 29, 56, 96, 117
Limuru Declaration 126
Lindell, I. 91, 139
Linz, J. 116
lived experience 38, 153
living informally 45–66
 causal factors in living informally 52–4
 characteristics of 10–11
 clientelism 104
 contextual factors 53
 emerging alternative theories 158–60
 governing informally 97, 99, 100
 informal neighbourhoods 3–4, 10, 11, 25, 40–1, 45–66, 104
 multi-voice understandings of 185, 189
 responses to 111–33
 top-down informal governance 102
loan sharks 97, 150
lobbying 100
local governments 14, 15, 37, 117
 see also state roles
Lombard, M. 10, 11, 12, 43, 51, 56, 58, 65, 89, 95, 104, 121, 157
London 25–6, 27, 43, 64, 65
longitudinal research 175, 176, 187
López, A. 51–2
Lucknow 32
lynch-mob justice 97–8

M

Mabin, A. 164
Madrid 64
Malecón 2000 139, 141–2
Maloney, W.F. 71, 184
Manchester 27, 157, 160, 168, 173, 189
Mangin, W. 29, 35
Manila 47
mapping technology 175, 192
marginality, myth of 32–3, 174
'marginality' as alternative to informality 158
market evictions 55, 116
Marx, C. 2, 157
Marxist political economy 70, 137, 156, 186
Mary Barton (Gaskell, 1848) 173
massification of production 69
Matin, I. 150, 151

Matos Mar, J. 28
Mayne, A. 17, 28, 37
McFarlane, C. 40, 42, 62, 75, 98, 104, 128, 129, 155, 163, 169, 186
McGranahan, G. 120
Mearns, A. 26, 27
media representations 16, 65
membership organizations 147, 148
Menon, G. 47
Meth, P. 10, 11, 12, 37, 89
methodological considerations 174–6
Mexico 65, 91, 104, 120, 121, 127, 142
Mexico City 34, 48, 50, 53, 56, 81, 96, 116, 158, 175
micro-credits 135, 150, 151
micro-entrepreneurialism 34, 64, 137, 148, 149, 150–1
microfinance 148, 151
micro-flats 64
middle- and high-income communities 40, 46, 62–4, 188
middle and high-value developments 55
migrant workers 75
Millennium Development Goals 10–11, 116, 120, 165
Mills, C.W. 12, 91
Miraftab, F. 100
'missing middle' 63
Mistry, R. 74, 106, 172, 183
Mitlin, D. 15, 53, 54, 59, 60, 92, 104, 106, 123, 127, 129, 131, 150, 169, 179–80
Moatasim, F. 63
mobile money transfer 151
modernization 69, 138, 139
moral problems 26, 30
Morar Carioca 122
Moser, C. 34, 35, 38, 57, 58, 70, 97, 98, 118, 137, 175, 178
motivations for informal work 72
Moulaert, F. 160
movies 75, 175
M-Pesa 151
Mukuru informal neighbourhood 3, 64, 89, 100–1, 104, 105, 111, 128, 149, 188
multi-actor responses 14, 183–92
multi-sector responses 190
Mumbai 39, 40, 47, 50, 62, 104, 130, 162, 174
Muungano wa Wanavijiji 100, 149, 168
Mwau, B. 64
Myers, G.A. 93

N

Nairobi 3, 50, 57, 63, 64, 89, 93, 104, 105, 111, 128, 149, 168, 188
Namibia 131
National Association of Street Vendors in India 147
National Slum Dwellers Federation of India 127
Nazha, N. 99
neighbourhood associations 99, 100
neoliberalization 14, 38, 100, 113
Netherlands 102

Neuwirth, R. 173–4
New Public Management 114
New Urban Agenda (NUA) 14, 114, 155–6, 164–6, 175, 188
New York 16, 26–7
NGOs (non-government organizations) 14, 97, 100, 125, 126, 129, 144–5, 147, 169–72, 189
Nicaragua 148
Nigeria 97, 104, 116, 131
Nima, Accra 31, 69
non-enforcement of regulations 53, 62
Nthambi Jimmy, E. 63

O

occupation of land 56
  see also land acquisition; land invasion/squatting; tenure security
Odongo, L. 194n1
Ohnsorge, F. 82
older people 79
Omeogun, A.O. 139, 140
Operation Murambatsvina 115
Orangi Pilot 124–5
'ordinary cities' 41
organized crime 62, 150
organized disorder 102
organizing logic, informality as 40–1
origins of urban informality 24–8
Osborne, M. 192
Ostrom, E. 130, 131
'othering' 157
Our World in Data 59
outsourcing 70–1, 137
overcrowding 26, 43, 57, 126
over-regulation 71
Özdemirli, Y.K. 104–5

P

Painter, J. 12
Pakistan 63, 123, 124–5, 131
Palestine 101
Parnell, S. 113
participatory research methods 178–9
Patel, K. 118
Patel, S. 156
patronage 12, 53, 91–2, 104
pavement dwelling 47
Payne, G. 62, 119, 120, 121, 122
Peake, L. 34, 118
peripheral land 25, 55, 56, 119, 160, 186, 190
Perlman, J. 32, 35, 158, 175
permacrisis 190, 191
Peru 28, 29, 56, 96, 117, 120
Philadelphia 64
photography 16
pirating 29, 59
place-specific planning 147–50, 190
planning consultations 111
planning ethics 177–8
planning regulations 41, 53, 101, 139, 147–50
platform-based employment 75–6, 78, 185, 192

poetry 8–9, 178
policing 97
policy and practice-based accounts of informality 17
politics
  causal factors of living informally 53
  co-production 131
  governing informally 6, 12, 89–109
  and informality 90–2
  political appointments 91
'politics of redress' 98–9
Ponte Tower, Johannesburg 48
'popular economy' 17, 85, 162–3
popular urbanization 158–60
population growth 52, 79
Porter, L. 93, 165, 166
Portes, A. 70, 137, 184
positionality (of researchers) 177
postcolonialism
  colonial legacies 186
  governing informally 90, 92–5, 96, 186
  planning regulations 139
  postcolonial urban theory 41–2, 65
  theory 5
  working informally 137
Potter, R. 5
Pritchett, L. 94, 95
privatization 52, 120
PRODEL (Local Development Programme) 148, 151
property ownership 34
  see also asset accumulation
protected markets 70
provincialization of urban theory 156
public spaces and informal economic activity 149–50
'pulling strings' 2, 6

Q

quiet encroachment 38, 98–9, 146, 147, 189
Quiros-Romero, G. 82–3

R

race
  domestic workers 75
  racial segregation 25, 41, 93
  working informally 137
Rakodi, C. 95
Rakowski, C.A. 35
Rankin, K. 177
Rao, V. 164
rapid urbanization 90, 111
Raval, N. 192
reciprocity 34, 35
recovery house movement 64
Red Light District, Amsterdam 102
refugee camps 97, 187
regularization 62, 112, 114, 122–3
regulation
  democratic reform 137
  and the desire for invisibility 18
formalization 142–3
governing informally 12, 94, 96
housing 28
hyperregulation 102–3
informal work 151
legalist approaches 71, 138
non-enforcement of regulations 53, 62
over-regulation 71
planning regulations 41, 53, 101, 139, 147–50
protected markets 31
regulatory non-compliance 53
subdivision 56–7
voluntarist approaches 71
rental housing 50, 64
representations 6, 15–18
research ethics 176–80
research methods 174–6
Resident Welfare Associations 106
resistance 38, 158
responses to informality, analyzing 13–15
'return of the slum' 36–7
revanchist responses to informal work 138–42
Right to the City 163
Riis, J. 15, 16, 26–7, 28
Rio de Janeiro 56, 122, 139, 169–72, 175, 189
Roberts, G.D. 174
Robinson, J. 41, 42, 138, 156, 186
Rocco, R. 163
Roma 75
romanticization 16, 38
Rome 64
Romero, G. 126, 127
Romero, J.L. 33–4, 126
Roy, A. 36, 38, 40–1, 62, 101, 137, 156, 185, 186
Royston, L. 55, 56
rural-urban migration 47, 69, 70, 79
Russia 91

S

Salazar, C. 34
Samper, J. 49, 175
San Francisco 43
sanitation 59, 111, 113, 118, 124–5, 131
Santiago 56, 96
São Paulo 48–9, 100, 159
Sassen, S. 139
Satterthwaite, D. 15, 34, 46, 47, 48, 49, 52, 53, 54, 56, 58, 60, 113, 117–18, 119, 123, 129, 131, 166
savings groups 127–8, 150, 151, 168
Schmid, C. 156, 157, 175
Schneider, F. 81–2
schools 149, 152–3
security services 97
Self-Employed Women's Association 147
self-employment 70, 75, 77–8
self-help processes
  20th century policy debates 33, 34
  emerging alternative theories 161, 185, 189
  governing informally 96–7

living informally 45, 57, 59, 60, 113, 116, 123, 131
self-reliance 38
self-sufficiency 137
Sen, A. 58
sensationalism 16
services to informal neighbourhoods
  basic services 59, 118, 126, 131
  Cali 52
  clientelism 105
  collaboration to achieve 59–60
  community-based organizations (CBOs) 128–9
  co-production 131
  data collection 128
  housing quality 57
  incremental 46
  informal provision of 149
  regularization 122, 124
  sanitation 59, 111, 113, 118, 124–5, 131
  security services 97
  settlement upgrading 117
  sewerage and waste management 59, 118, 122
  street lighting 46, 60, 118
  UN-Habitat definition of informal neighbourhoods 49
  water supplies 29, 59, 97, 113, 118, 128
settlement upgrading 117
sewerage and waste management 59, 118, 122
Shack/Slum Dwellers International (SDI) 18, 100, 126, 127–9, 149, 150, 168, 189
Shantaram (Roberts, 2004) 174
Silver, J. 163
Simone, A. 38, 84, 85, 156, 158, 163, 186
Sinclair, U. 173–4
Singer, H. 69
'sites of critical analysis' 9–10, 41, 184
Skinner, C. 135, 139, 150
slavery 92
Slough 42
'slums' 3, 10, 15–16, 25–30, 35–41, 48
Smith, N. 139
Smith, P. 75, 81
social and solidarity economy 160–2, 190
social infrastructure 163
social investments 84
social networks 92
social processes, informal neighbourhoods as 40–1
social production of habitat (SPH) 126–7
Society for the Promotion of Area Resource Centres (SPARC) 47
South Africa
  colonial legacies 186
  embracing informal work 144–5, 146
  eradication policies 37, 115–16
  eviction 139, 140, 147
  global value chains 84–5
  Homeless People's Federation 127
  informal neighbourhoods 58, 118
  micro-flats 64
  savings groups 168

'slums' 37, 115
working informally 68
South Asia
  domestic workers 75
  gig economy 78
  inner-city informal housing 48
  pavement dwelling 47
  vertical slums 63–4
Southern urban theory 5, 16–17, 42, 65, 156 7, 164, 190
South-North comparisons/learning 42, 65, 166, 169, 186, 189
South-South comparisons 42, 186
Special Planning Areas 101, 104, 149, 188
'squatting'/land invasion 28, 56, 97, 98, 104, 117
Staab, S. 142
state roles
  affordable housing 111
  co-production 129–31
  governing informally 90, 94, 96, 163–4
  informality as state (in)action 40–3
  living informally 54, 114–23
  New Urban Agenda 164–6
  working informally 137
stereotypes 30, 37, 38
Stokes, C. 29
street lighting 46, 60, 118
street vending 72, 79, 98, 102, 139, 144, 146, 147, 152, 162
Streule, M. 158
Structural Adjustment Programmes 36, 52, 80
structuralist approaches 9, 17, 35, 70, 136–7, 184
'subaltern urbanism' 38
subcontracting 67, 73, 84
subdivision 56–7
subletting 49, 50, 58
surplus labour 69
surveillance 192
survival activities 11, 70, 165
suspension of order 12
Sustainable Cities and Communities 188
Sustainable Development Goals 4, 10, 36, 59, 120, 142, 164, 165, 166, 175, 188
Swanson, K. 139, 141–2

T

Ta no Mapa 175
Tanzania 152
Tassi, N. 84, 150
tenement housing 48, 64
tenure security 28–9, 46, 50, 55–7, 62, 113, 118–20, 122, 185
Texaco (Chamoiseau, 1998) 174
Texas 43
Thailand 139
title legalization 34, 119–20
Tomas, F. 34
top-down versus bottom-up responses 14–15, 96, 101–7, 138–43, 164–6, 188–9
tourism 139

INDEX

trade unions 99, 147, 161
trading informally 102
  see also street vending
'traditional' governance 93
transcending informal urbanism 41–3
transdisciplinary lens 6, 36
Tshwane 84, 85
Turkey 102, 104
Turner, J. 33, 35, 96, 117, 175

U

ubiquity of informality 40
UK 2, 12, 43, 65, 91, 173
UN 126
underemployment 69
unemployment 69, 106
UN-Habitat
  citizen-led responses 125
  conferences 113, 164, 188
  definition of informal neighbourhoods 10, 49, 53, 55, 57, 59
  eviction 140
  Global Campaign for Security of Tenure (1999) 113, 120
  Global Report on Human Settlements 36
  Human Settlements Programme 3
  international governance 14, 112, 164, 188
  New Urban Agenda (NUA) 164
  services provision 117
  working informally 148, 149, 151, 152
United Nations
  2030 Agenda for Sustainable Development 164
  'Cities without Slums' 37
  Millennium Development Goals 10–11, 116, 120, 165
  Sustainable Development Goals 4, 10, 36, 59, 120, 142, 164, 165, 166, 175, 188
United States 12, 65, 75, 91, 173–4
Universal Declaration of Human Rights 151
universalism 156, 165, 185
University of Manchester 31
University of Nairobi 31
unskilled/low-skilled work 69, 76
upgrading 33, 118–19, 122, 128–30, 149
urban development 40
urban informal neighbourhoods 49–51
urban planners, training of 152–3
Urban Popular Economies Collective 162
'urban reform coalitions' 169
Urban Resource Centre 123, 124–5
urban revitalization 139, 141–2
urban theory 156–8
  see also Southern urban theory
'urban villages' 50
urbanization 25–6, 28–30, 36, 56, 90, 94, 111

V

Valencia, S.C. 146
van Ballegooijen, J. 163

van Blerk, L. 176
Vancouver Declaration on Human Settlements 113
Vanek, J. 5, 6, 11, 73, 77, 78
Vargas Falla, A.M. 146
Varley, A. 37, 49, 62, 121, 122, 158
vertical slums 63–4
Villa El Salvador 117
violence 23, 30, 37, 75, 99, 100, 107
Vitamin B 2, 6
vocabularies, new 157
voluntarist approaches 35, 70, 71, 184

W

Wade, P. 75
Waibel, M. 155
Ward, C. 64
water supplies 29, 59, 97, 113, 118, 128
Watson, V. 41, 42, 93, 96, 135, 139, 152, 156, 177, 186
Webb, J. 91
Wegmann, J. 42–3, 65
Weinstein, L. 62, 63, 104
Werna, E. 117, 118, 119
WIEGO (Women in Informal Employment: Globalizing and Organizing), 72, 76, 81, 144, 148, 152, 161–2, 189
Williams, R. 157
Wirth, L. 195n3
women 12, 31, 75, 77–8, 127, 128, 161–2, 166–7
word cloud 2
workers' rights 151
working informally 67–87
  20th century policy debates 30–2
  embracing 144–53
  emerging alternative theories 160–3
  governing informally 94
  incorporation into economic analysis 31–2
  interrelated dimensions 5–6, 7, 11–12, 185, 189
  responses to 135–54
World Bank 33, 36, 52, 112, 113, 114, 116, 117, 119, 164, 188
'world class cities' 135, 139, 185
World Health Organization 59
Wright, E.O. 137

X

Xalapa 33, 50, 56, 61, 104

Y

Yelling, J.A. 26, 28
Yiftachel, O. 42, 93, 101–2, 115, 137, 186
young people 78
Yu, S. 82

Z

Zanzibar 93
Zeiderman, A. 157
Zimbabwe 115
zoning regulations 63, 99, 102